P9-APZ-884

Ancient Law

CLASSICS OF ANTHROPOLOGY
Ashley Montagu, Editor

Ancient Law

Its Connection With the Early History of Society, and Its Relation to Modern Ideas

HENRY SUMNER MAINE

Foreword by Lawrence Rosen

UNIVERSITY OF ARIZONA PRESS
Tucson

About the Author

SIR HENRY SUMNER MAINE (1822—88), the noted English
jurist and historian, was a pioneer in the historical-
comparative study of civilizations. After having served
as reader to the Inns of Court and as professor of civil
law at Cambridge University, Maine received a royal
appointment as legal member of the viceroy's council
in India, where he helped codify Indian law. From
1869 until his death, Maine served as professor of
jurisprudence at Oxford University and as master of
Trinity Hall and professor of international law at Cambridge University. Maine's influence on the history of
jurisprudence continues to this day.

Entered, according to Act of Congress,
in the year 1864, by Charles Scribner

THE UNIVERSITY OF ARIZONA PRESS
Copyright © 1986
The Arizona Board of Regents
All Rights Reserved
Manufactured in the U.S.A.

Library of Congress Cataloging-in-Publication Data

Maine, Henry Sumner, Sir, 1822— 1888.
Ancient law.

(Classics of anthropology)
Reprint. Originally published: New York: Holt, 1864.
Bibliography: p.
Includes index.
1. Law, Ancient.   2. Law, Primitive.   3. Comparative
law.   I. Title.   II. Series: Classics of anthropology
(Tucson, Ariz.)
K190.M35   1986   340.5'3   86-6929
ISBN 0-8165-1006-7 (alk. paper)

CONTENTS

FOREWORD

Lawrence Rosen

THE enduring importance of Sir Henry Maine's *Ancient Law* resides both in its place in the history of western legal scholarship and in its ongoing capacity to stimulate insights and debates for more than a century and a quarter. Like many classics it has, of course, been more often cited than read; but when, in successive generations, interest in the book has been rekindled, readers who expect it to contain only a simple evolutionary thesis or well-known interpretation of Roman legal development are surprised by the richness of its detail and the range of its suggestions. Indeed, much of the book's appeal results from its combination of stylistic clarity and bold assertion, and, if at times its axiomatic statements may not have survived the discoveries of later scholarship, it is a measure of its seminal appeal that new readers constantly find in it new ideas.

Maine began his study of legal history at a time when the quest for historical antecedents was enlivening a host of

contemporary intellectual concerns. Studies in the physical
and biological sciences were beginning to demonstrate that
the structure of the earth and its many life forms had developed through a number of antecedent steps. At the same
time, legal studies, far from recognizing the importance of the
historical dimension, were almost wholly oriented either toward the evocation of timeless principles of natural law or
to the timely enactment of legislative programs that would
eliminate the undesirable fluctuations in the political order
through rational application of fixed rules and procedures.
When, following the completion of his undergraduate degree,
Maine stayed on at Cambridge, first as a tutor in classics but
soon after as Regius Professor of Civil law, it was in an
environment in which the study of law was not a systematized
university subject but a practical concern for which occasional
attendance at the Inns of Court was central.

Maine had lectured occasionally in London, and in 1854 he
resigned his Cambridge professorship to teach more regularly
at the Inns of Court. He was already beginning to demonstrate,
in his teaching and his early writings, that he was opposed to
the dominant legal ideology of the day, the ahistorical and
utilitarian theories of Jeremy Bentham and John Austin. Bentham argued that the greatest good would accrue to the
greatest number if legislative reforms were fashioned with this
end, rather than the preservation of tradition, constantly in
sight, while Austin furthered his master's ideas by claiming
that law emanated from the command of a territorial sovereign
and it was the jurist's task to examine these positive laws and
give them scientific application. By contrast, Maine told his
students that the implications of legal reform and judicial

decisions could only be appreciated in the light of the law's historical development and that the development of any one system of law was linked to that of others in a series of evolutionary stages. Maine had, moreover, signaled in his earliest journalistic pieces that he believed that progress from one stage to another was marked by the greater freedom of the individual to form his own contractual ties, and that the political environment most conducive to such development was one in which an aristocratic elite would ensure that neither the will of a sovereign nor that of the masses could limit such contractual possibilities. When, therefore, in 1861 Maine published *Ancient Law,* he sought to demonstrate to the legal profession that one cannot understand how law affects society without considering its historical dimensions and to educate the general reader to an awareness of the law as an ingredient in the course of human progress.

Maine begins *Ancient Law* by drawing an analogy from the field of geology. "The early forms of jural conceptions . . . are to the jurist," says Maine, "what the primary crusts of the earth are to the geologist. They contain, potentially, all the forms in which law has subsequently exhibited itself." Yet as one excavates through the different ages of the law, what one finds are not immutable precepts but changing institutions and beliefs. At the earliest stage the idea of law, says Maine, is not that of a command, nor even yet of something that has achieved sufficient regularity properly to be called a custom, but isolated assessments of fact that have no clear order. Only in a later stage, when monarchies become hereditary and aristocrats usurp the office of heroic kings, does custom become fixed by particular elites who can identify isolated practices as possessing an enduring heritage. These customs, in turn, may become embodied in codes whose conceptual underpinnings become subject to elaboration by a process of analogic extension. It is at this point that societies begin to diverge in a most crucial way. In societies that remain stationary, "instead of the civilisation expanding the law, the law has limited civilisation." But, for progressive societies, extension of the law comes about through the use of legal fictions, the amelioration of rigidified rules by the use of ideas of equity, and by the overt process of legislation. Each has its unintended consequences, for each creates "a new language and a new train of thought" which may run contrary to the existing system. In Rome, the archetype of an ancient system of law, legal fictions expanded innovative commercial relations, equity leveled social irregularities, and the legislative acts of the Praetor bureaucratized the monarchy. Thus, Maine argues, it is not necessary to rely on philosophical speculation about how, as a matter of natural law, humanity developed the rules by which it lives, for a careful examination of history can show the actual stages through which this progression has occurred.

Although he never indicates what, if any, universal forces prompt the shift from one stage of legal development to another, Maine does suggest that such change occurs very slowly because human nature, being constant, resists alteration in moral and social beliefs, and because social attachments, being of long duration, are often strengthened by a number of political and economic institutions. Natural law scholars, Rousseauian romanticists, and utilitarian reformers see humanity as comprised of free individuals who have been forced to give up their total freedom as society itself is born and develops. Maine, however, argued that the course of human history, as revealed by comparative legal studies, is one in which the collectivity came first and the gradual freeing of the individual came later. Indeed, so much was the collectivity the basic unit of society that an individual's identity, position, and property were wholly subsumed in his status as a member of the group. Far from being a collection of individuals, primitive society was, says Maine, composed of a number of families each of which operated like a corporation inasmuch as its organization and resources perdured irrespective of the movement or death of any of its members. Over the course of time, particularly as the result of elite domination of the legal order, opportunities were afforded individuals to transmit their property and arrange their economic ties on a personal, contractual basis rather than as representatives of a corporate group. And it is this process, this shift from collective to individual legal capabilities, that Maine articulated in his most famous general proposition: "the movement of the progressive societies has hitherto been a movement from Status to Contract." In order to support this proposition and to show how this shift implies changes in the moral, cultural, and political domains of "progressive societies," Maine turns his attention to the laws affecting inheritance, property, contracts, and crime.

In primitive and archaic societies, Maine says, it was not possible to transmit property individually because one's goods belonged to the group as a whole. Rather, what was passed was one's social position. Thus intestate succession, which prescribes the socially defined person to whom each share in the patrimony will pass, is older than testamentary succession, which could only come about as individuals were no longer identified solely in terms of family roles. Again, Maine uses this example to suggest that, causality aside, such a change could not have occurred just because it possessed some utilitarian value or rational merit; it could only have occurred if people's moral and ideological beliefs had, for whatever reasons, changed so that individuals could freely transmit property without society being harmed. The same analysis is applied by Maine to the history of property law. For property, he says, was originally based on the control of common resources by the patriarchal family, and only the extension of individual powers through the application of legal change could bring property within the control of freely contracting persons. At each point, then, it is contract that is crucial, and Maine further exemplifies this process by tracing how, in the context of Roman law, the formalism of direct exchange gave way to the true contract, as promises became linked to the moral duty to honor a commitment rather than remaining an impersonal duty to adhere to the strict formalities of ritualized exchange.

Thus, in each instance of substantive legal change, Maine tries to show how a host of social and ideational features cohere in a single process. He argues, for example, not just that contract changed relationships but that, in the Roman case, once contract developed the terms it engendered became those through which discussions of moral and political life came to be recast. For Maine, history revealed the actual course of legal development as well as the stages through which societies must pass if progress is to occur. But, as much as he suggested a certain uniformity of progress, he was no less concerned to show that ideas, institutions, and social relations reciprocally influence one another and that it is these systemic ties, rather than inevitable lines of development, that a study of legal history can reveal to the would-be reformer or logic-oriented jurist.

The central themes of *Ancient Law* have occasioned considerable discussion as well as a certain amount of misunderstanding. Perhaps the most contested aspect of the book is its evolutionary orientation. It is true that *Ancient Law* appeared just one year after Darwin's *Origin of Species* and that the same publisher issued both books, but there is no indication that Maine was actually influenced by Darwin's work. Indeed, Maine's work has properly been characterized as only mildly evolutionary: he formulated a distinct set of stages and processes by which legal development occurs, but he did not articulate either an appreciation of the variation of features in a given population or a belief in the manifest superiority of all later forms over earlier ones. In this regard he was very much a man of his time: he saw human societies as evincing different stages in a universal process but, as he noted in his Rede Lecture at Cambridge in 1875, he also believed that "the new does not wholly consist of positive additions to the old; much of it is merely the old very slightly modified, very slightly displaced, and very superficially recombined." Even in his dictum about status and contract he is careful to say that the progression from the former to the latter has only characterized events "*hitherto*" the present day. Thus, as much as Maine supported the views of the Whig party, particularly in its policies toward India, he did not always agree with the Whig view of what constituted progress. And although his antipathy to popular democracy and nostalgia for aristocratic rule became more evident in his later publications, Maine used evolutionary ideas not solely to criticize the political positions of his day but to undercut the prevailing view that legal systems are mainly the result of the sovereign's command or the dictates of natural law.

Indeed, the political implications of Maine's studies are vital to an understanding of his work. For, as much as Maine was concerned with the history of law, he was no less bent on showing that sovereign power is not the key determinant of progress at all stages. Custom, morality, and innate human inertia play equally important roles, and, even if Maine never specifies the precise forces at work in legal and political change, his emphasis on corporate groups, individual contract, and the role of progressive elites went a long way toward rescuing law from its perceived role as simply the expression of the power of the sovereign.

Maine's use of comparative materials, while distinguishing his work from the narrow concerns of British writers with their own common law tradition, has, like his use of evolutionary ideas, found both supporters and detractors. Some of his arguments about the history of property, further elaborated in *Village Communities in the East and West*, have been undermined by more recent scholarship, which has demonstrated that landholding arrangements are often more diverse in other societies than Maine had represented them. Some anthropologists, notably Max Gluckman in his *Ideas in Barotse Jurisprudence*, have, however, offered support for Maine's thesis that landholding is indistinguishable from personal status in many pre-industrial societies and that succession is not to particular goods but to a social role that affects control over those goods. And, although Maine said little more of religion that that it was inextricably bound to the force of law in archaic societies and took on broader aspects of morality only as societies progressed, he did suggest the need to consider the relation of law, political structure, and religion to one another at a time when E. B. Tylor was just beginning to formulate his ideas and James G. Frazer was still a young student.

Ancient Law was an instant success, and the impact of the book was as significant to the course of Maine's own subsequent activities as it has been on the practical and scholarly work of its many readers. Maine had long shown an interest in the law of India and in British policies on the subcontinent, and the success of his book, with its frequent references to Hindu law, won him an appointment in 1862 as the Legal Member of the governor-general's Council of India. During his seven years in India, Maine sought to increase the scope of contractual freedom afforded individual Indians since freedom from familial constraint would, he felt, contribute most to India's overall progress. His efforts to establish native small claims courts, to restrict the imposition of European terms on contracts with native growers, and to allow greater opportunity for individuality through the use of testamentary succession met with uneven success. Yet each effort grew out of the general principles set forth in *Ancient Law*, and each new experience in India confirmed his belief in the importance of political power in transforming societies through law, even as he found himslf increasingly convinced that such change would be slow to come and would depend greatly on local historical circumstances.

In the years following his return to England, where he

taught law at Oxford and Cambridge and served on the Secretary of State's Council of India, Maine continued to develop the themes of *Ancient Law*. In *Village Communities* (1871) he pursued the argument that collective ownership of property, whether under feudalism in the West or territorial aggregates in the East, is an integral step on the uneven way toward the development of private ownership. In *Lectures on the Early History of Institutions* (1875), he argued that power increasingly cumulates in the center but that the survival of governmental forms, in parts of Europe and India, in which the legislator lacks the power to bring about reform simply by his command proves that legal and political change often depend on social and cultural practice. In *Dissertations on Early Law and Custom* (1883), he argued that the matriarchal societies posited by L. H. Morgan and J. F. McLennan as the original forms of human organization probably developed after patriarchal systems, and that, in any event, his own concern was not with the "absolute origin of human society" or some predetermined future but with the actual design of legal development. And in *Popular Government* (1885), he asserted that popular democracy constitutes a new form of despotism in which a legislature not led by an educated elite interferes with social progress by imposing limitations on the freedom of contract of the individual. When he died in 1888, Maine had, therefore, completed a body of work that powerfully asserted a number of historical generalizations and demonstrated the usefulness of comparative analysis. The implications of that work have continued to have their effects in a number of different domains.

Maine had, for example, argued that collective property-holding preceded individual possession and that the ties that groups of men formed in relation to such property were deeply intertwined with their moral and religious lives. The free proprietor may have been the embodiment of the progressive ethic, but Maine saw this not as the expression of a natural law principle but of an historical process. By thus contextualizing collective property Maine's work provided an intellectual foundation for a major scholarly and political debate about the role of collective landholding in nineteenth-century Italy. As Paolo Grossi shows in *An Alternative to Private Property,* Maine's ideas formed the basis for the argument that private property was actually an undesirable aspect of a system of social relations in which dominant control over goods proceeds from an ethic that shows no respect for the positive fulfillment of obligations to others. It was, therefore, in terms set down by Maine that the discussion by Italian politicians and academics proceeded, and it was to a degree as a result of his work that legislation was passed that ensured partial recognition of collective landholding in post-unification Italy.

In the fields of anthropology and law the impact of Maine's work has been no less diverse. In legal studies the evolutionary approach embodied in Maine's writings acted as a major stimulus to the work of Oliver Wendell Holmes and Roscoe Pound, while his early attack on legal positivism influenced the studies of such diverse scholars as George Chapman Gray, Arthur Corbin, and James Henry Wigmore. Similarly, in anthropology, Maine's work directed the attention of later scholars to the importance of studying kinship, the need to consider the relation of legal formalism to its religious base, and the value of considering the impact of collective identity on individual responsibility. If the precise information he possessed about Roman law or primitive social arrangements has been superceded, in many instances, by more rigorous studies, it remains strikingly true that the terms of discourse first set down in *Ancient Law* and many of the general statements contained therein continue to vitalize current debate.

Each new generation of readers thus brings to *Ancient Law* its own concerns. If universal schemes of legal development or a concentration on historicist observation appeal less to modern readers than to their predecessors, other issues may now compete for our attention. Maine's emphasis on the relation of legal institutions to the ideas of a given society led him to suggest that, as the language by which social and ethical issues are discussed comes to be captured by those who codify and create laws, philosophical and social thought take on a shape distinctive to that mode of discourse. Contemporary readers might, therefore, be stimulated to rethink the role of law in particular historical situations, concentrating not on institutional change alone but on the systemic repercussions that ensue when a broad range of cultural issues come to be articulated in the language of the law. Similarly, Maine's idea that western social life has been characterized by a shift from status to contract raises intriguing questions about the repercussions for ideological and political development if social welfare laws create status-like entitlements in a society in which the concept of contract has come to prevail. And in an age when many find problematic the entire question of objective analysis in history, ethnography, and law, the work of Sir

Henry Maine forms a fascinating case study in the role that an investigator's own political and social background plays in the formation of scholarly ideas.

In a letter composed several years after the book's publication, an American reader tells how he experienced a sense of "intellectual ecstasy" as he read through *Ancient Law* on the New Year's day of 1864. Modern readers may not agree with the writer's sentiment that "no novel that I ever read enchained me more. . . . It has suggested to me many new and startling views of social progress." But we may find, as did that earlier letter-writer, that Sir Henry Maine's *Ancient Law* can still provoke new ideas simply because it "suggests far more than it says. Almost every proposition in it may be made the foundation of a long train of thought."

SELECT BIBLIOGRAPHY

Maine's Writings

"Roman Law and Legal Education," *Cambridge Essays* (1856; reprinted in *Village Communities,* 3rd ed. 1876); *Ancient Law* (1861); *Village Communities in the East and West* (1871); *Lectures on the Early History of Institutions* (1875); "The Effects of Observation of India on Modern European Thought" (The Rede Lecture, reprinted in *Village Communities,* 3rd ed. 1876); *Dissertations on Early Law and Custom* (1883); *Popular Government* (1885); *International Law: The Whewell Lectures* (1888).

Secondary Literature

BIOGRAPHIES: George Feaver, *From Status to Contract: A Biography of Sir Henry Maine, 1822 −1888,* London: Longmans, 1969 (contains a full bibliography of Maine's writings); Sir M. E. Grant Duff, *Sir Henry Maine: A Brief Memoir of His Life with Some of His Indian Speeches and Minutes*, New York: Henry Holt, 1892.

CRITICISM: E. Donald Elliott, "The Evolutionary Tradition in Jurisprudence," *Columbia Law Review*, v. 85 (January 1985), pp. 38−94; Max Gluckman, *Ideas in Barotse Jurisprudence*, New Haven: Yale University Press, 1965; Paolo Grossi, *An Alternative to Private Property: Collective Property in the Juridicial Consciousness of the Nineteenth Century*, Chicago: University of Chicago Press, 1981; E. A. Hoebel, "Maine, Henry Sumner," in *International Encyclopedia of the Social Sciences*, v. 9 (1968), pp. 530−33; Adam Kuper, "Ancestors: Henry Maine and the Constitution of Primitive Society," in *History and Anthropology*, v. 1 (1985), pp. 265−86; Sally Falk Moore, *Law as Process: An Anthropological Approach*, London: Routledge & Kegan Paul, 1978; Sir Frederick Pollock, "Sir Henry Maine and His Work," in his *Oxford Lectures*, London: Macmillan and Co., 1890, pp. 147−68; Robert Redfield, "Maine's *Ancient Law* in the Light of Primitive Societies," *Western Political Quarterly*, v. 3 (1950), pp. 574−89; Peter Stein, *Legal Evolution: The Story of an Idea*, Cambridge: Cambridge University Press, 1980; Stephen G. Utz, "Maine's *Ancient Law* and Legal Theory," *Connecticut Law Review*, v. 16 (1984), pp. 821−52; Alan Watson, *The Evolution of Law*, Baltimore: Johns Hopkins University Press, 1985.

INTRODUCTION

Theodore W. Dwight, LL.D.
Columbia College, New York

———

THE work of Professor Maine on "Ancient Law" is almost the only one in the English language in which general jurisprudence is regarded from the historical point of view. The text books prepared by lawyers both in England and this country, have only aimed to present a view of legal history, so far as it was necessary for practical purposes. The professed treatises on the "History of the English Law," such as those of Reeves and Crabbe, make no claim to philosophical deductions, and while the former is especially accurate and reliable, it is written in a manner altogether dry and uninteresting. Mr. Maine's work is vitalized throughout by the true spirit of philosophy. It is not, however, a philosophy which bases itself on an inspection of the present condition of society. It is founded on facts derived from the most patient and thorough historical investigation. It is to be hope that he, or some other equally competent person, will do that for the English common law, which has already been done in so masterly a manner for " ancient law." It is a remarkable fact that many of the early books of the common law are nearly inaccessible to the student. Some of them are in manuscript, hidden away in legal libraries. Those which are printed are composed in a language now obsolete, and with abbreviations which the general scholar does not easily understand. Mr. Wallace, of Philadelphia, in his learned work on the English Reporters has pointed out that the Parliament of England could do no more important work, than to reproduce in an accessible and intelligible form, these antique works which illustrate the early common law. He has truly said, that no philosophical knowledge of the law can ever be had without reference to its origin and history. Has not the time arrived when the materials for a comprehensive view of the common law should be furnished to the scholars of England?

Mr. Maine's work may be said to consist of two parts; the first part, embracing four chapters, contains the philosophy of legal history. No more accurate and profound generalization was probably ever made in jurisprudence, than that which sums up the agencies of legal progress: Fiction, Equity, and Legislation. Its truth strikes the attention of one versed only in the English common law. The first two agencies, especially, accomplished all the

early advancement in that system of jurisprudence
It is through them that public opinion gradually
modified the law. Without them, the English nation
would have remained stationary, or have been
driven to a revolution. Sometimes fiction affects
the law without consciousness on the part of the
judge. Instances of this are given by Mr. Maine.
At other times, the judiciary cover their intent to
alter the law with a thin and transparent veil of
fiction. When the English Parliament had passed
the Statute of Entailments, by which the nobility
expected to secure their landed possessions to their
families, the judges, who did not sympathize with
the legislature, eluded its effect by a fictitious legal
proceeding, called a common recovery. It came to
be a rule that no express words could be used in
creating an entailment, which would prevent its
destruction by this pretended action.

It was an early complaint, that by the growth
of Equity, the " heart of the common law was eaten
out." An excellent illustration of its workings is
derived from the law of trusts. The ancient common law made the validity of a conveyance depend
upon a visible act. The owner gave the intended
purchaser a clod of earth, or other symbol of possession. The ownership thus created admitted of
no qualification. The *visible* owner was to all in
tents and purposes the *actual* proprietor. On this
simple conception, Equity grafted the notion of
' uses." An owner of land could transfer it to an

indifferent person by a visible symbol, and charge the transferree to hold it for the use of another. The "conscience" of the transferree was said to be affected by this transaction, and he was equitably bound to perform the trust imposed upon him. This obligation could only be enforced in a Court of Chancery, the presiding judge being an ecclesiastic. That Court was supposed to proceed upon those principles which affect the moral sense. In all the old law Abridgments, Chancery law is found under the title "Conscience." Chief Justice Fortescue, in the reign of Henry VI., A. D. 1453, derives Equity from the two words *con-scio*, which he explains to mean the case where men have the same knowledge as God possesses, that is, they know His will as nearly as possible by reason. He further remarks that a man may have a claim at common law, when by "conscience" he would be condemned. In another case, occurring in the year 1474, the Chancellor said that a case before him must be determined according to the *law of nature* in the Chancery.*

When this principle came to be fully established, rights were recognized in one court, which were denied in the other. Thus in the case under contemplation, the transferree of the land was said to have the *legal title*, and the owner of the " *use* "

* Year Book, 13 Ed. IV. fol. 9, case 5. This is an earlier recognition of the duty of modern Courts of Equity to follow the Roman 'law of nature " than any noticed by Mr. Maine

an *equitable* interest, and the Court of Chancery substantially protected him in the enjoyment of the rights of ownership. He could, in general, insist on having the legal title made over to him by a formal conveyance. This doctrine was soon seized upon to create other modifications of property. For example, no owner of land could, by the common law, dispose of it by will, except in certain localities where a custom permitting a will prevailed. An evasion of this rule of law could be made through uses. If a man wished to make a will, he transferred his land to another to hold to his use. This person was in conscience bound to hold it for the grantor, who was said to have a "use." He could make a will of the use, and the devisee could then, by a resort to Chancery, compel the grantee to give him a deed of the land. If the grantor died without making a will, the "use" descended to his heir, who could in like manner exact a deed from the grantee. For many years, men were in the constant practice of evading in Equity the legal rule that an owner of land could not make a will. Every intelligent person knew of this double rule, but no steps were taken to remove the anomaly. Even Parliament passed special statutes facilitating the exercise by the king of the power to make a will in accordance with this device.

The time came when the fact was recognized that the difference between law and equity upon this and other points connected with uses was a mere form. The third agency indicated by Mr. Maine then interferes. Legislation corrects the anomaly He who has the use, is declared to be the owner of the land, and a statute is passed conferring the power to make wills.

When the statute of uses is brought before the courts, a narrow construction is adopted. It is decided that certain uses shall not be turned into legal ownership. Chancery seizes upon these rejected uses, and upholds them as trusts, fastening itself on the " conscience " of the legal owner. These trusts had become in certain cases purely formal, when after three centuries, the legislature of New York carries out the principle of the original statute, and declares that by no device shall there be a mere formal trust in land.

This topic might be pursued to an indefinite length, and many similar instances summoned from English legal history. Mr. Maine deserves the cre dit of being the first to give body and form to the principle, which every student of law perceives as soon as it is stated to him.

The second part of his book is equally striking. It contains an account of the origin and progress of leading rules in legal science. In its method, it is in direct antagonism to the loose declamatory style in which many discourse of legal principles. The work throughout has a high and cheerful tone. It maintains the steady progress of mankind in jurisprudence from an age of formalities and cere monies to an era of simplicity and symmetrical levelopment. It asserts the continuity of the human race, and we are permitted to feel nearly every link of the chain which binds the men of our day to the nations of the remotest antiquity.

The chapters on conveyances, wills, and contracts have an especial value, and will serve to dispel many erroneous views concerning transactions which make up a large part of the business of human life.

In the hope of facilitating the use of this book in law schools and colleges, the writer has prepared an abstract of its contents. He only vouches for its general accuracy. The special qualifications and limitations of the principal propositions must, of course, be sought in the body of the work. It is confidently believed that this treatise is worthy of the careful study of all young men who desire to make the law an honorable pursuit, and not a mere trade or calling. It may also be warmly commended to the general scholar, who cannot fail to derive instruction and stimulation from its weighty and earnest words.

I.

THE earliest notion of law is not an enunciation of a principle, but a judgment in a particular case. When pronounced, in the early ages, by a king, it was assumed to be the result of a direct divine

inspiration. Afterward came the notion of a cus
tom which a judgment affirms, or punishes its
breach. In the outset, however, the only authoritative statement of right and wrong is a judicial
sentence rendered after the facts have occurred. It
does not presuppose a law to have been violated,
but is breathed for the first time by a higher power
into the judge's mind at the moment of adjudication.

When aristocracies succeeded to the power of
the kings, they became depositaries and administrators of law, without claiming direct inspiration for
each sentence. They monopolize the knowledge of
law. *Customary* law now exists, which is assumed
to be precisely known to the privileged order or
caste. This is the era of true unwritten law. Before the invention of writing, this was the only
expedient by which there could be an approximation
to an accurate preservation of the customs of a race
or tribe.

Next we arrive at the era of the Codes, of which
the Twelve Tables are best known. Everywhere
law graven on tablets takes the place of usages
announced by the oligarchy. This movement was
not due to any notion of the superiority of codification, but to the fact that writing was a better
depositary of law than the memory of individuals.
The importance of the codes can not be denied.
They afforded protection against the frauds of the
oligarchy and the debasement of the national institutions. A great mark of distinction between the

Romans and the Hindoos consists in the fact that the Romans had a code early in their history, while customs were wholesome, and before that usage which was reasonable had generated that which was unreasonable.

As soon as a code is produced, there is no longer a spontaneous development of law. Hereafter, investigations must be confined to progressive races of men. With these, social necessities and social opinion are always more or less in advance of law. Law is stable; society is progressive. How shall this gulf be narrowed which has a perpetual tendency to re-open?

There are three agencies with which law is brought into harmony with society—Legal Fiction, Equity, and Legislation. Their historic order follows this arrangement. (1) By Legal Fiction is meant an assumption which conceals or affects to conceal the fact that a rule of law has undergone alteration, the letter remaining unchanged, but its operation being modified. This is a rude device absolutely necessary in the early stages of society; but fictions have had their day. (2) The next instrumentality by which law is adapted to social wants is called *Equity*. This is a body of rules existing by the side of the original law, founded on distinct principles, and claiming incidentally to supersede the civil law by virtue of a superior sanctity in its principles. This doctrine of Equity is found in the Roman law, and in the English law under the direction of the

Court of Chancery. It differs on the one hand from fiction, for its interference with the law is open and avowed, and on the other from legislation, for it does not lay claim to authority on the prerogative of any external person or body, but rests only on the special nature of its principles. (3) Next in order is Legislation. This derives its authority from an external body or person. It is not necessarily governed by any principle. The external body may legislate in the wantonness of caprice, or its action may be dictated by some principles of equity. In either case, its binding power depends solely upon its external authority.

In the youth and infancy of a nation it is a rare thing for legislation to be called into action for the general reform of private law. Its development must depend on the first two agencies which have been described.

Having thus stated the difference between these terms, the method in which they act upon positive law may now be noticed. This will be best disclosed by illustrations.

(1) *Fiction.* A striking instance of fiction is found in the case law of England. When a case is about to be decided under the common law, the assumption on the argument is that its decision will call only for the application of principles and distinctions which have long since been allowed. It is assumed that there is a rule of law which will govern the question now litigated, and which may be dis-

covered by the exercise of sufficient skill and knowledge. As soon as the case *has* been decided, a new
train of thought is adopted, and it is admitted that
the decision has modified the law. Though the law
has been changed, men fail to notice that the old
rule has been repealed. Even lawyers convey the
paradoxical proposition that, except by equity and
statute law, nothing has been added to the basis
of common law since it was first constituted. They
maintain that its rules, with some assistance from the
Court of Chancery and Parliament, are co-extensive
with the interests of modern society.

A similar illustration may be derived from the
Roman law. " The Responsa prudentum," or answers
of the learned in the law, consisted of explanations
of authoritative written documents. It was *assumed*
that the written law was binding, but the responses
practically modified and even overruled it. A great
variety of rules was thus supposed to be educed
from the Twelve Tables, which were not in fact to
be found there. They could be announced by any
jurisconsult whose opinions might, if he were distinguished, have a binding force nearly equal to enactments of the legislature. The responses were not
published by their author, but were recorded and
edited by his pupils, and to this fact the world is
indebted for the educational treatises, called Institutes
or Commentaries, which are among the most remarkable features of the Roman system. The distinction
between the " responses " and the " case law " of

England should be noticed. The one consists of expositions by the *bar*, and the other by the *bench*. It might have been expected that such a system would have *popularized* the law. This was not the fact. Weight was only attached to the responses of conspicuous men who were masters of the principles as well as details of jurisprudence. The great development of legal principles at Rome was due to this method of producing law. Under the English system no judge can enunciate a principle until an actual controversy arises to which the rule can be applied; under the Roman theory, there was no limit to the question to which a response might be given, except the skill and ingenuity of the questioner. Every possible phase of a legal-principle could thus be examined, and the result would show the symmetrical product of a single master mind. This method of developing law nearly ceased at the fall of the republic. The Responses were systematized and reduced into compendia. The right to make responses was limited by Augustus to a few jurisconsults. The edict of the Prætor became a source of law, and a great school of jurists, containing such men as Ulpian, Paulus, Gaius, and Papinian, arose, who were authors of treatises rather than of responses.

(2) *Equity*. The theories of Equity obtained an early currency, both in Rome and in England.

(A) *Equity Law of England.* A discussion of
the jurisprudence of the English Court of Chancery
would require a separate treatise. It is complex in
its texture, and derives its materials from heterogeneous sources, such as the canon law, Roman law
and the mixed systems of jurisprudence and morals
constructed by the publicists of the low countries.
It was greatly controlled in its growth by the necessity of conforming itself to the analogies of the
common law, although it claimed in many respects
to override it on the strength of an intrinsic ethical
superiority.

(B) *Equity Law of Rome.*—(*a*) *Its General
Principles.* The Equity of Rome was a much simpler structure and its development can be more
easily traced. The Roman legal system consisted
of two ingredients: one, the law which the people
enacts for itself, called the *civil law*, and the other
that which natural reason appoints for all men, and
which is called the *Law of Nations*, because all
men use it. This latter element is elsewhere called
the Law of Nature, and is said to be the offspring
of natural equity as well as of natural reason.

It was a peculiar feature in Roman history that
the fortunes of the republic were greatly affected
by the presence of foreigners. This fact is partly
attributable to a disposition to seek refuge in a
strong government from the instability of unsettled
society, and partly to the active commercial relations

which were had with Carthage and the interior of Italy. The alien, however, had no share in the purely Roman institutions. He could not make a strictly Roman conveyance nor bring a formal legal action. Controversies involving his interests could not be decided by pure Roman civil law. The Roman lawyers in this difficulty resorted to the expedient of selecting the rules of law common to Rome and to the different Italian communities in which the foreigners were born. This common element was called the *Jus Gentium*, or the law common to all nations. The result was that whenever a particular usage was seen to be practised by a large number of separate races, it was set down as a part of the law common to all nations.

It must not be supposed that the early Roman lawyer had any special respect for this law. It was forced on his attention by a political necessity. He was attached to the civil law with its ceremonies and formalities, and cared no more for the "law of nations" than for the foreigners for whose benefit it was intended. The "law of nations" must not be confounded with international law, or the law *between* nations.

At a later period, the law of nations was considered as the model to which all law ought as nearly as possible to conform. This result was brought about by the Greek theory of a law of nature. Under this theory, nature denoted the physical world regarded as the result of some original element or law. The later sects added the moral to the physical world in the conception of nature. It was not merely the phenomena of human society, but phenomena resolvable into some general and simple laws Greek Philosophers imagined that but for some accident, the human race would have conformed itself to simple rules of conduct, and have lived according to *nature*. This was the end for which man was created; it was the substance of the stoic philosophy. On the subjugation of Greece, this philosophy made the most rapid progress in Roman society. The Roman lawyers were the leading disciples of the new school, who affected the stoic principles of life according to nature. The alliance of the lawyers with the philosophers lasted for centuries. The influence of the stoic philosophy is not to be measured by the specific legal rules which it contributed to jurisprudence, but by the single assumption that the old *jus gentium* was the lost code of nature, and that the equity jurisprudence of the prætor was the restoration of a type from which law had departed. From this moment, the law improved with great rapidity. The simplicity and symmetry associate with the conception of nature were regarded as the characteristics of a good legal system. Ceremonies and useless formalities disappeared, and finally the law assumed its present shape under the superin tendence of Justinian.

The point of contact between the law of nations and the law of nature was equity. Some have derived this term from a Greek word which indicates the principle of equal distribution. We prefer that origin which gives it the sense of *levelling*. The civil law of Rome recognized many arbitrary distinctions between classes of men and property. The neglect of these distinctions was that feature of the law of nature which is depicted in equity. It was at first applied to foreign litigants without ethical meaning, and to the early Romans was without doubt extremely distasteful. When the " law of nature" was fully recognized a different view prevailed. Nature implied symmetrical order, and equity came to have associations with the idea of equal distribution. This may be inferred from the language of Cicero, and it is the first stage of a transmutation of the conception of equity which has been carried on by nearly every ethical system of later times.

b. The formal instrumentality by which the law of nations and of nature was incorporated into the Roman law.

After the expulsion of the Tarquins, the supreme judicial office devolved on the prætor. He had an undefined supremacy over law and legislation which had always attached to ancient sovereigns. This indefinite portion of his functions was the more important on account of the multitude of persons who were not indigenous Romans, and who would have been without remedies, had not the prætor under-taken to decide upon their rights.   It was a rule at Rome. as a matter of precaution, that every magis-trate having indefinite powers should publish, on commencing his year of office, an edict or proclama-tion in which he declared the manner in which his department would be administered. The prætor was governed by this rule.   It soon became the practice for each prætor to publish his predecessor's edict, with such modifications as he deemed neces-sary. The proclamation obtained the name of the *edictum perpetuum,* or the *continuous* or *unbroken* edict.   The practice of increasing the edict, ceased in the reign of the Emperor Hadrian, under the magistracy of Salvius Julianus, and the perpetual edict was then called the edict of Julianus.

It might seem at first thought that there was no limit by which this extensive power was con-fined, and that the action of the prætor might be-come dangerous to social order.   Practically, his power was restrained by the ideas and views of the legal profession to which he belonged.   At first his intervention was dictated by simple concern for the safety of the State.   Afterward, he used the "re-sponses" as a means of applying fundamental prin-ciples. Still subsequently, he acted under the influ-ence of Greek philosophical theories which marked out the line of his progress.

After the edict of Julianus, the equity jurispru

dence of Rome was developed by the labors cf a succession of great lawyers who flourished between the reign of Hadrian and that of Alexander Severus. Their treatises chiefly took the form of commentaries on the edict. The same tribunal administered law and equity. As soon as an equitable rule was evolved, the prætor applied it by the side of the old rule, which was substantially repealed without any act of the legislature. Although there was no complete fusion of law and equity, yet the latter supplied the jurist with all his materials for generalization, with all his methods of interpretation, with his elucidations of first principles, and with the great mass of limiting rules which seriously control the application of every legislative act.

In the reign of Alexander Severus, the power of growth in Roman equity was exhausted. Then follow imperial constitutions, and finally the attempts to codify the unwieldy mass of Roman jurisprudence, the most celebrated of which is the Corpus Juris of Justinian.

(c). *Features common to English and Roman equity.* These systems of jurisprudence had two features in common. First, each of them tended to exactly the same state in which the old common law was when equity first interfered with it. When the moral principles adopted by courts of equity have been carried out to their legitimate consequences, the system becomes rigid and unexpansive, and as liable to fall behind moral rules as a strict legal code. This happened at Rome, in the reign of Alexander Severus. The same period arrived in England during the chancellorship of Lord Eldon, whose task it was to explain and harmonize the jurisprudence of his court. Its morality is not the morality of our own day, but of past centuries. Further improvement is not to be had by this agency, but by legislation. Second : in each of these systems there was a false assumption upon which the claim of the superiority of the equitable rule was founded. The moral progress made was explained as the recovery of a lost perfection, and as a return to a state from which the race had lapsed. The Roman lawyers accounted for the improvement in their jurisprudence by the Greek doctrine of a natural society. In England, the claim of equity to override the common law, was explained by a supposed paternal authority vested in the king, enabling him to superintend the administration of justice. Another mode of expressing the same idea was that equity flowed from the king's conscience. The true reason was overlooked, that there was an improvement in the moral standard of the community.

(*d*). *Modern History of the Law of Nature* The Roman theory of the law of nature, though deficient in philosophical precision, was very important to mankind. There are two dangers to which law and society are liable in their infancy. One of them is that law may be too rapidly developed. This occurred with the codes of the Greek com munities. If the Romans were in danger of it, they had adequate protection in their theory of natural law. It kept before the mental vision a type of perfect law, to which there might be an indefinite approximation. This system was not entirely the product of imagination, but it was supposed to underlie existing law. Unlike the modern notion of a law of nature, its functions were remedial, not revolutionary or anarchical.

The other liability to which the infancy of so-ciety is exposed, is the identification of law with religion. The perfection of law has been considered as consisting in an adherence to the plan marked out by the original legislator. The great advantage which the Romans possessed, was that through their theory of natural law they had a distinct object to aim at, like that which Bentham gave to English lawyers, when he announced that the true object of jurisprudence was to secure the general good of the community. It was not from motives of philanthropy, but from a sense of simplicity and symmetry, that the Roman lawyers held up the law of nature as an ideal and perfect law.

The influence of the Roman theory of "natural law" in modern times has been very great. It is the source of most of the special ideas as to law, politics, and society which France during the last hundred years has diffused over the Western world. From various causes, natural law in the eighteenth century had become the common law of France. Its influence would probably have been checked by Montesquieu's "Spirit of the Laws," had not Rousseau appeared. In all his speculations, the central figure is man in a supposed state of nature. It is the theory of the Roman lawyers inverted. The subject of contemplation is not the law of nature, but the state of nature. Though Rousseau's philosophy in its grosser forms has fallen low in general esteem, yet in its disguises it still possesses popularity and power. The doctrines of nature and her law have preserved their energy by allying themselves with political and social tendencies. They enter largely into the ideas which radiate from France over the civilized world. From this source is derived the doctrine of the fundamental equality of human beings. The proposition in the Roman law, that all men are equal, is a legal rule; in modern times, it is a political dogma. In the American Declaration of Independence, the French assumption that "all men are born equal," is joined with the English idea that "all men are born free."

The greatest function of the Law of Nature was discharged in giving birth to International Law and the Law of War. The principal postulates of international law are : first, that there is a determinable law of nature; next, that Natural Law is binding on states. As a corollary from the second proposi-

tion, the several states must be absolutely equal
Third, in reference to acquisition of property, sove
reigns are related to each other like a group of
Roman proprietors. This may be resolved into the
propositions that sovereignty is territorial, and that
sovereigns as *between themselves* are absolute owners
of the state's territory. The doctrine of territorial
sovereignty, by which is meant the view which connects sovereignty with the possession of a limited
portion of the earth's surface, is the product of feudalism. Without this doctrine, Grotius' labors upon
international law would have been in vain. The
existence of an imperial power ruling over the states
of Europe, even in theory, would not have admitted
of the application of the principles of natural law
It was essential that they should be insulated and
independent of each other in order that they might
be equal. Had there been a common superior over
them, the notion of positive law would have been
introduced and the natural law excluded.

((3) *Legislation.* The Statute Law of Rome was
scanty during the republic, but voluminous under
the empire. In the youth of a nation, the interference of the legislative body is commonly directed
to the removal of some abuse, or the decision of
some quarrel between classes and dynasties. In
this way society was settled after a great civil com-
motion. The true period of statute law does not
begin till the establishment of the empire, and in

the reign of the second emperor considerable approximation had been made to that condition of the law
with which men are familiar at the present day.

II.

The true method of investigating the principles
of ancient law has often been overlooked. That
which has hitherto stood in the place of science has
been for the most part a series of guesses. The
mistake which has been committed is analogous to
the error of one who, in investigating the laws of
the material universe, should commence by contemplating the existing physical world as a whole,
instead of beginning with the particles which are
its simplest ingredients. Our proper course is to
penetrate as far up as we can in the histories of
primitive societies.

There are only three sources of knowledge upon
the rudiments of the social state: (a) accounts by
contemporary observers; (b) records which particular races have preserved concerning their primitive
history; (c) ancient law. An instance of the first
kind is the Germania of Tacitus. The amount of
testimony from the first two sources is exceedingly
small. Contempt, negligence, pride of race, and the
religious sentiment of a newer age, have each in their
turn impaired the value of such accounts as we have.
These suspicions do not attach to ANCIENT LAW

c

Much of this was preserved because it was old, and those who retained it offered no account of it except that it had come down to them from their ancestors. Inquiries may therefore be confined to the effect of evidence derived from comparative jurisprudence.

This evidence establishes that view of the race which is known as the PATRIARCHAL THEORY. This theory is based on the Scriptural history of the Hebrew patriarchs. All known societies were originally organized on this model. The eldest male parent is absolutely supreme in his household. His dominion extends to life and death, and is as unqualified over his children as over his slaves. The flocks and herds of the children are the flocks and herds of the father. These he holds in a representative rather than in a proprietary character.

When society came to be formed, it was not as now a collection of individuals, but an aggregation of families. The unit of an ancient society was the family; of a modern society, the individual. Law is scanty, because it is supplemented by the despotic commands of the heads of households. It is ceremonious, because the transactions to which it pays regard resemble international concerns much more than the quick play of intercourse between individuals. On this simple society, fiction soon began to operate. New comers were incorporated into it by the law of Adoption, which consists in feigning themselves to be of the same stock as the people on which they were engrafted. When this fiction

ceased to operate, these societies became aristocracies, and a new law came into play, viz., *Local Contiguity.*

The leading developments of this organization
will now be indicated.

1. *The life-long Authority of the Father over the
Person and Property of his Descendants.* This authority the Romans called *Patria Potestas*, or as it
may be briefly termed, "the child under power."
There is an important distinction to be noticed
between the relations created by public and by
private law. In reference to the public, the son
"under power" was as free as his father; in all the
relations created by private law, he lived under a
domestic despotism. The progress of civilization as
to this subject is best shown in the Roman law.

The early Roman law adopted the most rigid
form of this doctrine. While in the later period
of the empire, the power over the *person* became
nominal, that over the property was always exercised to the full extent sanctioned by law. The
father could enjoy the whole of the son's acquisitions
and the benefit of his contracts. The first innovation upon this rule took place in the acquisitions of
soldiers on service; afterward, the earnings of persons in the civil employments of the state were
secured to them. Even in the latest days of the
empire, the father was entitled to a life interest in
the acquisitions of his child.

This power of the father imposed upon him a corresponding duty. He was liable for the wrong ful acts of his son while under power. He had a *representative* ownership which was coëxtensive with his liability to provide for all the members of the brotherhood out of a common fund. This was a duty enforced rather by instinct and habit, than by definite sanctions.

The universality of "power" (patria potestas) may be shown by the examination of some other topics of ancient law. Among these, the most prominent is kinship. The Romans regarded kinship as Agnatic or Cognatic. Cognates are those whom we term blood relations, being all such persons as trace their descent from the legitimate marriage of a single pair. Agnates are those blood relations who trace their connection exclusively through males. This distinction will be made clear by the following table:

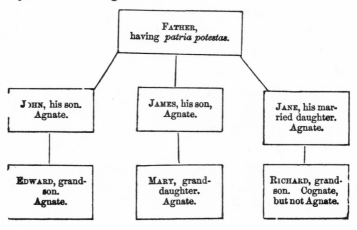

All the children of male Agnates, whether male or female, are themselves Agnates; all the children of female Agnates are Cognates to their mother's father and his other descendants. Under some systems of jurisprudence, as for example the Roman, Agnatic kindred may be introduced into the family by the fiction of Adoption. This arrangement of relationship appears entirely arbitrary. Its true principle is the "power" of the father. Wherever "power" (potestas) begins, relationship begins. The reason why descendants of a female were excluded from Agnatic relationship was, because after marriage her children fell under the power of her husband. The same person could not be under two jurisdictions.*

The doctrine of Agnation has much historical

* The question of Agnatic and Cognatic relationship has recently excited interest in connection with the acceptance by Maximilian, Archduke of Austria, of the position of Emperor of Mexico. A family law imposes on every Archduchess contracting marriage, the obliga tion of signing for herself, or her descendants, an act of renunciation of any pretension to the eventual succession to the Austrian throne, and to certain other rights. A family council resolved to apply the principle of this law to Maximilian, claiming that the acceptance of the foreign throne was analogous in its effect to a marriage by an Archduchess. The Archduke objected on the ground that he was the first Agnate to the Emperor Francis Joseph, and, on his death without a male heir, entitled to the Austrian throne. He urged that while a princess on her marriage loses her quality of Agnate to such an extent, that her heirs are only entitled to the title of Cognates, he still retained, though Emperor of Mexico, his title of Agnate. The matter was compromised by a renunciation for himself and his heirs of all right to the throne of Austria, so long as the new Mexican dynasty shall continue to reign.—*Memorial Diplomatique*, quoted in New York *Times*, April 28 1864.

importance. It can be traced to modern law. It explains the harsh rule of the common law of Eng land, that brothers of the half blood cannot inherit from each other. This doctrine in ancient law was properly confined to children of the same mother by different fathers (uterine brothers). In Eng land, through a want of knowledge of the origin of the rule, it was extended to brothers having the same father, but different mothers (consanguineous brothers). The position of woman in the ancient law is also explained by the patria potestas. The Agnatic bond was not released in her case by the death of her parent. She could never become the head of a family, as her brother might be. When her father died, she came under perpetual guardian ship to her nearest male relatives. This rule of ancient law disappeared from the matured jurispru dence of the Roman Empire.

At this point, we observe a remarkable contrast between ancient and modern law. Under the early system, woman was subordinated to her relatives; under the modern, to her husband. There are in fact three periods of jurisprudence to be noticed: the early Roman law, the later Roman law, and modern systems. Under the early Roman law, marriage could be contracted in three forms, one of which was religious, and the other two, civil. In view of the law, the wife became her husband's *daughter*, and he exercised over her the patria potestas. He could appoint guardians over her whose authority continued after his death. In the later Roman law, a form of marriage was recognized, which left the wife theoretically under the care of guardians whom her parents had appointed, but practically, when that guardianship became obsolete, under no control whatever. In modern law, there is a twofold element. The later Roman jurispru dence has been adopted so far as to emancipate unmarried women from the control of their male relatives; while married women, through the influence of religious sentiment and early notions prevalent among the dominant races from which modern nations have sprung, are governed by the rules of an imperfect civilization. Those systems of law are the most severe upon married women, which borrowed their rules from the canon law, or which came latest in contact with European civilization, as for instance, the Scandinavian.

A clear understanding of the patria potestas may be obtained from the position of married women in the English law. The details upon this topic will be found in a note.*

* A summary of the common law concerning the disabilities of married women, and the duties of their husbands.

I. THE HUSBAND'S RIGHT OVER THE WIFE'S PROPERTY, WHICH MIGHT CONSIST OF REAL ESTATE, LEASES, RIGHTS OF ACTION, OR PERSONAL PROPERTY.

a. As to her real estate, he became life tenant for the joint lives of himself and wife. He was entitled to the profits of the land, and they could be seized by his creditors. If any children of the marriage were born alive during the wife's life, he had an estate for his own

The doctrine of patria potestas is still further
illustrated by the law of guardianship concerning

life, though he outlived his wife. He was then called tenant by the
courtesy of England.

b. Her leases belonged to him absolutely in case he survived his
wife. If she survived, they belonged to her. Any disposition of them
by him during marriage, would defeat her right of survivorship.

c. Her rights of action became his absolutely, if he reduced them
to possession while the wife was living. By this was meant a receipt
of their amount, either by payment or collection through a lawsuit,
or by sale to a purchaser for valuable consideration. They could
even be taken by his creditors for the payment of debts, although in
that case, if not reduced to possession, they would revert to the wife,
if she survived her husband. If the wife died before the claims were
collected, the husband received them as *administrator*, in which case,
after payment of her debts, the surplus belonged to him absolutely.
If the wife survived, the uncollected claims belonged to her.

d. Her personal property of a tangible nature vested in the husband absolutely at the moment of marriage.

II. The Wife's Capacity to Contract.

The wife had no power to make a contract. Her legal personality
was merged in that of her husband. She could not deal with her
husband, for husband and wife were in law one person. If she dealt
with third parties, the transaction could only be supported on the
ground that she was her husband's agent. Her earnings belonged
to him, and he could collect them by action. In one or two cases, the
wife might act as a single woman. These were where her husband
was an alien, always living abroad, or he had been banished, or
had abjured the realm.

III. Other Disabilities.

A wife could not convey her land except by the fictitious judicial
proceedings called fine and recovery. She could not make a will of her
land, for she was excepted from the Statute of Wills. Nor could she
make a testament of personal property, except by the permission of
her husband. She could not be a witness against or for her husband,
either in a civil or criminal case. Her domicile followed that of the
husband. The husband, being entitled to her services, could bring
actions against one who harbored the wife, or who wrongfully inflicted
an injury upon her person. There were in some instances two
actions: one by the husband and wife for the personal injury done
to the wife, and one by the husband alone for the injury occasioned

male orphans. A person whose wardship had terminated by the death of his father or grandfather was placed at his fifteenth year in the full enjoyment of personal and proprietary independence. This rule does not depend upon any consideration of public convenience, but upon the ground that the child was supposed to be capable of becoming a parent himself. Guardianship ended with puberty. This was soon found to be an inconvenient rule, and a statute was passed creating a new kind of

by the loss of service. The entire pecuniary results of these actions belonged to him.

IV. DUTIES OF THE HUSBAND.

a. He was under a duty to maintain his wife in accordance with her rank and station. She became in such a case, presumptively, the husband's agent; and under proper circumstances, she could incur bills with tradesmen, which could be collected from the husband.

b. He was bound to pay her debts contracted before marriage This duty resulted from the fact that her legal personality was merged in his. It followed, that he must be sued with her, while both lived. He would then be compelled to pay her debts, though he had received nothing from her. If she died before an action were brought, he could only be sued as administrator, and be liable to the extent of the assets which he received in that character from her estate.

c. He was liable for the wife's wrongs committed after marriage. If she was guilty of slander or libel, the damages could be collected from him by action. He might be sent to jail if the judgment was not paid.

d. He was presumptively responsible for her felonious acts, and could be indicted for crimes of that grade committed by the wife in his presence. He could, however, introduce evidence to rebut the presumption.

These principles were affected by the rules adopted in Courts of Equity, which are not within the view of this note. They have been largely modified in the several States of this country by legislation. They are the law of most of the United States, except so far as they have been changed by statute.

guardian (Curator) to protect the infant against intellectual incapacity.

Finally, the slave was also included in the family This was well for him, as he was not degraded to the footing of inanimate property. He had in the last resort a capacity for inheritance. Those states which have adopted the rules of the Roman law have left the slave not so intolerably wretched as those which have adopted a different theory.

The movement of the progressive societies has been, in one respect, uniform. There has been a gradual dissolution of family dependency, and the growth of individual obligation has taken its place. The tie between man and man which replaces those rights and duties which have their origin in the family is contract. It was the tendency of former law to fix the condition or "status" of persons by positive rules; in modern times, the condition of persons is commonly the immediate or remote result of agreement. The movement has been from *status* to *contract*.

2. *Testamentary Succession.* The conception of a will in modern times is taken from Roman testamentary jurisprudence. It came into the English law through the medium of the church. Wills of personal property were administered in the ecclesiastical courts, which applied, though in an imperfect manner, the principles of Roman jurisprudence The English law of testamentary succession is thus

a modified form of the rules under which Roman inheritances were administered.

At this point, one may see the advantages of a historical treatment of the subject. Men who should simply reason upon a will would argue that it would take effect at death only; that it would be secret; and revocable during the testator's life. None of these characteristics originally belonged to a will. It was not secret, nor revocable, and took effect during the testator's life.

Many jurists have asserted that the right to make a will is conferred by the law of nature. They would imply either that the right is universal or that nations are prompted to it by an original instinct or impulse. On the contrary, experience teaches us that it is not universal, and history discloses to us that in all the early societies, the condition of jurisprudence in which testamentary privileges are not allowed precedes that in which they are permitted to supersede the rights of kindred by blood.

This subject can only be understood by glancing at the doctrine of *Universal Succession*. By "universal succession" is meant the case where one is invested with the legal character of another, subject to all his liabilities and entitled to all his rights. He becomes the representative of the person to whom he succeeds. Under the Roman law, at the death of a person, his heir became by inheritance his "universal successor." We cannot perhaps easily comprehend this notion, for we have no instances in modern law of this kind of succession. Even in a bankruptcy, the assignee who takes all the debtor's assets, does not assume his responsibilities. If he did, we would have the notion of a "universal succession."

Now, the theory of a will in ancient law was to put the devisee in the position of a universal successor. He was the representative of the testator as completely as the heir was of an intestate. Though the testator had ceased to live, his legal personality continued in his successor. An executor in our law only partially resembles such a successor, for he only takes the personal property, and is responsible only to the extent of the assets which he receives.

What, then, is the true theory of an ancient succession? Recur for a moment to the idea of the *family*. It was a corporation, with the patriarch at its head. He was the representative of its rights and obligations. When he died, the family—the corporation—did not die. Another representative took his position with all the corporate rights and duties. This feature of the law of family was ultimately transferred to the individual, and when society was resolved into its component parts, it continued to be the rule that on the death of an individual, his heirs or testamentary successors took his own legal position. We may state the position of the testator with sufficient accuracy if we describe him as a corporation sole, as a king, who never dies is a corporation sole.

When a Roman citizen died without a will, his heirs did not merely represent him. They continued his civil existence. This theory of universal succession is peculiar to Roman jurisprudence.

A will at the outset was a proceeding by which the devolution of a family was regulated. It was a mode of declaring the person who was to have the chieftainship in succession to the testator. This view explains the connection between wills and the *sacra* or family rites. No testament was allowed to distribute an inheritance without a strict apportionment of the expenses of these religious ceremonies among the co-heirs. Doubtless, Intestate Inheritance was more ancient than Testamentary Succession, and testaments were at first only allowed to take effect on failure of the persons entitled by blood relationship. In fact, the only methods of continuing a family where there was no succession of kindred, was either a will or adoption. In the Hindoo law the place filled by wills is occupied by Adoptions. To the Romans belongs the invention of a will.

We are thus enabled to explain the primitive Roman will, which was executed in the Comitia Curiata, or Parliament of Patricians, when assembled for private business. The key to this proceeding is to be sought in the ancient law of intestate succession. The order of descent was as follows: *first*,

the direct descendants who had not been emancipa,
ted; *second*, the nearest Agnate, the nearest person
under the same power (patria potestas) as the deceased; *third*, on the failure of these, the inheritance
devolved on the *gentiles* or the collective members
of the dead man's *gens* or House. This House was
composed of all the Roman Patricians who bore the
same name, and who were supposed to be descended
from a common ancestor. As the Parliament consisted of a representation of these very Houses, the
object of bringing the will before it was to determine
whether the testator had any *gentiles* whose claims
were affected by his will. It might be rejected or
allowed, according as the circumstances of the case
might demand.

The modern will was derived from a transaction
which was a conveyance *inter vivos*. It was a complete and irrevocable alienation of the testator's
family and substance to the person intended to be
his heir. It was derived from the *Mancipium* or
Mancipation. This transaction required the presence
of a vendor and vendee as well as five witnesses,
together with a person called a *libripens*, who held
a pair of scales to weigh the money employed in
the proceeding. The testator assumed the place of
a vendor, and the intended successor pretended to
strike the scales with a piece of money. By this
proceeding he became, in contemplation of law, the
purchaser of all the testator's property and privi
leges, and assumed all his obligations. This trans-

action vested the property in the heir immediately, even though the testator survived; and the latter could only continue to govern his household by the sufferance of the former. It was the abdication of the corporator in favor of his successor. When the Twelve Tables were established, the testator could not give any legacies which would bind the "uni versal successor." The doctrine finally came into vogue that he must take the inheritance subject to any burdens imposed upon it by the testator, which might be created, as legacies, either orally or in writing.

In the course of jurisprudence, the Prætors or judges introduced another kind of will depending on Equity. The requirements of the Mancipatory Will were observed so far as they furnished security against fraud. Seven witnesses were present; the will was recited, and each of the witnesses affixed his seal to the outside. This kind of will did not confer the legal title to the inheritance. It gave the "successor" an equitable right to the property, which, after a year of undisturbed possession, by force of a principle known as prescription (usucapion), ripened into a legal right to the property.

The Mancipatory Will was not displaced by the will of the Prætor. At the time of the Empire, an indifferent person was made the "purchaser" of the testator's rights, who was called the *emptor familiæ*. The person who was to receive the actual benefit was named by the testator. Wills thus became secret

A will then consisted of two parts: the conveyance and a publication. By the "publication" the testa tor declared his intentions either orally or in writing. The conveyance having now degenerated into a mere form, the intention was regarded as the principal feature in the transaction, and wills became revocable.

At the time of Justinian, a will was introduced into the Eastern Empire, which combined the two already described, but it was employed in that empire only, and the mancipatory testament, with all 'ts forms of conveyance, continued to be used in Western Europe, far down into the middle ages.

3. *Differences between Ancient and Modern Succession.*—There are some differences between ancient and modern ideas on this subject, which should be noticed. Though the text of the Twelve Tables allows the utmost liberty of testation, yet a will does not seem to have been regarded by the Romans as a means of disinheriting a family. The principal value of the power of testation was deemed to be the assistance it gave in making provision for a family, and in dividing the property more fairly than would have been done by the law of intestate succession. There was a strange dread of intestacy among the Romans. It is difficult to account for this sentiment at first thought. A close examination will reveal its origin. The Roman law consisted of two parts: the civil law, and the equity law By

the civil law, only three classes of persons were
called to the succession—unemancipated children,
the nearest class of Agnatic kindred, or members
of the *gens* or family to which the intestate belonged. The emancipated sons had no share in the
inheritance. So if a man died childless, it might
happen that all his property would devolve on a
class of persons with whom he had no connection,
except the fiction which assumed that all members
of a *gens* or class had descended from a common
ancestor. There was thus a conflict between natural affection and legal theories, and men felt an
enthusiasm for an institution which permitted them
to escape from the thraldom of legal rules, and to
give their property to the objects of their love.

The Prætor by his equity law ultimately permitted some persons to succeed who were not included in the civil law, but the sentiment which had
caused a will to be so much regarded in the mind
of a Roman outlived the necessity which had called
it forth.

The opposite view, which values a will because
it enables the testator to divert his property from
his family, or to distribute it among his relations in
such form or proportions as he may desire, is of
modern origin. It can be unhesitatingly traced to
the influence of Primogeniture. When the law had
established that all the land should pass to one of
the heirs, to the exclusion of the rest, it was easy to
reach the result that the excluded persons had no

D

claim upon the other items of property. Primo
geniture itself is modern. There is not the faintest
trace of it among the Romans, or other ancient na
tions. Among the Hindoos, when a son is born, he
acquires a vested right in his father's property,
which cannot be sold without a recognition of his
joint ownership. It may even be divided during the
father's life, between him and his children. Similar
principles prevailed among the ancient Romans. The
history of primogeniture thus becomes exceedingly
obscure.

The origin of primogeniture must be sought in
the beneficiary gifts of the barbarian chieftains who
invaded the Roman Empire. Similar gifts were made
on a great scale by Charlemagne, and were grants
of Roman provincial land to be holden by the
beneficiary on condition of military service. Originally held at the pleasure of the grantor, the gran-
tees ultimately succeeded in causing them to become
hereditary. They sometimes descended to the
eldest son, and in other cases a different rule prevailed. The method of descent depended upon
agreement. Similar phenomena occur when the
feudal law impressed itself on all estates of land.
Primogeniture once admitted as to some estates, was
seen to possess some marked advantages, and spread
with great rapidity over Europe, largely through
the instrumentality of family settlements.

The question recurs, why should primogeniture
diffuse itself so rapidly? Doubtless it had an his-

toric origin in some ancient theories based on the idea that, whenever political power or public office passes by succession, it follows the rule of primogeniture. Proofs of this are found in the Hindoo law. It spread rapidly, because European society had retrograded. Civil society having no coherence men threw themselves on a patriarchal institution older than existing organizations. It was a source of strength to hold the entire property together for the use of the family. Power was concentrated in a single hand. After a time the notion that the land was held for the behoof of the whole family wore away. The refined idea that uncontrolled power over property is equivalent to ownership came in contact with the patriarchal theory, and the eldest son became legal proprietor of the inheritance. The younger brother ceased to participate in the property of his kinsman, and became the priest, soldier, or dependant.

There are two forms of primogeniture, of which that already described is the normal one. In the Celtic societies, the *eldest line* succeeds. An uncle may inherit rather than an infant son of the last owner. This is principally true in the case of devolution of political power, such as the chieftainship of a clan. This modification was doubtless derived from the fact that it is better to be governed by a grown-up chieftain than by a child, and that a younger brother is much more likely to have reached maturity than any of an elder brother's descendants.

4. *The Early History of Property.*—Historica▴
investigations lead us to depart from the idea
shadowed forth in Roman jurisprudence and adopted
by Blackstone and others, that the origin of property is to be traced to occupancy. This notion i
found in the later Roman law, and is the product of
a refined jurisprudence and of a settled condition
of the laws. It does not arise until the rights of
property have gained a sanction from long practical
inviolability, and is occasioned by the presumption
that everything ought to have an owner. This
view is directly contradicted by history. The social
compact, which admits occupancy, is made by *individuals.* Ancient law, however, knows nothing of
individuals. It is concerned only with families and
groups of beings. This notion of occupancy as a
natural right has had a powerful influence on
modern law. From it, some of the great rules of
international law have been derived, such as the right
of capture in war, and the claim to new countries
by discovery. As an account of the origin of property it possesses no historical value.

We cannot look for the germ of the right of
property in the Roman law. We must go to an
older system, and inspect the customs of the Hindoos. The village community is there an organized
patriarchal society and an assemblage of co-proprietors. Co-ownership by the family was the original
law of property. At the present time, co-ownership is
regarded as the exceptional condition. In its simplest

form, the "community" was a body of kindred
holding a domain in common. It was, however,
more than a brotherhood of relatives. It is an
organized society, with a common fund and complete
machinery for internal government.

More complicated forms also appear. Men of
foreign extraction are admitted, and the purchaser
of a share may become a member of the brotherhood. The fiction is still preserved that all these
persons had a common parentage. If a family becomes extinct, its share returns to the common stock.
We have here a reproduction of the Roman gens or
clan. Similar inferences are derived from recent
researches into Russian villages which closely resemble ancient types.

From these various communities we may get
some conception of the manner in which the right
of individual property grew up. It was chiefly
formed by the gradual disentanglement of the sep
arate rights of individuals from the blended rights
of a community. It would appear that ownership
followed the law which has already been noticed
in respect to the family. As the family became dis-
integrated, ownership became several as well as
joint.

The difficulties in the way of the transfer of
property in ancient times were very great. Conveyances, being transactions between organized companies of men rather than individuals, were in a high
degree ceremonious, requiring many symbolical acts

and a great number of witnesses. Not an item of this ceremony could be safely omitted, not a gesture, not a syllable, not a witness. If there were an omission, the conveyance was void.

The change gradually produced was due to a classification of property. One kind of property was considered of more dignity than another, and demanded more form. The transfer of the other class of objects could be made more simply. After a time the superior convenience of the simple rules leads to their extension to more dignified objects, and the ceremonious forms become obsolete. The classification of objects was often quite arbitrary. It is in vain to attempt to refer it to any philosophical principle. It must simply be viewed historically. The most probable explanation is that those articles were especially honored which were first known to each community. Other articles were placed on a lower standing, because the knowledge of their value did not exist until after the classification was made. The Romans in this spirit divided all property into *res mancipi* and *res nec mancipi*, or, in other words, property which could only be sold by the ceremony called " Mancipation " and property which could be transferred without that form. [This is much the same as if we should classify all property into that which can be sold by deed, and that which can be transferred without a deed.] The *res mancipi* were Italian lands, slaves, and beasts of burden. They are the instruments of agricultural labor, and were never extended. The *res nec mancipi* admitted of indefinite expansion. Such property was transferred by simple delivery. As its items increased in number and importance, the advantages of the simpler forms became apparent, and finally the cumbersome ceremony of mancipation entirely disappeared, and delivery became the one great conveyance of the law.

It is true, however, that there were some positive restrictions on alienation, which could not be overcome in this manner. In some countries, property could only be transferred with the consent of children; in others, alienation was altogether prohibited. In some, inherited property could not be sold, while one's own acquisitions were transferable Very extensive classifications of this kind are found among the ancient Germans. Ultimately there was only one distinction of importance, that between land and chattels, land being considered of more importance than personal objects of enjoyment.

Another mode in which the trammels of ancient law were relaxed, was by prescription. It was a positive rule of the Twelve Tables, that commodities which had been for a very short period in possession of a person became his property. This was a most useful security against a cumbrous system of conveyance. If the act of mancipation had been performed in an irregular manner, after two years of possession, the title became perfect. This was an exceedingly important principle, because it quickly

healed all defects in the title to objects of enjoy
ment.

Still another method was by collusive action.
The plaintiff in a fictitious action, claimed that the
property belonged to him. The defendant, who
was the real owner, made no defence, whereupon
the court adjudged that the property belonged to
the plaintiff. This was quite analogous to the fictitious action in the common law of England, which
was employed to destroy entailments, and known
as a Common Recovery.

The influence of courts of law and their procedure upon property has been very great. We can
only notice the importance of the legal distinction
between property and possession. In the Roman
law, the word possession did not merely convey the
idea of physical detention, but it also included the
intent to insist upon the ownership of the thing
detained. Such possessors were protected by the
Prætor's interdict or injunction, which was ultimately
moulded into a shape fitted to try conflicting claims
to a disputed possession. Ultimately, owners vin-
dicated their claims to property by the same proceeding. In the same way, the old real actions of
the English common law, whose office was to try
the title to land, have been superseded by the possessory action of ejectment, which is now employed
to try not only the question of possession, but also
of ownership.

Courts of Equity have also acted powerfully upon

property, by means of the distinction taken between legal and equitable ownership. The Courts of Equity in England, as well as in Rome, created new rights in various forms. This is a topic too extensive to be followed. It has been alluded to, merely fo. the purpose of showing that the peculiar notions of *feudal* ownership are not to be traced to the equity law of the Roman Prætor. The true origin of feudal ownership is the *emphyteusis*, or perpetual rent of the Roman law. The lessee was there treated as a true proprietor, and could not be disturbed, so long as his rent was paid. The owner of the rent could reënter upon the land, if payment was not made. He also had a right of preëmption in case of sale. There is clear evidence that this system was introduced into Germany, in favor of Roman veterans, who settled upon the land, with an agreement to render garrison duty, as a substitute for the ordinary quitrent. The special services rendered to the feudal lord, which were not common to the Roman quitrent, were doubtless borrowed from the relation of patron and client.

5. *The History of Contract.*—The present condition of society makes it difficult to comprehend the early history of contract. The archaic rules of imperative law have almost everywhere given way to obligations founded on contract. The mind is apt to transfer this condition to ancient times, and even to have misgivings whether morality is advan-

cing. This feeling is often occasioned by some special instances of stupendous fraud. The fact, however, is that social morality has advanced from a rude to a highly refined conception, and we look upon rights growing out of the repose of confidence in others, as entitled to the protection of the penal law.

Jurists have been led into the same error as other thinkers. Even the later Roman lawyers regarded those contracts, which involved no other ingredient than that of assent, as of earlier origin than those which were made ceremoniously, and looked upon them as contracts, known to man in a state of nature. This twofold error was adopted by Rousseau. He regarded the earlier ages as the times of innocence, which had given way to modern degeneracy, and based his speculations on the theory of a "social contract." English lawyers laid hold of this theory, and, careless of its historical relations, insisted on the "social contract" as an historical fact.

This theory has but little influence at the present time, partly because it is not satisfactory, and partly because men have ceased to theorize altogether. Men love to analyze society as it exists, and reach no results from an omission to call in the assistance of history. The patriarchal origin of society leaves but little room for the notion of contract. Under that system, two members of a family cannot contract with each other, nor can the family itself be bound by the engagements of its subordinate members. One family may contract with another, but only in the most ceremonious manner. The duty resulting from one man's reliance on the word of another is one of the slowest conquests of civilization. There is nothing in early times like the interposition of law to compel the performance of a promise. That promise only is sanctioned which is accompanied with a ceremonial; and if the ceremonies be performed, the promise will be carried out, though obtained through duress or deception. This strictness slowly gives way—steps in the ceremony are dispensed with or simplified, some contracts of the most practical importance are separated from the rest, and entered into without cumbrous forms. Ultimately the mental engagement is principally regarded. The Romans distinguished between the two classes of cases, calling the ceremonious engagements, *contracts*, and those in which no ceremonies were necessary, *pacts*. In the progress of jurisprudence, contracts were absorbed by pacts.

The progress of this change it is important to notice. The early term for contracts was *nexum*, and the parties to a contract were said to be connected by a strong bond or chain. The definition of *nexum* is "every transaction with the copper and balance." This is also the definition of a conveyance. We thus have a contract confounded with a conveyance. This view is in entire opposition to modern notions. We carefully distinguish between the proprietary rights created by *conveyances* and the obligations created by *contracts*. In the ancient law, the same forms were used in a conveyance as were employed in a contract. After a time, the notion of a contract is disengaged from that of a conveyance. Conveyances are called by a new name, *mancipation*, while *nexum* designates the ceremony when applied to a contract. The process may be conjectured to have taken place in this manner: If, for example, the transaction concerned the sale of a slave, the purchaser was present with his money, and a third person with scales to weigh it. While the transfer was being made, the bond (nexum) continued, but when the sale was completed, the " bond " was at an end. If the slave was transferred, but the money was *not paid*, the " nexum " continued on the purchaser's part, but not on that of the seller. If neither party completed the transaction, the ordinary *executory contract* of sale is made. Under this view, a contract was regarded as an *incomplete conveyance*. If this view be correct, we reach a conclusion in direct opposition to that of many modern theorists, who regard contracts as of paramount importance in the early law. We also see why the ancient law was so severe upon debtors, and why it gave such extravagant powers to creditors. Indebtedness was considered as an anomaly, and looked upon with disfavor, for accord ing to principle, the price of a commodity should have been paid when the sale was made.

It is necessary, however to analyze more closely, and to distinguish between contracts and pacts. A pact was only the engagement of individuals, without those solemnities which were necessary to a contract. An *obligation* must have been attached by law to a pact before it became a contract. It is very important to notice, that in the old law, an engagement does not constitute a contract. An obligation must be annexed by the law in the plenitude of its power. The law bound the parties together, and the *chain* could only be broken by a legal process. It is singular that *obligation* meant the right to have a debt paid, as well as the duty to pay it.

In the later Roman law, pacts were nearly in every case connected with legal obligations, but in tracing the history of the subject, we find in the course of its development, the contract classified into four kinds : verbal, literal, real, and consensual. These names were given from the formalities which were required beyond mere consent.

(1). *The Verbal Contract.*—Here a particular form of words must be employed. This was doubtless the most ancient form of contract. It involved the necessity of a question and an answer. The question was always put by the promisee, and the answer given by the promisor. It was technical in its form, and must be scrupulously followed.

Though not framed for any reasons of convenience, it had its practical advantages. It arrested the promisor's attention, and fixed his mind on the *exact* engagement which he was making. This is in direct opposition to modern theories, for we look at a contract from the point of view of the promisor. The person who asks the question, is called the *stipulator*, and the act of asking it and receiving the answer, *stipulatio.*

(2). *The Literal Contract.*—This consisted of the entry of the amount due on the debit side of a ledger. This contract depended on the great regularity of ancient book-keeping. It was the practice for each member of a family, after entering items of receipt and expenditure in a waste book, to transfer them to a general ledger. It is not known whether the entry in the creditor's books was sufficient to constitute the contract, or whether it was also necessary that the debtor should make a corresponding statement. At all events, if a proper entry was made, formalities essential in the verbal contract were not required. We thus have a second relaxation of the rigid law of early contracts.

(3). *Real Contracts.*—The delivery of the thing agreed upon, raised an obligation on the part of the receiver to complete the contract. This view was a great departure from the law of " ceremonious " contracts, and for the first time introduced the element of moral obligation into this branch of law.

(4). *Consensual Contracts.*—These very important contracts depend for their validity, purely upon mutual assent. There are four of this class, which embraces those contracts that are the most important in the intercourse of life. No formalities are requisite. The law attaches its obligation or chain to the mere assent or pact. The mere consent draws with it the obligation in the same manner, as the question, book entry, and delivery attract it in other contracts. Contracts belonging to this class are agency, sale, partnership, and letting and hiring (bailment). The great importance and frequency of these transactions, without doubt, led the Romans to relieve them from all technical rules. This was doubtless the case with other nations, so that these contracts were deemed to be contracts by the "law of nations," and ultimately by the "law of nature," until the singular notion prevailed, that the earlier the civilization, the simpler the contract.

From this time forward, consent came to be regarded as the principal ingredient in a contract. The "consensual" contracts were looked upon with peculiar favor. Although the Prætors could not extend their number, it was determined to give *equitable* actions in every case in which a pact was founded on a consideration. In this way new consensual contracts were introduced, although not so termed. If they were without consideration, the Prætors would not enforce them. It was then necessary to make the contract formal, by means of "question and answer."

This history of the progress of Roman law, is probably typical of all ancient law in its progress up to a certain point. Some of its features are exclusively Roman, such as the nature of "Obligation" and the "Theory of Natural Law."

The influence of Jurisprudence upon other branches of science has been remarkable. It is especially noticeable in Politics, Moral Philosophy, and Theology. That part of the law which has been most extensively influential, is the law of obligation, or contract, and the law of wrongs (delicts). In politics, from a confusion of distinct legal notions was derived the error which attributed political rights and duties to an original compact between the governors and governed. The law furnished a body of words and phrases, which approximated in meaning to the ideas which were forming on the subject of political obligation.

In Moral Philosophy, ancient law has been more directly laid under contribution. As long as ethical science concerned itself with the practical rules of conduct, it was affected by Roman law. Moral Philosophy was originally incorporated with Theology. Its relation to Jurisprudence was less close when it came to be cultivated by the great Spanish moralists. "Moral Theology" then degenerated into

Casuistry. Under the guidance of Protestants, a new science of Moral Philosophy abandoned the path which the " Moral Theologians " had followed, and Roman law again exercised its influence on ethical inquiry.

There is no branch of knowledge which has been so little affected by Roman law as Metaphysics. Discussions upon metaphysical questions were conducted in Greek, or in a dialect constructed to give expression to Greek conceptions. The problems of Metaphysics which have been most strongly agitated in Western Europe, betray a legal parentage. No Greek-speaking people has ever been seriously perplexed by the question of free will and necessity. No such people ever showed the smallest capacity for producing a philosophy of law. The problem of free will arises when we contemplate a metaphysical conception under a legal aspect. This conception was theological before it became philosophical. Note the difference between the various topics of theological speculation in the two branches of the Roman Empire. The Greek mind engaged in profound controversies as to the divine person, the divine substance and the divine nature. The Western Church discussed the nature of sin, and its transmission by inheritance, the atonement, the antagonism between free will and divine Providence. Why are these problems so strikingly different? We answer unhesitatingly that in the West, theological speculation had passed from a region of Greek

E

metaphysics to Roman law.   The substratum of law
in Western theology lies exceedingly deep. Though
for a time its doctrines were almost buried under
Aristotelian philosophy, yet at the Reformation
they were extricated. It is difficult to say whether
the system of Calvin or of Arminius has the more
marked legal character.

Besides, the Roman law of contracts had a strong
influence upon institutions. Feudalism is com-
pounded of barbaric usage and Roman law. While
it resembled in some respects a Hindoo village community, it is in other respects quite different. The
Hindoo communities gathered together by instinct,
and new comers were introduced by fiction. The
feudal obligation was created by contract. The
feudal communities were, for this reason, more
durable and varied in character than the ancient
societies. Some would hold that the variety of
modern civilization is due to the exuberant and
erratic genius of Germanic races. In opposition to
this error, it may be asserted that the Roman Empire bequeathed to society the legal conception to
which all this variety is attributable. The one
striking and characteristic fact in the customs and
institutions of barbaric races is their extreme uniformity.

6. *Delict or Crime*—All known collections of
ancient law are characterized by a feature which
broadly distingu'shes them from matured systems

of jurisprudence. The proportion of civil to criminal law is very different in the two cases. The
elder the system, the fuller and more minute the
penal legislation. The poverty of civil law is due
to the plan on which the family is organized. There
is no corresponding limitation in reference to penal
law, and it is also probable that the infancy of nations is a period of ungoverned violence.

This early penal law is not a true criminal law.
In all matured systems, a sharp distinction is drawn
between crimes and wrongs. In the one, the act is
regarded with reference to the State ; in the other,
with reference to the individual injured. In ancient
law, the act was only regarded with reference to the
individual. He proceeds by a civil action, and
recovers compensation in the shape of money. In
the Twelve Tables, the chief civil wrong is *theft*.
Those offences which are now termed crimes, were
treated exclusively as torts or wrongs. The same
fact is perceived in the consolidated laws of the
Germanic tribes. In the infancy of jurisprudence,
the citizen depends for protection against violence
or fraud, not on the law of crime, but on the law of
tort. It should also be noticed that sins are known
to primitive societies. There were in the Athenian
and Roman States laws punishing sins as well as
torts. The ordinances against the former were based
on the conception of an offence against God; the
provisions against the latter, on the conception of
an offence against one's neighbor. The idea of an

offence against the *State* did not at first produce a
true criminal jurisprudence.

The conception of a wrong done to the State,
however, was not wanting. The State was thought
to suffer a personal injury, and avenged itself on
the criminal by a single act. Every offence was
punished by a special act of the legislative power.
The *trial* of an offender was wholly irregular. The
proceeding was the same in form as the enactment
of an ordinary statute. After regular criminal
procedure came into vogue, the people still retained
the power of punishing offences by a special law.

It may be urged that the State has from the
earliest period compelled the wrong doer to compound for his wrong, and that this interference must
have depended upon the fact that it was injured. The
State, however, only interfered in the character of
arbitrator between two litigants, and received compensation for its trouble and loss of time. This is
shown by the sums paid in the progress of an action
in the Roman law (Sacramenta), and by the subjects described by Homer on the shield of Achilles.
It is still further shown by the fact that the court,
in awarding damages, took a its guide the measure
of vengeance likely to be exacted by the aggrieved
person under all the circumstances. This is the explanation of the different penalties imposed on
offenders caught in the act of committing crime, and
on those detected after considerable delay. The
·nen of ancient times had none of the scruples of

modern judges in discriminating between the degrees of criminality which belong to offences falling within the same description. They look only at the impulses of the injured person, and follow the rise and fall of his passions.

The earliest criminal tribunals were mere committees of the legislature. The popular assembly delegated its functions to a commission quite analogous to the committee of a modern legislative body, except that it did not report to the legislature, but itself rendered a final decision. Some of these commissions resembled modern standing committees, and were appointed regularly every year. There was no true criminal law at Rome, until B. C. 149. A Calpurnian law then provided a permanent commission for the trial of offences under that act, and judges were selected from particular classes, and renewed in conformity with definite rules. This was a regular criminal judicature. These commissions were always regarded as mere committees of the popular assembly. Two important consequences followed. One was that the legislature could always try the case as a special offence, and the other that the punishment of death could not be inflicted by the commission, because it could have no greater powers than the legislative body whence it emanated, which could not itself inflict death.

Two additional peculiarities should be mentioned; the great number of Roman tribunals, and the capricious classification of crimes. Both of these are explained by the historical account already given. As each commission for the trial of crime had its origin in a distinct statute, which was passed to meet an existing emergency, the commissions were naturally very numerous, and without any connection. It became very difficult to draw any exact lines between the different commissions. This result was not only inconvenient but oppressive, for if there was doubt as to the particular statute under which a crime should be ranged, an alleged criminal could be indicted before several commissions, so that if he was acquitted by one, he could be condemned by another. Though this anomaly was abolished by the Emperors, yet the classification of crimes remained remarkably capricious. The only principle on which acts were associated, was that they had been made criminal offences at the same time, and by the same statute. Thus perjury was classed with cutting, wounding, and poisoning, because a law of Sylla had given jurisdiction over these forms of crime to the same commission. Finally, criminal law was extended by a new description of offences called *crimina extraordinaria*. These were offences originally treated merely as wrongs. In the progress of social ideas, the injured party was allowed to pursue them as crimes; adopting a mode of redress differing from the ordinary procedure.

The theory and practice of criminal justice under the Empire has had a powerful effect on modern

society. There was at first committed to the Senate
an extensive criminal jurisdiciton; it was ultimately
transferred to magistrates, nominated by the Emperor, with an appeal to the Imperial Privy Council.
From this source was derived the doctrine, familiar
to modern peoples, that the sovereign is the fountain
of all justice, and the depositary of all grace. This
theory was the fruit of the centralization of the Empire. It saved modern society from passing through
the series of changes illustrated by the history of
the commissions (*quœstiones*). The development
of criminal law was hastened by two causes; the
memory of the Roman Empire, and the influence
of the Church. Two assumptions were contended
for by the Church, one that each feudal ruler might
be assimilated to the Roman magistrates spoken of
by St. Paul, and the other that the offences which
he was to chastise were those selected in the Mo-
siac commandments. Thus heresy and perjury were
ecclesiastical offences, and the Church only admitted
the co-operation of the secular arm; while murder
and robbery were under the jurisdiction of civil
rulers, not by the accident of their position, but as
an express ordinance of God.

Ancient Law

ANCIENT LAW.

—•—

CHAPTER I.

ANCIENT CODES.

THE most celebrated system of jurisprudence known
to the world begins, as it ends, with a Code. From
the commencement to the close of its history, the
expositors of Roman Law consistently employed
language which implied that the body of their
system rested on the Twelve Decemviral Tables,
and therefore on a basis of written law. Except
in one particular, no institutions anterior to the
Twelve Tables were recognised at Rome. The
theoretical descent of Roman jurisprudence from a
code, the theoretical ascription of English law to
immemorial unwritten tradition, were the chief
reasons why the development of their system differed from the development of ours. Neither the
ory corresponded exactly with the facts, but each
produced consequences of the utmost importance.

I need hardly say that the publication of the

Twelve Tables is not the earliest point at which we
can take up the history of law. The ancient Roman
code belongs to a class of which almost every civil
ised nation in the world can show a sample, and
which, so far as the Roman and Hellenic worlds
were concerned, were largely diffused over them at
epochs not widely distant from one another. They
appeared under exceedingly similar circumstances,
and were produced, to our knowledge, by very
similar causes. Unquestionably, many jural phenomena lie behind these codes and preceded them
in point of time. Not a few documentary records
exist which profess to give us information concerning the early phenomena of law; but, until philology
has effected a complete analysis of the Sanskrit literature, our best sources of knowledge are undoubtedly the Greek Homeric poems, considered of course
not as a history of actual occurrences, but as a description, not wholly idealised, of a state of society
known to the writer. However the fancy of the
poet may have exaggerated certain features of the
heroic age, the prowess of warriors and the potency
of gods, there is no reason to believe that it has
tampered with moral or metaphysical conceptions
which were not yet the subjects of conscious observation; and in this respect the Homeric literature
is far more trustworthy than those relatively later
documents which pretend to give an account of
times similarly early, but which were compiled under philosophical or theological influences. If by

any means we can determine the early foims of jural conceptions, they will be invaluable to us. These rudimentary ideas are to the jurist what the primary crusts of the earth are to the geologist. They contain, potentially, all the forms in which law has subsequently exhibited itself. The haste or the prejudice which has generally refused them all but the most superficial examination, must bear the blame of the unsatisfactory condition in which we find the science of jurisprudence. The inquiries of the jurist are in truth prosecuted much as inquiry in physics and physiology was prosecuted before observation had taken the place of assumption. Theories, plausible and comprehensive, but absolutely unverified, such as the Law of Nature or the Social Compact, enjoy a universal preference over sober research into the primitive history of society and law; and they obscure the truth not only by diverting attention from the only quarter in which it can be found, but by that most real and most important influence which, when once entertained and believed in, they are enabled to exercise on the later stages of jurisprudence.

The earliest notions connected with the conception, now so fully developed, of a law or rule of life, are those contained in the Homeric words "Themis" and "Themistes." "Themis," it is well known, appears in the later Greek pantheon as the Goddess of Justice, but this is a modern and much developed idea, and it is in a very different sense that Themis

is described in the Iliad as the assessor of Zeus. It
is now clearly seen by all trustworthy observers of
the primitive condition of mankind that, in the infancy of the race, men could only account for sustained or periodically recurring action by supposing
a personal agent. Thus, the wind blowing was a
person and of course a divine person; the sun
rising, culminating, and setting was a person and a
divine person; the earth yielding her increase was
a person and divine. As, then, in the physical
world, so in the moral. When a king decided a
dispute by a sentence, the judgment was assumed to
be the result of direct inspiration. The divine
agent, suggesting judicial awards to kings or to
gods, the greatest of kings, was *Themis*. The peculiarity of the conception is brought out by the use
of the plural. *Themistes*, Themises, the plural of
Themis, are the awards themselves, divinely dictated to the judge. Kings are spoken of as if they
had a store of "Themistes" ready to hand for use;
but it must be distinctly understood that they are
not laws, but judgments, or, to take the exact Teutonic equivalent, "dooms." "Zeus, or the human
king on earth," says Mr. Grote, in his History of
Greece, "is not a law-maker, but a judge." He is
provided with Themistes, but, consistently with
the belief in their emanation from above, they cannot be supposed to be connected by any thread of
principle; they are separate, isolated judgments.

Even in the Homeric poems, we can see that

these ideas are transient. Parities of circumstance were probably commoner in the simple mechanism of ancient society than they are now, and in the succession of similar cases awards are likely to follow and resemble each other. Here we have the germ or rudiment of a custom, a conception posterior to that of Themistes or judgments. However strongly we, with our modern associations, may be inclined to lay down *à priori* that the notion of a Custom must precede that of a judicial sentence, and that a judgment must affirm a Custom or punish its breach, it seems quite certain that the historical order of the ideas is that in which I have placed them. The Homeric word for a custom in the embryo is sometimes "Themis" in the singular —more often "Dike," the meaning of which visibly fluctuates between a "judgment" and a "custom" or "usage." *Νόμος,* a Law, so great and famous a term in the political vocabulary of the later Greek society, does not occur in Homer.

The notion of a divine agency, suggesting the Themistes, and itself impersonated in Themis, must be kept apart from other primitive beliefs with which a superficial inquirer might confound it. The conception of the Deity dictating an entire code or body of law as in the case of the Hindoo laws of Menu, seems to belong to a range of ideas more recent and more advanced. "Themis" and "Themistes" are much less remotely linked with that persuasion which clung so long and so tenaciously to

the human mind, of a divine influence underlying
and supporting every relation of life, every social
institution. In early law, and amid the rudiments
of political thought, symptoms of this belief meet
us on all sides. A supernatural presidency is supposed to consecrate and keep together all the cardi-
nal institutions of those times, the State, the Race,
and the Family. Men, grouped together in the different relations which those institutions imply, are
bound to celebrate periodically common rites and
to offer common sacrifices ; and every now and then
the same duty is even more significantly recognised
in the purifications and expiations which they perform, and which appear intended to deprecate punishment for involuntary or neglectful disrespect.
Everybody acquainted with ordinary classical literature will remember the *sacra gentilicia*, which
exercised so important an influence on the early
Roman law of adoption and of wills. And to this
hour the Hindoo Customary Law, in which some of
the most curious features of primitive society are stereotyped, makes almost all the rights of persons and
all the rules of succession hinge on the due solemni-
sation of fixed ceremonies at the dead man's funeral,
that is, at every point where a breach occurs in the
continuity of the family.

Before we quit this stage of jurisprudence, a
caution may be usefully given to the English student. Bentham, in his " Fragment on Government,"
and Austin, in his " Province of Jurisprudence De-

termined," resolve every law into a *command* of
the lawgiver, an *obligation* imposed thereby on the
citizen, and a *sanction* threatened in the event of
disobedience; and it is further predicated of the
command, which is the first element in a law, that
it must prescribe, not a single act, but a series or
number of acts of the same class or kind. The
results of this separation of ingredients tally exactly
with the facts of mature jurisprudence; and, by a
little straining of language, they may be made to
correspond in form with all law, of all kinds, at all
epochs. It is not, however, asserted that the notion
of law entertained by the generality is even now
quite in conformity with this dissection; and it is
curious that, the farther we penetrate into the primitive history of thought, the farther we find ourselves from a conception of law which at all resembles a compound of the elements which Bentham
determined. It is certain that, in the infancy of
mankind, no sort of legislature, not even a distinct
author of law, is contemplated or conceived of.
Law has scarcely reached the footing of custom; it
is rather a habit. It is, to use a French phrase, " in
the air." The only authoritative statement of right
and wrong is a judicial sentence after the facts, not
one presupposing a law which has been violated,
but one which is breathed for the first time by a
higher power into the judge's mind at the moment
of adjudication. It is of course extremely difficult
for us to realise a view so far removed from us in

point both of time and of association, but it will become more credible when we dwell more at length
on the constitution of ancient society, in which every
man, living during the greater part of his life under
the patriarchal despotism, was practically controlled
in all his actions by a regimen not of law but of caprice. I may add that an Englishman should be
better able than a foreigner to appreciate the historical fact that the " Themistes " preceded any conception of law, because, amid the many inconsistent
theories which prevail concerning the character of
English jurisprudence, the most popular, or at all
events the one which most affects practice, is certainly a theory which assumes that adjudged cases
and precedents exist antecedently to rules, principles, and distinctions. The " Themistes " have too,
it should be remarked, the characteristic which, in
the view of Bentham and Austin, distinguishes
single or mere commands from laws. A true law
enjoins on all the citizens indifferently a number of
acts similar in class or kind; and this is exactly the
feature of a law which has most deeply impressed
itself on the popular mind, causing the term " law "
to be applied to mere uniformities, successions, and
similitudes. A *command* prescribes only a single
act, and it is to commands, therefore, that " Themistes " are more akin than to laws. They are
simply adjudications on insulated states of fact, and
do not necessarily follow each other in any orderly
sequence.

The literature of the heroic age discloses to us
law in the germ under the " Themistes " and a little
more developed in the conception of " Dike."   The
next stage which we reach in the history of juris
prudence is strongly marked and surrounded by the
utmost interest.   Mr. Grote, in the second part and
second chapter of his History, has fully described
the mode in which society gradually clothed itself
with a different character from that delineated by
Homer.   Heroic kingship depended partly on divinely given prerogative, and partly on the possession of supereminent strength, courage, and wisdom.
Gradually, as the impression of the monarch's sacredness became weakened, and feeble members occurred in the series of hereditary kings, the royal
power decayed, and at last gave way to the dominion of aristocracies.   If language so precise can be
used of the revolution, we might say that the office
of the king was usurped by that council of chiefs
which Homer repeatedly alludes to and depicts.
At all events from an epoch of kingly rule we come
everywhere in Europe to an era of oligarchies ; and
even where the name of the monarchical functions
does not absolutely disappear, the authority of the
king is reduced to a mere shadow.   He becomes a
mere hereditary general, as in Lacedæmon, a mere
functionary, as the King Archon at Athens, or a
mere formal hierophant, like the *Rex Sacrificulus*
at Rome.   In Greece, Italy, and Asia Minor, the
dominant orders seem to have universally consisted

of a number of families united by an assumed relationship in blood, and, though they all appear at
first to have laid claim to a quasi-sacred character,
their strength does not seem to have resided in
their pretended sanctity. Unless they were prema-
turely overthrown by the popular party, they all
ultimately approached very closely to what we
should now understand by a political aristocracy.
The changes which society underwent in the communities of the further Asia occurred of course at
periods long anterior in point of time to these revolutions of the Italian and Hellenic worlds; but their
relative place in civilisation appears to have been
the same, and they seem to have been exceedingly
similar in general character. There is some evidence
that the races which were subsequently united under
the Persian monarchy, and those which peopled the
peninsula of India, had all their heroic age and their
era of aristocracies; but a military and a religious
oligarchy appear to have grown up separately, nor
was the authority of the king generally superseded.
Contrary, too, to the course of events in the West,
the religious element in the East tended to get the
better of the military and political. Military and
civil aristocracies disappear, annihilated or crushed
into insignificance between the kings and the sacerdotal order; and the ultimate result at which we
arrive is, a monarch enjoying great power, but cir-
cumscribed by the privileges of a caste of priests.
With these differences, however, that in the East

aristocracies became religious, in the West civil or
political, the proposition that a historical era of aristocracies succeeded a historical era of heroic kings
may be considered as true, if not of all mankind, at
all events of all branches of the Indo-European
family of nations.

The important point for the jurist is that these
aristocracies were usually the depositaries and administrators of law. They seem to have succeeded
to the prerogatives of the king, with the important
difference, however, that they do not appear to have
pretended to direct inspiration for each sentence.
The connection of ideas which caused the judgments
of the patriarchal chieftain to be attributed to su-
perhuman dictation still shows itself here and there
in the claim of a divine origin for the entire body
of rules, or for certain parts of it, but the progress
of thought no longer permits the solution of particular disputes to be explained by supposing an extra-
human interposition. What the juristical oligarchy
now claims is to monopolise the *knowledge* of the
laws, to have the exclusive possession of the principles by which quarrels are decided. We have in
fact arrived at the epoch of Customary Law. Customs or Observances now exist as a substantive
aggregate, and are assumed to be precisely known
to the aristocratic order or caste. Our authorities
leave us no doubt that the trust lodged with the
oligarchy was sometimes abused, but it certainly
ought not to be regarded as a mere usurpation or

engine of tyranny. Before the invention of writing,
and during the infancy of the art, an aristocracy invested with judicial privileges formed the only expedient by which accurate preservation of the customs of the race or tribe could be at all approximated to. Their genuineness was, so far as possible,
insured by confiding them to the recollection of a
limited portion of the community.

The epoch of Customary Law, and of its custody
by a privileged order, is a very remarkable one.
The condition of jurisprudence which it implies has
left traces which may still be detected in legal and
popular phraseology. The law, thus known exclusively to a privileged minority, whether a caste, an
aristocracy, a priestly tribe, or a sacerdotal college,
is true unwritten law. Except this, there is no such
thing as unwritten law in the world. English case-
law is sometimes spoken of as unwritten, and there
are some English theorists who assure us that if
code of English jurisprudence were prepared, we
should be turning unwritten law into written—a
conversion, as they insist, if not of doubtful policy,
at all events of the greatest seriousness. Now, it is
quite true that there was once a period at which the
English common law might reasonably have been
termed unwritten. The elder English judges did
really pretend to knowledge of rules, principles, and
distinctions which were not entirely revealed to the
bar and to the lay-public. Whether all the law
which they claimed to monopolise was really un-

written, is exceedingly questionable; but at all events, on the assumption that there was once a large mass of civil and criminal rules known exclu- sively to the judges, it presently ceased to be unwrit ten law. As soon as the Courts at Westminster Hall began to base their judgments on cases recorded, whether in the year books or elsewhere, the law which they administered became written law. At the present moment a rule of English law has first to be disentangled from the recorded facts of ad- judged printed precedents, then thrown into a form of words, varying with the taste, precision, and knowledge of the particular judge, and then applied to the circumstances of the case for adjudication. But at no stage of this process has it any character- istic which distinguishes it from written law. It is written case-law, and only different from code-law because it is written in a different way.

From the period of Customary Law we come to another sharply defined epoch in the history of ju- risprudence. We arrive at the era of Codes, those ancient codes of which the Twelve Tables of Rome were the most famous specimen. In Greece, in Italy, on the Hellenised sea-board of Western Asia, these codes all made their appearance at periods much the same everywhere, not, I mean, at periods identical in point of time, but similar in point of the relative progress of each community. Everywhere, in the countries I have named, laws engraven on tablets and published to the people take the place of usages

deposited with the recollection of a privileged oligarchy. It must not for a moment be supposed that
the refined considerations now urged in favour of
what is called codification had any part or place in
the change I have described. The ancient codes
were doubtless originally suggested by the discovery
and diffusion of the art of writing. It is true that
the aristocracies seem to have abused their monopoly
of legal knowledge ; and at all events their exclusive
possession of the law was a formidable impediment to
the success of those popular movements which began
to be universal in the western world. But, though
democratic sentiment may have added to their popularity, the codes were certainly in the main a direct
result of the invention of writing. Inscribed tablets
were seen to be a better depositary of law, and a
better security for its accurate preservation, than
the memory of a number of persons however
strengthened by habitual exercise.

The Roman code belongs to the class of codes I
have been describing. Their value did not consist
in any approach to symmetrical classifications, or to
terseness and clearness of expression, but in their
publicity, and in the knowledge which they furnished to everybody, as to what he was to do, and
what not to do. It is indeed true that the Twelve
Tables of Rome do exhibit some traces of systematic
arrangement, but this is probably explained by the
tradition that the framers of that body of law called
in the assistance of Greeks who enjoyed the later

Greek experience in the art of law-making. The
fragments of the Attic Code of Solon show, how
ever, that it had but little order, and probably the
laws of Draco had even less.   Quite enough too
remains of these collections, both in the East and
in the West, to show that they mingled up religious
civil, and merely moral ordinances, without any
regard to differences in their essential character;
and this is consistent with all we know of early
thought from other sources, the severance of law
from morality, and of religion from law, belonging
very distinctly to the *later* stages of mental progress.

   But, whatever to a modern eye are the singularities of these Codes, their importance to ancient
societies was unspeakable. The question—and it was
one which affected the whole future of each community—was not so much whether there should be
a code at all, for the majority of ancient societies
seem to have obtained them sooner or later, and, but
for the great interruption in the history of jurisprudence created by feudalism, it is likely that all
modern law would be distinctly traceable to one or
more of those fountain-heads.   But the point on
which turned the history of the race was, at what
period, at what stage of their social progress, they
should have their laws put into writing.   In the
western world the plebeian or popular element in
each State successfully assailed the oligarchical monopoly, and a code was nearly universally obtained
early in the history of the Commonwealth.   But, in

the East, as I have before mentioned, the ruling
aristocracies tended to become religious rather than
military or political, and gained, therefore, rather
than lost in power; while in some instances the
physical conformation of Asiatic countries had the
effect of making individual communities larger and
more numerous than in the West; and it is a known
social law that the larger the space over which a
particular set of institutions is diffused, the greater
is its tenacity and vitality.   From whatever cause,
the codes obtained by Eastern societies were obtained, relatively, much later than by Western, and
wore a very different character.   The religious
oligarchies of Asia, either for their own guidance, or
for the relief of their memory, or for the instruction
of their disciples, seem in all cases to have ultimately
embodied their legal learning in a code ; but the
opportunity of increasing and consolidating their
influence was probably too tempting to be resisted.
Their complete monopoly of legal knowledge appears to have enabled them to put off on the world
collections, not so much of the rules actually observed
as of the rules which the priestly order considered
proper to be observed.   The Hindoo Code, called the
Laws of Menu, which is certainly a Brahmin compilation, undoubtedly enshrines many genuine observances of the Hindoo race, but the opinion of the
best contemporary orientalists is, that it does not,
as a whole, represent a set of rules ever actually ad
ministered in Hindostan.   It is, in great part, an

ideal picture of that which, in the view of the Brahmins, *ought* to be the law. It is consistent with human nature and with the special motives of their authors, that codes like that of Menu should pretend to the highest antiquity and claim to have emanated in their complete form from the Deity. Menu, according to Hindoo mythology, is an emanation from the supreme God; but the compilation which bears his name, though its exact date is not easily discovered, is, in point of the relative progress of Hindoo jurisprudence, a recent production.

Among the chief advantages which the Twelve Tables and similar codes conferred on the societies which obtained them, was the protection which they afforded against the frauds of the privileged oligarchy and also against the spontaneous depravation and debasement of the national institutions. The Roman Code was merely an enunciation in words of the existing customs of the Roman people. Relatively to the progress of the Romans in civilization, it was a remarkably early code, and it was published at a time when Roman society had barely emerged from that intellectual condition in which civil obligation and religious duty are inevitably confounded. Now a barbarous society practising a body of customs, is exposed to some especial dangers which may be absolutely fatal to its progress in civilisation. The usages which a particular community is found to have adopted in its infancy and in

2

its primitive seats are generally those which are on
the whole best suited to promote its physical and
moral well-being; and, if they are retained in their
integrity until new social wants have taught new
practices, the upward march of society is almost
certain.   But unhappily there is a law of development which ever threatens to operate upon unwritten usage.   The customs are of course obeyed by
multitudes who are incapable of understanding the
true ground of their expediency, and who are therefore left inevitably to invent superstitious reasons
for their permanence.   A process then commences
which may be shortly described by saying that
usage which is reasonable generates usage which is
unreasonable.   Analogy, the most valuable of instruments in the maturity of jurisprudence, is the
most dangerous of snares in its infancy.   Prohibi-
tions and ordinances, originally confined, for good
reasons, to a simple description of acts, are made to
apply to all acts of the same class, because a man
menaced with the anger of the gods for doing one
thing, feels a natural terror in doing any other thing
which is remotely like it.   After one kind of food
has been interdicted for sanitary reasons, the prohibition is extended to all food resembling it, though
the resemblance occasionally depends on analogies
the most fanciful.   So, again, a wise provision for
insuring general cleanliness dictates in time long
routines of ceremonial ablution; and that division
into classes which at a particular crisis of social his

tory is necessary for the maintenance of the national existence degenerates into the most disastrous and
blighting of all human institutions—Caste.   The
fate of the Hindoo law is, in fact, the measure of the
value of the Roman Code.   Ethnology shows us
that the Romans and the Hindoos sprang from the
same original stock, and there is indeed a striking
resemblance between what appear to have been
their original customs.   Even now, Hindoo jurisprudence has a substratum of forethought and sound
judgment, but irrational imitation has engrafted in
it an immense apparatus of cruel absurdities.   From
these corruptions the Romans were protected by
their code.   It was compiled while usage was still
wholesome, and a hundred years afterwards it might
have been too late.   The Hindoo law has been to a
great extent embodied in writing, but ancient as in
one sense are the compendia which still exist in
Sanskrit, they contain ample evidence that they
were drawn up after the mischief had been done.
We are not of course entitled to say that if the
Twelve Tables had not been published the Romans
would have been condemned to a civilisation as
feeble and perverted as that of the Hindoos, but
thus much at least is certain, that *with* their code
they were exempt from the very chance of so unhappy a destiny.

CHAPTER II.

LEGAL FICTIONS.

WHEN primitive law has once been embodied in a Code, there is an end to what may be called its spontaneous development. Henceforward the changes effected in it, if effected at all, are effected deliberately and from without. It is impossible to suppose that the customs of any race or tribe remained unaltered during the whole of the long—in some instances the immense—interval between their declaration by a patriarchal monarch and their publication in writing. It would be unsafe too to affirm that no part of the alteration was effected deliberately. But from the little we know of the progress of law during this period, we are justified in assuming that set purpose had the very smallest share in producing change. Such innovations on the earliest usages as disclose themselves appear to have been dictated by feelings and modes of thought which, under our present mental conditions, we are unable to comprehend. A new era begins, however, with the Codes. Wherever, after this epoch, we trace the course of legal modification we are able to attribute it to the conscious desire of improvement, or at all events of compassing objects other than those which were aimed at in the primitive times.

It may seem at first sight that no general propositions worth trusting can be elicited from the history of legal systems subsequent to the codes. The field is too vast. We cannot be sure that we have included a sufficient number of phenomena in our observations, or that we accurately understand those which we have observed. But the undertaking will be seen to be more feasible, if we consider that after the epoch of codes the distinction between stationary and progressive societies begins to make itself felt. It is only with the progressive societies that we are concerned, and nothing is more remarkable than their extreme fewness. In spite of oveerwhlming evidence, it is most difficult for a citizen of western Europe to bring thoroughly home to himself the truth that the civilisation which surrounds him is a rare exception in the history of the world. The tone of thought common among us, all our hopes, fears, and speculations, would be materially affected, if we had vividly before us the relation of the progressive races to the totality of human life. It is indisputable that much the greatest part of mankind has never shown a particle of desire that its civil institutions should be improved since the

moment when external completeness was first given
to them by their embodiment in some permanent
record. One set of usages has occasionally been
violently overthrown and superseded by another;
here and there a primitive code, pretending to a
supernatural origin, has been greatly extended, and
distorted into the most surprising forms, by the perversity of sacerdotal commentators; but, except in a
small section of the world, there has been nothing
like the gradual amelioration of a legal system.
There has been material civilisation, but, instead of
the civilisation expanding the law, the law has limited the civilisation. The study of races in their primitive condition affords us some clue to the point at
which the development of certain societies has
stopped. We can see that Brahminical India has
not passed beyond a stage which occurs in the history of all the families of mankind, the stage at
which a rule of law is not yet discriminated from a
rule of religion. The members of such a society
consider that the transgression of a religious ordinance should be punished by civil penalties, and that
the violation of a civil duty exposes the delinquent
to divine correction. In China this point has been
past, but progress seems to have been there arrested, because the civil laws are coextensive with all
the ideas of which the race is capable. The difference between the stationary and progressive societies is, however, one of the great secrets which
inquiry has yet to penetrate. Among partial ex-

planations of it I venture to place the considerations
urged at the end of the last chapter. It may further
be remarked that no one is likely to succeed in
the investigation who does not clearly realise that
the stationary condition of the human race is the
rule, the progressive the exception. And another
indispensable condition of success is an accurate
knowledge of Roman law in all its principal stages.
The Roman jurisprudence has the longest known
history of any set of human institutions. The character
of all the changes which it underwent is tolerably
well ascertained. From its commencement
to its close, it was progressively modified for the
better, or for what the authors of the modification
conceived to be the better, and the course of improvement
was continued through periods at which
all the rest of human thought and action materially
slackened its space, and repeatedly threatened to
settle down into stagnation.

I confine myself in what follows to the progressive
societies. With respect to them it may be laid
down that social necessities and social opinion are
always more or less in advance of Law. We may
come indefinitely near to the closing of the gap between
them, but it has a perpetual tendency to reopen.
Law is stable; the societies we are speaking
of are progressive. The greater or less happiness
of a people depends on the degree of promptitude
with which the gulf is narrowed.

A general proposition of some value may be ad

vanced with respect to the agencies by which Law
is brought into harmony with society. These in
strumentalities seem to me to be three in number,
Legal Fictions, Equity, and Legislation. Their his
torical order is that in which I have placed them.
Sometimes two of them will be seen operating together, and there are legal systems which have escaped the influence of one or other of them. But
I know of no instance in which the order of their
appearance has been changed or inverted. The
early history of one of them, Equity, is universally
obscure, and hence it may be thought by some that
certain isolated statutes, reformatory of the civil
law, are older than any equitable jurisdiction. My
own belief is that remedial Equity is everywhere
older than remedial Legislation; but, should this
be not strictly true, it would only be necessary to
limit the proposition respecting their order of sequence to the periods at which they exercise a sustained and substantial influence in transforming the
original law.

I employ the word " fiction " in a sense considerably wider than that in which English lawyers are
accustomed to use it, and with a meaning much more
extensive than that which belonged to the Roman
" fictiones." Fictio, in old Roman law, is properly a
term of pleading, and signifies a false averment on
the part of the plaintiff which the defendant was
not allowed to traverse; such, for example, as an
averment that the plaintiff was a Roman citizen

when in truth he was a foreigner.   The object of
these " fictiones " was, of course, to give jurisdiction,
and they therefore strongly resembled the allega-
tions in the writs of the English Queen's Bench and
Exchequer, by which those Courts contrived to
usurp the jurisdiction of the Common Pleas:—the
allegation that the defendant was in custody of the
king's marshal, or that the plaintiff was the king's
debtor, and could not pay his debt by reason of the
defendant's default.   But I now employ the expres
sion "Legal Fiction" to signify any assumption
which conceals, or affects to conceal, the fact that a
rule of law has undergone alteration, its letter remaining unchanged, its operation being modified.
The words, therefore, include the instances of fictions which I have cited from the English and Roman law, but they embrace much more, for I should
speak both of the English Case-law and of the Roman Responsa Prudentum as resting on fictions.
Both these examples will be examined presently.
The *fact* is in both cases that the law has been
wholly changed; the *fiction* is that it remains what
it always was.   It is not difficult to understand why
fictions in all their forms are particularly congenial
to the infancy of society.   They satisfy the desire
for improvement, which is not quite wanting, at the
same time that they do not offend the superstitious
disrelish for change which is always present.   At
a particular stage of social progress they are invaluable expedients for overcoming the rigidity of law

and, indeed, without one of them, the Fiction of Adoption which permits the family tie to be artifi-cially created, it is difficult to understand how soci-ety would ever have escaped from its swaddling clothes, and taken its first steps towards civilisation. We must, therefore, not suffer ourselves to be af-fected by the ridicule which Bentham pours on le-gal fictions wherever he meets them. To revile them as merely fraudulent is to betray ignorance of their peculiar office in the historical development of law. But at the same time it would be equally foolish to agree with those theorists who, discerning that fictions have had their uses, argue that they ought to be stereotyped in our system. There are several Fictions still exercising powerful influence on English jurisprudence which could not be dis-carded without a severe shock to the ideas, and con-siderable change in the language, of English practi-tioners; but there can be no doubt of the general truth that it is unworthy of us to effect an admit-tedly beneficial object by so rude a device as a legal fiction. I cannot admit any anomaly to be in-nocent, which makes the law either more difficult to understand or harder to arrange in harmonious order. Now, among other disadvantages, legal fic tions are the greatest of obstacles to symmetrical classification. The rule of law remains sticking in the system, but it is a mere shell. It has been long ago undermined, and a new rule hides itself under its cover. Hence there is at once a difficulty in knowing whether the rule which is actually operative should be classed in its true or in its apparent place, and minds of different casts will differ as to the branch of the alternative which ought to be se lected. If the English law is ever to assume an or· derly distribution, it will be necessary to prune away the legal fictions which, in spite of some recent legislative improvements, are still abundant in it.

The next instrumentality by which the adaptation of law to social wants is carried on I call Equity, meaning by that word any body of rules existing by the side of the original civil law, founded on distinct principles and claiming incidentally to supersede the civil law in virtue of a superior sanctity inherent in those principles. The Equity whether of the Roman Prætors or of the English Chancellors, differs from the Fictions which in each case preceded it, in that the interference with law is open and avowed. On the other hand, it differs from Legislation, the agent of legal improvement which comes after it, in that its claim to authority is grounded, not on the prerogative of any external person or body, not even on that of the magistrate who enunciates it, but on the special nature of its principles, to which it is alleged that all law ought to conform. The very conception of a set of principles, invested with a higher sacredness than those of the original law and demanding application independently of the consent of any external body, belongs to a much

more advanced stage of thought than that to which
legal fictions originally suggested themselves.

Legislation, the enactments of a legislature which,
whether it take the form of an autocratic prince or
of a parliamentary assembly, is the assumed organ
of the entire society, is the last of the ameliorating
instrumentalities. It differs from Legal Fictions
just as Equity differs from them, and it is also distinguished from Equity, as deriving its authority
from an external body or person. Its obligatory
force is independent of its principles. The legislature, whatever be the actual restraints imposed on it
by public opinion, is in theory empowered to impose what obligations it pleases on the members of
the community. There is nothing to prevent its
legislating in the wantonness of caprice. Legislation may be dictated by equity, if that last word be
used to indicate some standard of right and wrong
to which its enactments happen to be adjusted; but
then these enactments are indebted for their binding
force to the authority of the legislature, and not to
that of the principles on which the legislature acted;
and thus they differ from rules of Equity, in the
technical sense of the word, which pretend to a paramount sacredness entitling them at once to the
recognition of the courts even without the concurrence of prince or parliamentary assembly. It is
the more necessary to note these differences because
a student of Bentham would be apt to confound
Fictions, Equity, and Statute law under the single

head of legislation. They all, he would say, involve *law-making ;* they differ only in respect of the machinery by which the new law is produced. That is perfectly true, and we must never forget it ; but it furnishes no reason why we should deprive our selves of so convenient a term as Legislation in the special sense. Legislation and Equity are disjoined in the popular mind and in the minds of most lawyers ; and it will never do to neglect the distinction between them, however conventional, when important practical consequences follow from it.

It would be easy to select from almost any regularly developed body of rules examples of *legal fictions,* which at once betray their true character to the modern observer. In the two instances which I proceed to consider, the nature of the expedient employed is not so readily detected. The first authors of these fictions did not perhaps intend to innovate, certainly did not wish to be suspected of innovating. There are, moreover, and always have been, persons who refuse to see any fiction in the process, and conventional language bears out their refusal. No examples, therefore, can be better calculated to illustrate the wide diffusion of legal fictions, and the efficiency with which they perform their two-fold office of transforming a system of laws and of concealing the transformation.

We in England are well accustomed to the extension, modification, and improvement of law by a machinery which, in theory, is incapable of altering

one jot or one line of existing jurisprudence. The
process by which this virtual legislation is effected
is not so much insensible as unacknowledged. With
respect to that great portion of our legal system
which is enshrined in cases and recorded in law reports, we habitually employ a double language, and
entertain, as it would appear, a double and inconsistent set of ideas. When a group of facts come
before an English Court for adjudication, the whole
course of the discussion between the judge and the
advocate assumes that no question is, or can be,
raised which will call for the application of any
principles but old ones, or of any distinctions but
such as have long since been allowed. It is taken
absolutely for granted that there is somewhere a
rule of known law which will cover the facts of the
dispute now litigated, and that, if such a rule be
not discovered, it is only that the necessary patience,
knowledge or acumen, is not forthcoming to detect
it. Yet the moment the judgment has been rendered and reported, we slide unconsciously or una
vowedly into a new language and a new train of
thought. We now admit that the new decision *has*
modified the law. The rules applicable have, to use
the very inaccurate expression sometimes employed,
become more elastic. In fact they have been changed.
A clear addition has been made to the precedents,
and the canon of law elicited by comparing the
precedents is not the same with that which would
have been obtained if the series of cases had been

curtailed by a single example. The fact that the old rule has been repealed, and that a new one has replaced it, eludes us, because we are not in the habit of throwing into precise language the legal formulas which we derive from the precedents, so that a change in their tenor is not easily detected unless it is violent and glaring. I shall not now pause to consider at length the causes which have led English lawyers to acquiesce in these curious anomalies. Probably it will be found that originally it was the received doctrine that somewhere, *in nubibus* or *in gremio magistratuum*, there existed a complete, coherent, symmetrical body of English law, of an amplitude sufficient to furnish principles which would apply to any conceivable combination of circumstances. The theory was at first much more thoroughly believed in than it is now, and indeed it may have had a better foundation. The judges of the thirteenth century may have really had at their command a mine of law unrevealed to the bar and to the lay-public, for there is some reason for suspecting that in secret they borrowed freely, though not always wisely, from current compendia of the Roman and Canon laws. But that storehouse was closed as soon as the points decided at Westminster Hall became numerous enough to supply a basis for a substantive system of jurisprudence; and now for centuries English practitioners have so expressed themselves as to convey the paradoxical proposition that, except by Equity and Statute law, nothing has

been added to the basis since it was first constituted.
(We do not admit that our tribunals legislate; we
imply that they have never legislated ; and yet we
maintain that the rules of the English common law,
with some assistance from the Court of Chancery
and from Parliament, are coextensive with the complicated interests of modern society.)

A body of law bearing a very close and very instructive resemblance to our case-law in those particulars which I have noticed, was known to the
Romans under the name of the Responsa Prudentum, the "answers of the learned in the law." The
form of these Responses varied a good deal at different periods of the Roman jurisprudence, but
throughout its whole course they consisted of ex-
planatory glosses on authoritative written documents, and at first they were exclusively collections
of opinions interpretative of the Twelve Tables. As
with us, all legal language adjusted itself to the assumption that the text of the old Code remained
unchanged. There was the express rule. It overrode all glosses and comments, and no one openly
admitted that any interpretation of it, however eminent the interpreter, was safe from revision on appeal to the venerable texts. Yet in point of fact,
Books of Responses bearing the names of leading
jurisconsults obtained an authority at least equal to
that of our reported cases, and constantly modified,
extended, limited or practically overruled the provisions of the Decemviral law. The authors of the

new jurisprudence during the whole progress of its
formation professed the most sedulous respect for
the letter of the Code. They were merely explain‧
ing it, deciphering it, bringing out its full meaning;
but then, in the result, by piecing texts together, by
adjusting the law to states of fact which actually presented themselves and by speculating on its possible
application to others which might occur, by intro-
ducing principles of interpretation derived from the
exegesis of other written documents which fell
under their observation, they educed a vast variety
of canons which had never been dreamed of by the
compilers of the Twelve Tables and which were in
truth rarely or never to be found there.   All these
treatises of the jurisconsults claimed respect on the
ground of their assumed conformity with the Code,
but their comparative authority depended on the
reputation of the particular jurisconsults who gave
them to the world.   Any name of universally acknowledged greatness clothed a Book of Responses
with a binding force hardly less than that which
belonged to enactments of the legislature; and such
a book in its turn constituted a new foundation on
which a further body of jurisprudence might rest.
The Responses of the early lawyers were not however published, in the modern sense, by their au‧
thor. They were recorded and edited by his pupils,
and were not therefore in all probability arranged
according to any scheme of classification. The part
of the students in these publications must be care‧

fully noted, because the service they rendered to
their teacher seems to have been generally repaid
by his sedulous attention to the pupils' education.
The educational treatises called Institutes or Commentaries, which are a later fruit of the duty then
recognised, are among the most remarkable features
of the Roman system. It was apparently in these
Institutional works, and not in the books intended
for trained lawyers, that the jurisconsults gave to
the public their classifications and their proposals
for modifying and improving the technical phraseology.

In comparing the Roman Responsa Prudentum
with their nearest English counterpart, it must be
carefully borne in mind that the authority by which
this part of the Roman jurisprudence was expounded
was not the *bench*, but the *bar*. The decision of a
Roman tribunal, though conclusive in the particular
case, had no ulterior authority except such as was
given by the professional repute of the magistrate
who happened to be in office for the time. Properly speaking, there was no institution at Rome
during the republic analogous to the English Bench,
the Chambers of Imperial Germany, or the Parlia-
ments of Monarchical France. There were magistrates indeed, invested with momentous judicial
functions in their several departments, but the ten
ure of the magistracies was but for a single year, so
that they are much less aptly compared to a permanent judicature than to a cycle of offices briskly cir-

culating among the leaders of the bar. Much might
be said on the origin of a condition of things which
looks to us like a startling anomaly, but which was
in fact much more congenial than our own system
to the spirit of ancient societies, tending, as they
always did, to split into distinct orders which, how
ever exclusive themselves, tolerated no professional
hierarchy above them.

It is remarkable that this system did not produce certain effects which might on the whole have
been expected from it. It did not, for example,
popularise the Roman law,—it did not, as in some
of the Greek republics, lessen the effort of intellect
required for the mastery of the science, although its
diffusion and authoritative exposition were opposed
by no artificial barriers. On the contrary, if it had
not been for the operation of a separate set of
causes, there were strong probabilities that the Roman jurisprudence would have become as minute,
technical, and difficult as any system which has since
prevailed. Again, a consequence which might still
more naturally have been looked for, does not appear at any time to have exhibited itself. The jurisconsults, until the liberties of Rome were overthrown, formed a class which was quite undefined
and must have fluctuated greatly in numbers; nevertheless, there does not seem to have existed a doubt
as to the particular individuals whose opinion, in
their generation, was conclusive on the cases submitted to them. The vivid pictures of a leading

jurisconsult's daily practice which abound in Latin
literature—the clients from the country flocking to
his antechamber in the early morning, and the stu
dents standing round with their note-books to record the great lawyer's replies—are seldom or never
identified at any given period with more than one
or two conspicuous names. Owing too to the direct contact of the client and the advocate, the Roman people itself seems to have been always alive
to the rise and fall of professional reputation, and
there is abundance of proof, more particularly in
the well-known oration of Cicero, "Pro Muræna,"
that the reverence of the commons for forensic success was apt to be excessive rather than deficient.

We cannot doubt that the peculiarities which
have been noticed in the instrumentality by which
the development of the Roman law was first effected, were the source of its characteristic excellence,
its early wealth in principles. The growth and exuberance of principle was fostered, in part, by the
competition among the expositors of the law, an
influence wholly unknown where there exists a
Bench, the depositaries instrusted by king or commonwealth with the prerogative of justice. But
the chief agency, no doubt, was the uncontrolled
multiplication of cases for legal decision. The state
of facts which caused genuine perplexity to a country client was not a whit more entitled to form the
basis of the jurisconsult's Response, or legal decision, than a set of hypothetical circumstances pro-

pounded by an ingenious pupil. All combinations
of fact were on precisely the same footing, whether
they were real or imaginary. It was nothing to the
jurisconsult that his opinion was overruled for the
moment by the magistrate who adjudicated on his
client's case, unless that magistrate happened to rank
above him in legal knowledge or the esteem of his
profession. I do not, indeed, mean it to be inferred
that he would wholly omit to consider his client's
advantage, for the client was in earlier times the
great lawyer's constituent and at a later period his
paymaster, but the main road to the rewards of
ambition lay through the good opinion of his order,
and it is obvious that under such a system as I have
been describing this was much more likely to be
secured by viewing each case as an illustration of a
great principle, or an exemplification of a broad
rule, than by merely shaping it for an insulated
forensic triumph. It is evident that powerful influence must have been exercised by the want of any
distinct check on the suggestion or invention of possible questions. Where the data can be multiplied
at pleasure, the facilities for evolving a general rule
are immensely increased. As the law is administered among ourselves, the judge cannot travel out
of the sets of facts exhibited before him or before his
predecessors. Accordingly each group of circumstances which is adjudicated upon receives, to employ a Gallicism, a sort of consecration. It acquires
certain qualities which distinguish it from every

other case genuine or hypothetical. But at Rome,
as I have attempted to explain, there was nothing
resembling a Bench or Chamber of judges; and
therefore no combination of facts possessed any particular value more than another. When a difficulty
came for opinion before the jurisconsult, there was
nothing to prevent a person endowed with a nice
perception of analogy from at once proceeding to
adduce and consider an entire class of supposed
questions with which a particular feature connected
it. Whatever were the practical advice given to
the client, the *responsum* treasured up in the note-
books of listening pupils would doubtless contemplate the circumstances as governed by a great
principle, or included in a sweeping rule. Nothing
like this has ever been possible among ourselves,
and it should be acknowledged that in many criti-
cisms passed on the English law the manner in which
it has been enunciated seems to have been lost sight
of. The hesitation of our courts in declaring principles may be much more reasonably attributed to
the comparative scantiness of our precedents, voluminous as they appear to him who is acquainted
with no other system, than to the temper of our
judges. It is true that in the wealth of legal principle we are considerably poorer than several modern
European nations. But they, it must be remem-
bered, took the Roman jurisprudence for the foundation of their civil institutions. They built the
débris of the Roman law into their walls; but in

the materials and workmanship of the residue there
is not much which distinguishes it favourably from
the structure erected by the English judicature.

The period of Roman freedom was the period
during which the stamp of a distinctive character
was impressed on the Roman jurisprudence; and
through all the earlier part of it, it was by the Responses of the jurisconsults that the development of
the law was mainly carried on. But as we approach
the fall of the republic there are signs that the Responses are assuming a form which must have been
fatal to their farther expansion. They are becoming systematised and reduced into compendia. Q.
Mucius Scævola, the Pontifex, is said to have published a manual of the entire Civil Law, and there
are traces in the writings of Cicero of growing disrelish for the old methods, as compared with the
more active instruments of legal innovation. Other
agencies had in fact by this time been brought to
bear on the law. The Edict, or annual proclamation of the Prætor, had risen into credit as the
principal engine of law reform, and L. Cornelius
Sylla, by causing to be enacted the great group of
statutes called the *Leges Corneliæ*, had shown what
rapid and speedy improvements can be effected by
direct legislation. The final blow to the Responses
was dealt by Augustus, who limited to a few leading jurisconsults the right of giving binding opinions on cases submitted to them, a change which,
though it brings us nearer the ideas of the modern

world, must obviously have altered fundamentally
the characteristics of the legal profession and the
nature of its influence on Roman law. At a later
period another school of jurisconsults arose, the
great lights of jurisprudence for all time. But
Ulpian and Paulus, Gaius and Papinian, were not
authors of Responses. Their works were regular
treatises on particular departments of the law, more
especially on the Prætor's Edict.

The *Equity* of the Romans and the Prætorian
Edict by which it was worked into their system, will
be considered in the next chapter. Of the Statute
Law it is only necessary to say that it was scanty
during the republic, but became very voluminous
under the empire. In the youth and infancy of a
nation it is a rare thing for the legislature to be
called into action for the general reform of private
law. The cry of the people is not for change in
the laws, which are usually valued above their real
worth, but solely for their pure, complete and easy
administration ; and recourse to the legislative body
is generally directed to the removal of some great
abuse, or the decision of some incurable quarrel between classes or dynasties. There seems in the minds
of the Romans to have been some association between the enactment of a large body of statutes and
the settlement of society after a great civil commo-
tion. Sylla signalised his reconstitution of the republic by the Leges Corneliæ; Julius Cæsar contemplated vast additions to the Statute Law; Augustus caused

to be passed the all-important group of Leges Juliæ
nd among later emperors the most active promul
gators of constitutions are princes who, like Con
stantine, have the concerns of the world to readjust.
The true period of Roman Statute Law does not
begin till the establishment of the empire. The
enactments of the emperors, clothed at first in the
pretence of popular sanction, but afterwards ema-
nating undisguisedly from the imperial prerogative,
extend in increasing massiveness from the consolidation of Augustus's power to the publication of the
Code of Justinian. It will be seen that even in the
reign of the second emperor a considerable approximation is made to that condition of the law and
that mode of administering it with which we are all
familiar. A statute law and a limited board of expositors have arisen into being; a permanent court
of appeal and a collection of approved commentaries will very shortly be added; and thus we are
brought close on the ideas of our own day.

CHAPTER III.

THE theory of a set of legal principles entitled by their intrinsic superiority to supersede the older law, very early obtained currency both in the Roman State and in England. Such a body of principles, existing in any system, has in the foregoing chapters been denominated Equity, a term which, as will presently be seen, was one (though only one) of the designations by which this agent of legal change was known to the Roman jurisconsults. The jurisprudence of the Court of Chancery, which bears the name of Equity in England, could only be adequately discussed in a separate treatise. It is extremely complex in its texture, and derives its materials from several heterogeneous sources. The early ecclesiastical chancellors contributed to it, from the Canon Law, many of the principles which lie deepest in its structure. The Roman Law, more fertile than the Canon Law in rules applicable to secular disputes, was not seldom resorted to by a later generation of Chancery judges, amid whose recorded dicta we often find entire texts from the *Corpus Juris Civilis* imbedded, with their terms unaltered, though their origin is never acknowledged. Still more recently, and particularly at the middle and during the latter half of the eighteenth century, the mixed systems of jurisprudence and morals constructed by the publicists of the Low Countries appear to have been much studied by English lawyers, and from the chancellorship of Lord Talbot to the commencement of Lord Eldon's chancellorship these works had considerable effect on the rulings of the Court of Chancery. The system, which obtained its ingredients from these various quarters, was greatly controlled in its growth by the necessity imposed on it of conforming itself to the analogies of the common law, but it has always answered the description of a body of comparatively novel legal principles claiming to override the older jurisprudence of the country on the strength of an intrinsic ethical superiority.

The Equity of Rome was a much simpler structure, and its development from its first appearance can be much more easily traced. Both its character and its history deserve attentive examination. It is the root of several conceptions which have exercised profound influence on human thought, and through human thought have seriously affected the destinies of mankind.

The Romans described their legal system as consisting of two ingredients. "All nations," says the Institutional Treatise published under the authority of the Emperor Justinian, "who are ruled by laws and customs, are governed partly by their own particular laws, and partly by those laws which are common to all mankind. The law which a people enacts is called the Civil Law of that people, but that which natural reason appoints for all mankind is called the Law of Nations, because all nations use it." The part of the law "which natural reason appoints for all mankind" was the element which the Edict of the Prætor was supposed to have worked into Roman jurisprudence. Elsewhere it is styled more simply Jus Naturale, or the Law of Nature; and its ordinances are said to be directed by Natural Equity (*naturalis æquitas*) as well as by natural reason. I shall attempt to discover the origin of these famous phrases, Law of Nations, Law of Nature, Equity, and to determine how the conceptions which they indicate are related to one another.

The most superficial student of Roman history must be struck by the extraordinary degree in which the fortunes of the republic were affected by the presence of foreigners, under different names, on her soil. The causes of this immigration are discernible enough at a later period, for we can readily understand why men of all races should flock to the mistress of the world ; but the same phenomenon of a large population of foreigners and denizens meets us in the very earliest records of the Roman State. No

doubt, the instability of society in ancient Italy,
composed as it was in great measure of robber
tribes, gave men considerable inducement to locate
themselves in the territory of any community strong
enough to protect itself and them from external
attack, even though protection should be purchased
at the cost of heavy taxation, political disfranchise-
ment, and much social humiliation. It is probable,
however, that this explanation is imperfect, and that
it could only be completed by taking into account
those active commercial relations which, though they
are little reflected in the military traditions of the
republic, Rome appears certainly to have had with
Carthage and with the interior of Italy in pre-historic
times. Whatever were the circumstances to which
it was attributable, the foreign element in the commonwealth determined the whole course of its history, which, at all its stages, is little more than a
narrative of conflicts between a stubborn nationality
and an alien population. Nothing like this has been
seen in modern times ; on the one hand, because
modern European communities have seldom or never
received any accession of foreign immigrants which
was large enough to make itself felt by the bulk of
the native citizens, and on the other, because modern states, being held together by allegiance to a
king or political superior, absorb considerable bodies
of immigrant settlers with a quickness unknown to
the ancient world, where the original citizens of a
commonwealth always believed themselves to be

united by kinship in blood, and resented a claim to equality of privilege as a usurpation of their birth right. In the early Roman republic the principle of the absolute exclusion of foreigners pervaded the Civil Law no less than the constitution. The alien or denizen could have no share in any institution supposed to be coeval with the State. He could not have the benefit of Quiritarian law. He could not be a party to the *nexum* which was at once the conveyance and the contract of the primitive Romans. He could not sue by the Sacramental Action, a mode of litigation of which the origin mounts up to the very infancy of civilisation. Still, neither the interest nor the security of Rome permitted him to be quite outlawed. All ancient communities ran the risk of being overthrown by a very slight disturbance of equilibrium, and the mere instinct of self-preservation would force the Romans to devise some method of adjusting the rights and duties of foreigners, who might otherwise—and this was a danger of real importance in the ancient world—have decided their controversies by armed strife. Moreover, at no period of Roman history was foreign trade entirely neglected. It was therefore probably half as a measure of police and half in furtherance of commerce that jurisdiction was first assumed in disputes to which the parties were either foreigners or a native and a foreigner. The assumption of such a jurisdiction brought with it the immediate necessity of discovering some principles on which the questions to be adjudicated upon could be settled, and the principles applied to this object by the Roman lawyers were eminently characteristic of the time. They refused, as I have said before, to decide the new cases by pure Roman Civil Law. They refused, no doubt because it seemed to involve some kind of degradation, to apply the law of the particular State from which the foreign litigant came. The expedient to which they resorted was that of selecting the rules of law common to Rome and to the different Italian communities in which the immigrants were born. In other words, they set themselves to form a system answering to the primitive and literal meaning of Jus Gentium, that is, Law common to all Nations. Jus Gentium was, in fact, the sum of the common ingredients in the customs of the old Italian tribes, for they were *all the nations* whom the Romans had the means of observing, and who sent successive swarms of immigrants to Roman soil. Whenever a particular usage was seen to be practised by a large number of separate races in common it was set down as part of the Law common to all Nations, or Jus Gentium. Thus, although the conveyance of property was certainly accompanied by very different forms in the different commonwealths surrounding Rome, the actual transfer, tradition, or delivery of the article intended to be conveyed was a part of the ceremonial in all of them. It was, for instance, a part, though a subordinate part, in the

Mancipation or conveyance peculiar to Rome. Tradition, therefore, being in all probability the only common ingredient in the modes of conveyance which the jurisconsults had the means of observing was set down as an institution Juris Gentium, or rule of the Law common to all Nations. A vast number of other observances were scrutinised with the same result. Some common characteristic was discovered in all of them, which had a common object, and this characteristic was classed in the Jus Gentium. The Jus Gentium was accordingly a collection of rules and principles, determined by observation to be common to the institutions which prevailed among the various Italian tribes.

The circumstances of the origin of the Jus Gentium are probably a sufficient safeguard against the mistake of supposing that the Roman lawyers had any special respect for it. It was the fruit in part of their disdain for all foreign law, and in part of their disinclination to give the foreigner the advantage of their own indigenous Jus Civile. It is true that we, at the present day, should probably take a very different view of the Jus Gentium, if we were performing the operation which was effected by the Roman jurisconsults. We should attach some vague superiority or precedence to the element which we had thus discerned underlying and pervading so great a variety of usage. We should have a sort of respect for rules and principles so universal. Perhaps we should speak of the common ingredient as

being of the essence of the transaction into which it
entered, and should stigmatise the remaining apparatus of ceremony, which varied in different communities, as adventitious and accidental. Or it may
be, we should infer that the races which we were
comparing at once obeyed a great system of common institutions of which the Jus Gentium was the
reproduction, and that the complicated usages of
separate commonwealths were only corruptions and
depravations of the simpler ordinances which had
once regulated their primitive state. But the results
to which modern ideas conduct the observer are, as
nearly as possible, the reverse of those which were
instinctively brought home to the primitive Roman.
What we respect or admire, he disliked or regarded
with jealous dread. The parts of jurisprudence
which he looked upon with affection were exactly
those which a modern theorist leaves out of consideration as accidental and transitory; the solemn
gestures of the mancipation; the nicely adjusted
questions and answers of the verbal contract; the
endless formalities of pleading and procedure. The
Jus Gentium was merely a system forced on his attention by a political necessity. He loved it as little
as he loved the foreigners from whose institutions it
was derived and for whose benefit it was intended.
A complete revolution in his ideas was required before it could challenge his respect, but so complete
was it when it did occur, that the true reason why
our modern estimate of the Jus Gentium differs from

3

that which has just been described, is that both
modern jurisprudence and modern philosophy have
inherited the matured views of the later juriscon
sults on this subject. There did come a time when,
from an ignoble appendage of the Jus Civile, th
Jus Gentium came to be considered a great though
as yet imperfectly developed model to which all law
ought as far as possible to conform. This crisis arrived when the Greek theory of a Law of Nature
was applied to the practical Roman administration
of the Law common to all Nations.

The Jus Naturale, or Law of Nature, is simply
the Jus Gentium or Law of Nations seen in the light
of a peculiar theory. An unfortunate attempt to
discriminate them was made by the jurisconsult
Ulpian, with the propensity to distinguish characteristic of a lawyer, but the language of Gaius, a
much higher authority, and the passage quoted before from the Institutes, leave no room for doubt
that the expressions were practically convertible
The difference between them was entirely historical,
and no distinction in essence could ever be established between them. It is almost unnecessary to
add that the confusion between Jus Gentium, or Law
common to all nations, and *international law* is entirely modern. The classical expression for international law is Jus Feciale, or the law of negotiation
and diplomacy. It is, however, unquestionable
that indistinct impressions as to the meaning of Jus
Gentium had considerable share in producing the

modern theory that the relations of independent states are governed by the Law of Nature.

It becomes necessary to investigate the Greek conceptions of Nature and her law. The word φύσις, which was rendered in the Latin *natura* and our *nature*, denoted beyond all doubt originally the material universe contemplated under an as-pect which—such is our intellectual distance from those times—it is not very easy to delineate in modern language. Nature signified the physical world regarded as the result of some primordial element or law. The oldest Greek philosophers have been accustomed to explain the fabric of crea-tion as the manifestation of some single principle which they variously asserted to be movement, *force*, fire, moisture, or generation. In its simplest and most ancient sense, Nature is precisely the physical universe looked upon in this way as the manifestation of a principle. Afterwards, the later Greek sects, returning to a path from which the greatest intellects of Greece had meanwhile strayed, added the *moral* to the *physical* world in the con-ception of Nature. They extended the term till it embraced not merely the visible creation, but the thoughts, observances, and aspirations of mankind. Still, as before, it was not solely the moral phe-nomena of human society which they understood by *Nature*, but these phenomena considered as re-solvable into some general and simple laws.

Now, just as the oldest Greek theorists sup

posed that the sports of chance had changed the
material universe from its simple primitive form
into its present heterogeneous condition, so their
intellectual descendants imagined that but for un-
toward accident the human race would have conformed itself to simpler rules of conduct and a less
tempestuous life. To live according to *nature* came
to be considered as the end for which man was
created, and which the best men were bound to
compass. To live according to *nature* was to rise
above the disorderly habits and gross indulgences
of the vulgar to higher laws of action which nothing but self-denial and self-command would enable
the aspirant to observe. It is notorious that this
proposition—live according to nature—was the sum
of the tenets of the famous Stoic philosophy. Now
on the subjugation of Greece that philosophy made
instantaneous progress in Roman society. It possessed natural fascinations for the powerful class
who, in theory at least, adhered to the simple
habits of the ancient Italian race, and disdained to
surrender themselves to the innovations of foreign
fashion. Such persons began immediately to affect
the Stoic precepts of life according to nature—an
affectation all the more grateful, and, I may add, all
the more noble, from its contrast with the unbounded profligacy which was being diffused through the
imperial city by the pillage of the world and by the
example of its most luxurious races. In the front
of the disciples of the new Greek school, we might

be sure, even if we did not know it historically
that the Roman lawyers figured. We have abun
dant proof that, there being substantially but two
professions in the Roman republic, the military men
were generally identified with the party of move
ment, but the lawyers were universally at the head
of the party of resistance.

The alliance of the lawyers with the Stoic phi·
losophers lasted through many centuries. Some of
the earliest names in the series of renowned juris·
consults are associated with Stoicism, and ultimate·
ly we have the golden age of Roman jurisprudence
fixed by general consent at the era of the Antonine
Cæsars, the most famous disciples to whom that
philosophy has given a rule of life. The long
diffusion of these doctrines among the members of a
particular profession was sure to affect the art which
they practised and influenced. Several positions
which we find in the remains of the Roman juris·
consults are scarcely intelligible unless we use the
Stoic tenets as our key; but at the same time it is
a serious, though a very common, error to measure
the influence of Stoicism on Roman law by counting
up the number of legal rules which can be con·
fidently affiliated on Stoical dogmas. It has often
been observed that the strength of Stoicism resided
not in its canons of conduct, which were often re·
pulsive and ridiculous, but in the great though
vague principle which it inculcated of resistance to
passion. Just in the same way the influence or

jurisprudence of the Greek theories, which had their most distinct expression in Stoicism, consisted not in the number of specific positions which they con-tributed to Roman law, but in the single funda-mental assumption which they lent to it. After Nature had become a household word in the mouths of the Romans, the belief gradually prevailed among the Roman lawyers that the old Jus Gentium was in fact the lost code of Nature, and that the Prætor in framing an Edictal jurisprudence on the prin-ciples of the Jus Gentium was gradually restoring a type from which law had only departed to de-teriorate. The inference from this belief was imme-diate that it was the Prætor's duty to supersede the Civil Law as much as possible by the Edict, to re-vive as far as might be the institutions by which Nature had governed man in the primitive state. Of course there were many impediments to the amelioration of law by this agency. There may have been prejudices to overcome even in the legal profession itself, and Roman habits were far too tenacious to give way at once to mere philosophical theory. The indirect methods by which the Edict combated certain technical anomalies, show the cau-tion which its authors were compelled to observe, and down to the very days of Justinian there was some part of the old law which had obstinately re-sisted its influence. But on the whole, the progress of the Romans in legal improvement was astonish-ingly rapid as soon as stimulus was applied to it by

the theory of Natural Law. The ideas of simplification and generalization had always been associated with the conception of Nature; simplicity,
symmetry, and intelligibility came therefore to be
regarded as the characteristics of a good legal system, and the taste for involved language, multiplied
ceremonials, and useless difficulties disappeared altogether. The strong will and unusual opportunities of Justinian were needed to bring the Roman
law into its existing shape, but the ground plan of
the system had been sketched long before the imperial reforms were effected.

What was the exact point of contact between
the old Jus Gentium and the Law of Nature? I
think that they touch and blend through Æquitas,
or Equity in its original sense; and here we seem to
come to the first appearance in jurisprudence of this
famous term, Equity. In examining an expression
which has so remote an origin and so long a history
as this, it is always safest to penetrate, if possible,
to the simple metaphor or figure which at first
shadowed forth the conception. It has generally
been supposed that Æquitas is the equivalent of the
Greek ἰσότης, i. e. the principle of equal or propor-
tionate distribution. The equal division of numbers or physical magnitudes is doubtless closely entwined with our perceptions of justice; there are
few associations which keep their ground in the
mind so stubbornly or are dismissed from it with
such difficulty by the deepest thinkers. Yet in

tracing the history of this association, it certainly
does not seem to have suggested itself to very early
thought, but is rather the offspring of a compara
tively late philosophy. It is remarkable too that
the " equality " of laws on which the Greek democ-
racies prided themselves—that equality which, in
the beautiful drinking song of Callistratus, Harmo-
dius and Aristogiton are said to have given to
Athens—had little in common with the " equity "
of the Romans. The first was an equal administration of civil laws among the citizens, however
limited the class of citizens might be ; the last implied the applicability of a law, which was not civil
law, to a class which did not necessarily consist of
citizens. The first excluded a despot ; the last included foreigners, and for some purposes slaves.
On the whole, I should be disposed to look in
another direction for the germ of the Roman
" Equity." The Latin word " æquus " carries with
it more distinctly than the Greek " ἴσος " the sense
of *levelling*. Now its levelling tendency was exactly the characteristic of the Jus Gentium, which
would be most striking to a primitive Roman. The
pure Quiritarian law recognised a multitude of arbitrary distinctions between classes of men and
kinds of property ; the Jus Gentium, generalised
from a comparison of various customs, neglected the
Quiritarian divisions. The old Roman law estab
lished, for example, a fundamental difference between "Agnatic " and " Cognatic " relationship, that

is, between the Family considered as based upon common subjection to patriarchal authority and the Family considered (in conformity with modern ideas) as united through the mere fact of a common descent. This distinction disappears in the "law common to all nations," as also does the difference between the archaic forms of property, Things "Mancipi" and Things "nec Mancipi." The neglect of demarcations and boundaries seems to me, therefore, the feature of the Jus Gentium which was depicted in Æquitas. I imagine that the word was at first a mere description of that constant *levelling* or removal of irregularities which went on wherever the prætorian system was applied to the cases of foreign litigants. Probably no colour of ethical meaning belonged at first to the expression ; nor is there any reason to believe that the process which it indicated was otherwise than extremely distasteful to the primitive Roman mind.

On the other hand, the feature of the Jus Gentium which was presented to the apprehension of a Roman by the word Equity, was exactly the first and most vividly realised characteristic of the hypothetical state of nature. Nature implied symmetrical order, first in the physical world, and next in the moral, and the earliest notion of order doubtless involved straight lines, even surfaces, and measured distances. The same sort of picture or figure would be unconsciously before the mind's eye, whether it strove to form the outlines of the sup-

posed natural state, or whether it took in at a glance
the actual administration of the " law common to
all nations ; " and all we know of primitive thought
would lead us to conclude that this ideal similarity
would do much to encourage the belief in an identity of the two conceptions. But then, while the
Jus Gentium had little or no antecedent credit at
Rome, the theory of a Law of Nature came in surrounded with all the prestige of philosophical authority, and invested with the charms of association
with an elder and more blissful condition of the
race. It is easy to understand how the difference in
the point of view would affect the dignity of the
term which at once described the operation of the
old principles and the results of the new theory.
Even to modern ears it is not at all the same thing
to describe a process as one of " levelling " and to
call it the " correction of anomalies," though the
metaphor is precisely the same. Nor do I doubt
that, when once Æquitas was understood to convey an allusion to the Greek theory, associations
which grew out of the Greek notion of ἰσότης began
to cluster round it. The language of Cicero renders
it more than likely that this was so, and it was the
first stage of a transmutation of the conception of
Equity, which almost every ethical system which
has appeared since those days has more or less
helped to carry on.

Something must be said of the formal instrumentality by which the principles and distinctions

associated, first with the Law common to all Nations, and afterwards with the Law of Nature, were
gradually incorporated with the Roman law. At
the crisis of primitive Roman history which is
marked by the expulsion of the Tarquins, a change
occurred which has its parallel in the early annals
of many ancient states, but which had little in common with those passages of political affairs which
we now term revolutions. It may best be described
by saying that the monarchy was put into commission. The powers heretofore accumulated in the
hands of a single person were parcelled out among
a number of elective functionaries, the very name
of the kingly office being retained and imposed on
a personage known subsequently as the Rex Sac-
rorum or Rex Sacrificulus. As part of the change,
the settled duties of the supreme judicial office devolved on the Prætor, at the time the first functionary in the commonwealth, and together with these
duties was transferred the undefined supremacy
over law and legislation which always attached to
ancient sovereigns, and which is not obscurely related to the patriarchal and heroic authority they
had once enjoyed. The circumstances of Rome gave
great importance to the more indefinite portion of
the functions thus transferred, as with the establishment of the republic began that series of recurrent
trials which overtook the state, in the difficulty of
dealing with a multitude of persons who, not coming within the technical description of indigenous

Romans were nevertheless permanently located within Roman jurisdiction. Controversies between such persons, or between such persons and native born citizens, could have remained without the pale of the remedies provided by Roman law, if the Prætor had not undertaken to decide them, and he must soon have addressed himself to the more critical disputes which in the extension of commerce arose between Roman subjects and avowed foreigners. The great increase of such cases in the Roman Courts about the period of the first Punic War is marked by the appointment of a special Prætor, known subsequently as the Prætor Peregrinus, who gave them his undivided attention. Meantime, one precaution of the Roman people against the revival of oppression, had consisted in obliging every magistrate whose duties had any tendency to expand their sphere, to publish, on commencing his year of office, an Edict or proclamation, in which he declared the manner in which he intended to administer his department. The Prætor fell under the rule with other magistrates; but as it was necessarily impossible to construct each year a separate system of principles, he seems to have regularly republished his predecessor's Edict with such additions and changes as the exigency of the moment or his own views of the law compelled him to introduce. The Prætor's proclamation, thus lengthened by a new portion every year, obtained the name of the Edictum Perpetuum, that is, the *continuous* or *unbroken* edict. The immense length to which it extended, together perhaps with some distaste for its necessarily.disorderly texture, caused the practice of increasing it to be stopped in the year of Salvius Julianus, who occupied the magistracy in the reign of the Emperor Hadrian. The edict of that Prætor embraced therefore the whole body of equity jurisprudence, which it probably disposed in new and symmetrical order, and the perpetual edict is therefore often cited in Roman law merely as the Edict of Julianus.

Perhaps the first inquiry which occurs to an Englishman who considers the peculiar mechanism of the Edict is, what were the limitations by which these extensive powers of the Prætor were restrained? How was authority so little definite to be reconciled with a settled condition of society and law? The answer can only be supplied by careful observation of the conditions under which our own English law is administered. The Prætor, it should be recollected, was a jurisconsult himself, or a person entirely in the hands of advisers who were jurisconsults, and it is probable that every Roman lawyer waited impatiently for the time when he should fill or control the great judicial magistracy. In the interval, his tastes, feelings, prejudices, and degree of enlightenment were inevitably those of his own order, and the qualifications which he ultimately brought to office were those which he had acquired in the practice and study of his profession.

An English Chancellor goes through precisely the
same training, and carries to the woolsack the same
qualifications. It is certain when he assumes office
that he will have, to some extent, modified the law
before he leaves it; but until he has quitted his
seat, and the series of his decisions in the Law Reports has been completed, we cannot discover how
far he has elucidated or added to the principles
which his predecessors bequeathed to him. The influence of the Prætor on Roman jurisprudence differed only in respect of the period at which its
amount was ascertained. As was before stated, he
was in office but for a year, and his decisions rendered during his year, though of course irreversible
as regarded the litigants, were of no ulterior value.
The most natural moment for declaring the changes
he proposed to effect, occurred therefore at his en-
trance on the prætorship; and hence, when commencing his duties, he did openly and avowedly
that which in the end his English representative
does insensibly and sometimes unconsciously. The
checks on his apparent liberty are precisely those
imposed on an English judge. Theoretically there
seems to be hardly any limit to the powers of either
of them, but practically the Roman Prætor, no less
than the English Chancellor, was kept within the
narrowest bounds by the prepossessions imbibed
from early training, and by the strong restraints of
professional opinion, restraints of which the stringency can only be appreciated by those who have

personally experienced them. It may be added that the lines within which movement is permitted, and beyond which there is to be no travelling, were chalked with as much distinctness in the one case as in the other. In England the judge follows the analogies of reported decisions on insulated groups of facts. At Rome, as the intervention of the Prætor was at first dictated by simple concern for the safety of the state, it is likely that in the earliest times it was proportioned to the difficulty which it attempted to get rid of. Afterwards, when the taste for principle had been diffused by the Responses, he no doubt used the Edict as the means of giving a wider application to those funda-mental principles which he and the other practising jurisconsults, his contemporaries, believed them-selves to have detected underlying the law. Lat-terly he acted wholly under the influence of Greek philosophical theories, which at once tempted him to advance and confined him to a particular course of progress.

The nature of the measures attributed to Salvius Julianus has been much disputed. Whatever they were, their effects on the Edict are sufficiently plain. It ceased to be extended by annual additions, and henceforward the equity jurisprudence of Rome was developed by the labours of a succession of great jurisconsults who fill with their writings the inter-val between the reign of Hadrian and the reign of Alexander Severus. A fragment of the wonderfu

system which they built up survives in the Pandects of Justinian, and supplies evidence that their
works took the form of treatises on all parts of Roman law, but chiefly that of commentaries on the
Edict. Indeed, whatever be the immediate subject
of a jurisconsult of this epoch, he may always be
called an expositor of Equity. The principles of
the Edict had, before the epoch of its cessation,
made their way into every part of Roman jurisprudence. The Equity of Rome, it should be understood, even when most distinct from the Civil Law,
was always administered by the same tribunals.
The Prætor was the chief equity judge as well as
the great common law magistrate, and as soon as
the Edict had evolved an equitable rule the Prætor's court began to apply it in place of or by the
side of the old rule of the Civil Law, which was
thus directly or indirectly repealed without any express enactment of the legislature. The result, of
course, fell considerably short of a complete fusion
of law and equity, which was not carried out till
the reforms of Justinian. The technical severance
of the two elements of jurisprudence entailed some
confusion and some inconvenience, and there were
certain of the stubborner doctrines of the Civil Law
with which neither the authors nor the expositors
of the Edict had ventured to interfere. But at the
same time there was no corner of the field of jurisprudence which was not more or less swept over by
the influence of Equity   It supplied the jurist with

all his materials for generalisation, with all his methods of interpretation, with his elucidations of first principles, and with that great mass of limiting rules which are rarely interfered with by the legis-lator, but which seriously control the application of every legislative act.

The period of jurists ends with Alexander Sev-erus. From Hadrian to that emperor the improve-ment of law was carried on, as it is at the present moment in most continental countries, partly by approved commentaries and partly by direct legis-lation. But in the reign of Alexander Severus the power of growth in Roman Equity seems to be ex hausted, and the succession of jurisconsults comes to a close. The remaining history of the Roman law is the history of the imperial constitutions, and, at the last, of attempts to codify what had now be-come the unwieldy body of Roman jurisprudence. We have the latest and most celebrated experiment of this kind in the *Corpus Juris* of Justinian.

It would be wearisome to enter on a detailed comparison or contrast of English and Roman Equity; but it may be worth while to mention two features which they have in common. The first may be stated as follows. Each of them tended, and all such systems tend, to exactly the same state in which the old common law was when Equity first interfered with it. A time always comes at which the moral principles originally adopted have been carried out to all their legitimate consequences

5

and then the system founded on them becomes as
rigid, as unexpansive, and as liable to fall behind
moral progress as the sternest code of rules avowedly legal.   Such an epoch was reached at Rome in the
reign of Alexander Severus; after which, though
the whole Roman world was undergoing a moral
revolution, the Equity of Rome ceased to expand.
The same point of legal history was attained in
England under the chancellorship of Lord Eldon
the first of our equity judges who, instead of enlarging the jurisprudence of his court by indirect
legislation, devoted himself through life to explaining and harmonising it.   If the philosophy of legal
history were better understood in England, Lord
Eldon's services would be less exaggerated on the
one hand and better appreciated on the other than
they appear to be among contemporary lawyers.
Other misapprehensions too, which bear some practical fruit, would perhaps be avoided.   It is easily
seen by English lawyers that English Equity is a
system founded on moral rules; but it is forgotten
that these rules are the morality of past centuries—
not of the present—that they have received nearly
as much application as they are capable of, and
that, though of course they do not differ largely
from the ethical creed of our own day, they are not
necessarily on a level with it.   The imperfect theories of the subject which are commonly adopted
have generated errors of opposite sorts.   Many
writers of treatises on Equity, struck with the com-

pleteness of the system in its present state, commit
themselves expressly or implicitly to the paradoxical assertion that the founders of the chancery jurisprudence contemplated its present fixity of form
when they were settling its first bases.   Others,
again, complain—and this is a grievance frequently observed upon in forensic arguments—that the
moral rules enforced by the Court of Chancery fall
short of the ethical standard of the present day.
They would have each Lord Chancellor perform
precisely the same office for the jurisprudence which
he finds ready to his hand, which was performed
for the old common law by the fathers of English
equity.   But this is to invert the order of the agencies by which the improvement of the law is carried
on.   Equity has its place and its time ; but I have
pointed out that another instrumentality is ready
to succeed it when its energies are spent.

Another remarkable characteristic of both English and Roman Equity is the falsehood of the assumptions upon which the claim of the equitable to
superiority over the legal rule is originally defend-
ed.   Nothing is more distasteful to men, either as
individuals or as masses, than the admission of their
moral progress as a substantive reality.   This unwillingness shows itself, as regards individuals, in
the exaggerated respect which is ordinarily paid to
the doubtful virtue of consistency.   The movement
of the collective opinion of a whole society is too
palpable to be ignored, and is generally too visibly

for the better to be decried ; but there is the great
est disinclination to accept it as a primary phenomenon, and it is commonly explained as the recovery of a lost perfection—the gradual return to a
state from which the race had lapsed. This tendency to look backward instead of forward for the
goal of moral progress produced anciently, as we
have seen, on Roman jurisprudence effects the most
serious and permanent. The Roman jurisconsults,
in order to account for the improvement of their
jurisprudence by the Prætor, borrowed from Greece
the doctrine of a Natural state of man—a Natural
society—anterior to the organization of commonwealths governed by positive laws. In England,
on the other hand, a range of ideas especially congenial to Englishmen of that day, explained the
claim of Equity to override the common law by supposing a general right to superintend the administration of justice which was assumed to be vested
in the king as a natural result of his paternal authority. The same view appears in a different and
quainter form in the old doctrine that Equity flowed
from the king's conscience—the improvement which
had in fact taken place in the moral standard of the
community being thus referred to an inherent elevation in the moral sense of the sovereign. The
growth of the English constitution rendered such a
theory unpalatable after a time ; but, as the juris,
diction of the Chancery was then firmly established-
it was not worth while to devise any formal sub-

stitute for it. The theories found in modern manuals of Equity are very various, but all alike in
their untenability. Most of them are modifications
of the Roman doctrine of a natural law, which is
indeed adopted in terms by those writers who begin a discussion of the jurisdiction of the Court of
Chancery by laying down a distinction between
natural justice and civil.

CHAPTER IV.

IT will be inferred from what has been said that the theory which transformed the Roman jurisprudence had no claim to philosophical precision. It involved, in fact, one of those "mixed modes of thought" which are now acknowledged to have characterized all but the highest minds during the infancy of speculation, and which are far from undiscoverable even in the mental efforts of our own day. The Law of Nature confused the Past and the Present. Logically, it implied a state of Nature which had once been regulated by natural law; yet the jurisconsults do not speak clearly or confidently of the existence of such a state, which indeed is little noticed by the ancients except where it finds a poetical expression in the fancy of a golden age. Natural law, for all practical purposes, was something belonging to the present, something entwined with existing institutions, something which could be distinguished from

them by a competent observer. The test which
separated the ordinances of Nature from the gross
ingredients with which they were mingled was a
sense of simplicity and harmony; yet it was not
on account of their simplicity and harmony that
these finer elements were primarily respected, but
on the score of their descent from the aboriginal
reign of Nature. This confusion has not been successfully explained away by the modern disciples
of the jurisconsults, and in truth modern speculations on the Law of Nature betray much more
indistinctness of perception and are vitiated by
much more hopeless ambiguity of language than
the Roman lawyers can be justly charged with.
There are some writers on the subject who attempt
to evade the fundamental difficulty by contending
that the code of Nature exists in the future and is
the goal to which all civil laws are moving, but
this is to reverse the assumptions on which the old
theory rested, or rather perhaps to mix together
two inconsistent theories. The tendency to look
not to the past but to the future for types of perfection was brought into the world by Christianity.
Ancient literature gives few or no hints of a belief
that the progress of society is necessarily from
worse to better.

But the importance of this theory to mankind
has been very much greater than its philosophical
deficiencies would lead us to expect. Indeed, it
is not easy to say what turn the history of thought

and therefore, of the human race, would have taken, if the belief in a law natural had not become universal in the ancient world.

There are two special dangers to which law and society which is held together by law, appear to be liable in their infancy. One of them is that law may be too rapidly developed. This occurred with the codes of the more progressive Greek communities, which disembarrassed themselves with astonishing facility from cumbrous forms of procedure and needless terms of art, and soon ceased to attach any superstitious value to rigid rules and prescriptions. It was not for the ultimate advantage of mankind that they did so, though the immediate benefit conferred on their citizens may have been considerable. One of the rarest qualities of national character is the capacity for applying and working out the law, as such, at the cost of constant miscarriages of abstract justice, without at the same time losing the hope or the wish that law may be conformed to a higher ideal. The Greek intellect, with all its nobility and elasticity, was quite unable to confine itself within the strait waistcoat of a legal formula; and, if we may judge them by the popular courts of Athens, of whose working we possess accurate knowledge, the Greek tribunals exhibited the strongest tendency to confound law and fact. The remains of the Orators and the forensic commonplaces preserved by Aristotle in his Treatise on Rhetoric, show that ques tions of pure law were constantly argued on every consideration which could possibly influence the mind of the judges. No durable system of juris- prudence could be produced in this way. A com- munity which never hesitated to relax rules of written law whenever they stood in the way of an ideally perfect decision on the facts of particular cases, would only, if it bequeathed any body of judicial principles to posterity, bequeath one con- sisting of the ideas of right and wrong which hap- pened to be prevalent at the time. Such jurispru- dence would contain no framework to which the more advanced conceptions of subsequent ages could be fitted. It would amount at best to a philosophy, marked with the imperfections of the civilisation under which it grew up.

Few national societies have had their jurispru- dence menaced by this peculiar danger of precocious maturity and untimely disintegration. It is cer- tainly doubtful whether the Romans were ever seriously threatened by it, but at any rate they had adequate protection in their theory of Natural Law. For the Natural Law of the jurisconsults was dis- tinctly conceived by them as a system which ought gradually to absorb civil laws, without superseding them so long as they remained unrepealed. There was no such impression of its sanctity abroad, that an appeal to it would be likely to overpower the mind of a judge who was charged with the superin- tendence of a particular litigation   The value and

serviceableness of the conception arose from its
keeping before the mental vision a type of perfect
law, and from its inspiring the hope of an indefinite
approximation to it, at the same time that it never
tempted the practitioner or the citizen to deny the
obligation of existing laws which had not yet been
adjusted to the theory.   It is important too to observe that this model system, unlike many of those
which have mocked men's hopes in later days, was
not entirely the product of imagination.   It was
never thought of as founded on quite untested principles.   The notion was that it underlay existing
law and must be looked for through it.   Its functions were in short remedial, not revolutionary or
anarchical.   And this, unfortunately, is the exact
point at which the modern view of a Law of Nature has often ceased to resemble the ancient.

The other liability to which the infancy of society is exposed has prevented or arrested the progress
of far the greater part of mankind.   The rigidity of
primitive law, arising chiefly from its early associa
tion and identification with religion, has chained
down the mass of the human race to those views
of life and conduct which they entertained at the
time when their usages were first consolidated into
a systematic form.   There were one or two races
exempted by a marvellous fate from this calamity,
and grafts from these stocks have fertilised a few
modern societies; but it is still true that, over the
larger part of the world, the perfection of law has

always been considered as consisting in adherence to the ground plan supposed to have been marked out by the original legislator. If intellect has in such cases been exercised on jurisprudence, it has uniformly prided itself on the subtle perversity of the conclusions it could build on ancient texts, without discoverable departure from their literal tenour. I know no reason why the law of the Romans should be superior to the laws of the Hindoos, unless the theory of Natural Law had given it a type of excellence different from the usual one. In this one exceptional instance, simplicity and symmetry were kept before the eyes of a society whose influence on mankind was destined to be prodigious from other causes, as the characteristics of an ideal and absolutely perfect law. It is impossible to overrate the importance to a nation or profession of having a distinct object to aim at in the pursuit of improvement. The secret of Bentham's immense influence in England during the past thirty years is his success in placing such an object before the country. He gave us a clear rule of reform. English lawyers of the last century were probably too acute to be blinded by the paradoxical commonplace that English law was the perfection of human reason, but they acted as if they believed it, for want of any other principle to proceed upon. Bentham made the good of the community take precedence of every other object, and thus gave escape to a current which had long been trying to find its way outwards.

It is not an altogether fanciful comparison if we call the assumptions we have been describing the ancient counterpart of Benthamism. The Roman theory guided men's efforts in the same direction as the theory put into shape by the Englishman; its practical results were not widely different from those which would have been attained by a sect of law-reformers who maintained a steady pursuit of the general good of the community. It would be a mistake, however, to suppose it a conscious anticipation of Bentham's principles. The happiness of mankind is, no doubt, sometimes assigned both in the popular and in the legal literature of the Romans, as the proper object of remedial legislation, but it is very remarkable how few and faint are the testimonies to this principle compared with the tributes which are constantly offered to the overshadowing claims of the Law of Nature. It was not to anything resembling philanthropy, but to their sense of simplicity and harmony—of what they significantly termed "elegance"—that the Roman jurisconsults freely surrendered themselves. The coincidence of their labours with those which a more precise philosophy would have counselled has been part of the good fortune of mankind.

Turning to the modern history of the law of nature, we find it easier to convince ourselves of the vastness of its influence than to pronounce confidently whether that influence has been exerted for good or for evil. The doctrines and institutions

which may be attributed to it are the material of
some of the most violent controversies debated in
our time, as will be seen when it is stated that the
theory of Natural Law is the source of almost all the
special ideas as to law, politics, and society which
France during the last hundred years has been the
instrument of diffusing over the western world.
The part played by jurists in French history, and
the sphere of jural conceptions in French thought,
have always been remarkably large.   It was not indeed in France, but in Italy, that the juridical science
of modern Europe took its rise, but of the schools
founded by emissaries of the Italian universities in
all parts of the continent, and attempted (though
vainly) to be set up in our island, that established
in France produced the greatest effect on the fortunes of the country.   The lawyers of France immediately formed a strict alliance with the kings of the
houses of Capet and Valois, and it was as much
through their assertions of royal prerogative, and
through their interpretations of the rules of feudal
succession, as by the power of the sword, that the
French monarchy at last grew together out of the
agglomeration of provinces and dependencies.   The
enormous advantage which their understanding with
the lawyers conferred on the French kings in the
prosecution of their struggle with the great feuda-
tories, the aristocracy, and the church, can only be
appreciated if we take into account the ideas which
prevailed in Europe far down into the middle ages

There was, in the first place, a great enthusiasn. for
generalisation and a curious admiration for all general propositions, and consequently, in the field of
law, an involuntary reverence for every general
formula which seemed to embrace and sum up a
number of the insulated rules which were practised
as usages in various localities. Such general formulas it was, of course, not difficult for practitioners
familiar with the Corpus Juris or the Glosses to
supply in almost any quantity. There was, however,
another cause which added yet more considerably
to the lawyers' power. At the period of which we
are speaking, there was universal vagueness of ideas
as to the degree and nature of the authority residing
in written texts of law. For the most part, the
peremptory preface, *Ita scriptum est*, seems to have
been sufficient to silence all objections. Where a
mind of our own day would jealously scrutinise the
formula which had been quoted, would inquire its
source, and would (if necessary) deny that the body
of law to which it belonged had any authority to
supersede local customs, the elder jurist would not
probably have ventured to do more than question
the applicability of the rule, or at best cite some
counter-proposition from the Pandects or the Canon
Law. It is extremely necessary to bear in mind the
uncertainty of men's notions on this most important
side of juridical controversies, not only because it
helps to explain the weight which the lawyers
threw into the monarchical scale, but on account of

the light which it sheds on several curious historical problems. The motives of the author of the Forged Decretals and his extraordinary success are rendered more intelligible by it. And, to take a phenomenon of smaller interest, it assists us, though only partially to understand the plagiarisms of Bracton. That an English writer of the time of Henry III. should have been able to put off on his countrymen as a compendium of pure English law a treatise of which the entire form and a third of the contents were directly borrowed from the Corpus Juris, and that he should have ventured on this experiment in a country where the systematic study of the Roman law was formally proscribed, will always be among the most hopeless enigmas in the history of jurisprudence; but still it is something to lessen our surprise when we comprehend the state of opinion at the period as to the obligatory force of written texts, apart from all consideration of the source whence they were derived.

When the kings of France had brought their long struggle for supremacy to a successful close, an epoch which may be placed roughly at the accession of the branch of Valois-Angoulême to the throne, the situation of the French jurists was peculiar, and continued to be so down to the outbreak of the revolution. On the one hand, they formed the best instructed and nearly the most powerful class in the nation. They had made good their footing as a privileged order by the side of the feudal aristoc-

racy, and they had assured their influence by an
organisation which distributed their profession over
France in great chartered corporations possessing
large defined powers and still larger indefinite claims.
In all the qualities of the advocate, the judge, and the
legislator, they far excelled their compeers throughout Europe. Their juridical tact, their ease of expression, their fine sense of analogy and harmony,
and (if they may be judged by the highest names
among them) their passionate devotion to their
conceptions of justice, were as remarkable as the
singular variety of talent which they included, a
variety covering the whole ground between the opposite poles of Cujas and Montesquieu, of D'Agues-
seau and Dumoulin. But, on the other hand, the
system of laws which they had to administer stood
in striking contrast with the habits of mind which
they had cultivated. The France which had been
in great part constituted by their efforts was smitten
with the curse of an anomalous and dissonant jurisprudence beyond every other country in Europe.
One great division ran through the country and
separated it into *Pays du Droit Ecrit* and *Pays du
Droit Coutumier*, the first acknowledging the written Roman law as the basis of their jurisprudence,
the last admitting it only so far as it supplied general forms of expression, and courses of juridical
reasoning, which were reconcileable with the local
usages. The sections thus formed were again variously subdivided. In the *Pays du Droit Coutu-*

mier province differed from province, county from county, municipality from municipality, in the nature of its customs. In the *Pays du Droit Ecrit* the stratum of feudal rules which overlay the Roman law was of the most miscellaneous composition. No such confusion as this ever existed in England. In Germany it did exist, but was too much in harmony with the deep political and religious divisions of the country to be lamented or even felt. It was the special peculiarity of France that an extraordinary diversity of laws continued without sensible altera- tion while the central authority of the monarchy was constantly strengthening itself, while rapid ap- proaches were being made to complete administra- tive unity, and while a fervid national spirit had been developed among the people. The contrast was one which fructified in many serious results, and among them we must rank the effect which it pro- duced on the minds of the French lawyers. Their speculative opinions and their intellectual bias were in the strongest opposition to their interests and professional habits. With the keenest sense and the fullest recognition of those perfections of juris- prudence which consist in simplicity and uniformity, they believed, or seemed to believe, that the vices which actually invested French law were ineradica- ble ; and in practice they often resisted the reforma- tion of abuses with an obstinacy which was not shown by many among their less enlightened coun- trymen. But there was a way to reconcile these

6

contradictions. They became passionate enthusiasts
for Natural Law. The Law of Nature overleapt all
provincial and municipal boundaries; it disregarded
all distinctions between noble and burgess, between
burgess and peasant; it gave the most exalted place
to lucidity, simplicity, and system; but it committed
its devotees to no specific improvement, and did not
directly threaten any venerable or lucrative techni-
cality. Natural law may be said to have become
the common law of France, or, at all events, the
admission of its dignity and claims was the one
tenet which all French practitioners alike subscribed to. The language of the præ-revolution-
ary jurists in its eulogy is singularly unqualified,
and it is remarkable that the writers on the Customs, who often made it their duty to speak dis-
paragingly of the pure Roman law, speak even
more fervidly of Nature and her rules than the
civilians who professed an exclusive respect for the
Digest and the Code. Dumoulin, the highest of all
authorities on old French Customary Law, has some
extravagant passages on the Law of Nature; and
his panegyrics have a peculiar rhetorical turn which
indicates a considerable departure from the caution
of the Roman jurisconsults. The hypothesis of a
Natural Law had become not so much a theory
guiding practice as an article of speculative faith
and accordingly we shall find that, in the transformation which it more recently underwent, its weak

est parts rose to the level of its strongest in the esteem of its supporters.

The eighteenth century was half over when the most critical period in the history of Natural Law was reached. Had the discussion of the theory and of its consequences continued to be exclusively the employment of the legal profession, there would possibly have been an abatement of the respect which it commanded; for by this time the *Esprit des Lois* had appeared. Bearing in some exaggerations the marks of the excessive violence with which its author's mind had recoiled from assumptions usually suffered to pass without scrutiny, yet showing in some ambiguities the traces of a desire to compromise with existing prejudice, the book of Montesquieu, with all its defects, still proceeded on that Historical Method before which the Law of Nature has never maintained its footing for an instant. Its influence on thought ought to have been as great as its general popularity; but, in fact, it was never allowed time to put it forth, for the counter-hypothesis which it seemed destined to destroy passed suddenly from the forum to the street, and became the key-note of controversies far more exciting than are ever agitated in the courts or the schools. The person who launched it on its new career was that remarkable man who, without learning, with few virtues, and with no strength of character, has nevertheless stamped himself ineffaceably on history by the force of a vivid imagination, and

by the help of a genuine and burning love for his fel-
low-men, for which much will always have to be for-
given him.   We have never seen in our own generation—indeed the world has not seen more than once
or twice in all the course of history—a literature
which has exercised such prodigious influence over
the minds of men, over every cast and shade of intellect, as that which emanated from Rousseau between 1749 and 1762.   It was the first attempt to
re-erect the edifice of human belief after the purely
iconoclastic efforts commenced by Bayle, and in part
by our own Locke, and consummated by Voltaire;
and besides the superiority which every constructive
effort will always enjoy over one that is merely de-
structive, it possessed the immense advantage of ap-
pearing amid an all but universal scepticism as to
the soundness of all foregone knowledge in matters
speculative.   Now, in all the speculations of Rousseau, the central figure, whether arrayed in an English dress as the signatary of a social compact, or
simply stripped naked of all historical qualities, is
uniformly Man, in a supposed state of nature.   Every
law or institution which would misbeseem this
imaginary being under these ideal circumstances is
to be condemned as having lapsed from an original
perfection; every transformation of society which
would give it a closer resemblance to the world
over which the creature of Nature reigned, is ad-
mirable and worthy to be effected at any apparent
cost.   The theory is still that of the Roman law-

yers, for in the phantasmagoria with which the
Natural Condition is peopled, every feature and
characteristic eludes the mind except the simplicity
and harmony which possessed such charms for the
jurisconsult; but the theory is, as it were, turned up-
side down.   It is not the Law of Nature, but the
State of Nature, which is now the primary subject
of contemplation.   The Roman had conceived that
by careful observation of existing institutions parts
of them could be singled out which either exhibited
already, or could by judicious purification be made
to exhibit, the vestiges of that reign of nature whose
reality he faintly affirmed.   Rousseau's belief was
that a perfect social order could be evolved from
the unassisted consideration of the natural state, a
social order wholly irrespective of the actual condition of the world and wholly unlike it.   The
great difference between the views is that one bit-
terly and broadly condemns the present for its un-
likeness to the ideal past; while the other, assuming
the present to be as necessary as the past, does not
affect to disregard or censure it.   It is not worth
our while to analyse with any particularity that
philosophy of politics, art, education, ethics, and
social relation which was constructed on the basis
of a state of nature.   It still possesses singular fasci-
nation for the looser thinkers of every country, and
is no doubt the parent, more or less remote, of almost all the prepossessions which impede the employment of the Historical Method of inquiry, but

its discredit with the higher minds of our day is deep enough to astonish those who are familiar with the extraordinary vitality of speculative error. Perhaps the question most frequently asked nowadays is not what is the value of these opinions, but what were the causes which gave them such overshadowing prominence a hundred years ago. The answer is, I conceive, a simple one. The study which in the last century would best have corrected the misapprehensions into which an exclusive attention to legal antiquities is apt to betray was the study of religion. But Greek religion, as then understood, was dissipated in imaginative myths. The Oriental religions, if noticed at all, appeared to be lost in vain cosmogonies. There was but one body of primitive records which was worth studying— the early history of the Jews. But resort to this was prevented by the prejudices of the time. One of the few characteristics which the school of Rousseau had in common with the school of Voltaire was an utter disdain of all religious antiquities; and, more than all, of those of the Hebrew race. It is well known that it was a point of honour with the reasoners of that day to assume not merely that the institutions called after Moses were not divinely dictated, nor even that they were codified at a later date than that attributed to them, but that they and the entire Pentateuch were a gratuitous forgery, executed after the return from the Captivity. Debarred, therefore, from one chief security against speculative delusion, the philosophers of France, in their eagerness to escape from what they deemed a superstition of the priests, flung themselves headlong into a superstition of the lawyers.

But though the philosophy founded on the hypothesis of a state of nature has fallen low in general esteem, in so far as it is looked upon under its coarser and more palpable aspect, it does not follow that in its subtler disguises it has lost plausibility, popularity, or power. I believe, as I have said, that it is still the great antagonist of the Historical Method; and whenever (religious objections apart) any mind is seen to resist or contemn that mode of investigation, it will generally be found under the influence of a prejudice or vicious bias traceable to a conscious or unconscious reliance on a non-historic, natural, condition of society or the individual. It is chiefly, however, by allying themselves with political and social tendencies that the doctrines of Nature and her law have preserved their energy. Some of these tendencies they have stimulated, others they have actually created, to a great number they have given expression and form. They visibly enter largely into the ideas which constantly radiate from France over the civilised world, and thus become part of the general body of thought by which its civilisation is modified. The value of the influence which they thus exercise over the fortunes of the race is of course one of the points which our age debates most warmly, and it is beside the purpose of this treatise to discuss it. Looking back, however, to the period at which the theory of the state of nature acquired the maximum of political importance, there are few who will deny that it helped most powerfully to bring about the grosser disappointments of which the first French revolution was fertile. It gave birth, or intense stimulus, to the vices of mental habit all but universal at the time, disdain of positive law, impatience of experience, and the preference of à priori to all other reasoning. In proportion too as this philosophy fixes its grasp on minds which have thought less than others and fortified themselves with smaller observation, its tendency is to become distinctly anarchical. It is surprising to note how many of the *Sophismes Anarchiques* which Dumont published for Bentham, and which embody Bentham's exposure of errors distinctively French, are derived from the Roman hypothesis in its French transformation, and are unintelligible unless referred to it. On this point too it is a curious exercise to consult the *Moniteur* during the principal eras of the Revolution. The appeals to the Law and State of Nature become thicker as the times grow darker.

There is a single example which very strikingly illustrates the effects of the theory of natural law on modern society, and indicates how very far are those effects from being exhausted. There cannot, I conceive, be any question that to the assumption of the Law Natural we owe the doctrine of the fundamental equality of human beings. That " all

men are equal" is one of a large number of legal
provisions which, in progress of time, have become
political. The Roman jurisconsults of the Antonine era lay down that "omnes homines naturâ
æquales sunt," but in their eyes this is a strictly juridical axiom. They intend to affirm that under
the hypothetical Law of Nature, and in so far as
positive law approximates to it, the arbitrary distinctions which the Roman Civil Law maintained
between classes of persons cease to have a legal existence. The rule was one of considerable importance to the Roman practitioner, who required to
be reminded that, wherever Roman jurisprudence
was assumed to conform itself exactly to the code
of Nature, there was no difference in the contemplation of the Roman tribunals between citizen
and foreigner, between freeman and slave, Agnate
and Cognate. The jurisconsults who thus expressed
themselves most certainly never intended to censure
the social arrangements under which civil law fell
somewhat short of its speculative type; nor did
they apparently believe that the world would ever
see human society completely assimilated to the
economy of nature. But when the doctrine of human equality makes its appearance in a modern
dress it has evidently clothed itself with a new
shade of meaning. Where the Roman jurisconsult
had written "æquales sunt," meaning exactly what
he said, the modern civilian wrote "all men are
equal" in the sense of "all men ought to be equal."

The peculiar Roman idea that natural law coexisted
with civil law and gradually absorbed it, had evidently been lost sight of, or had become unintelligible,
and the words which had at most conveyed a theory
concerning the origin, composition and development of human institutions, were beginning to express the sense of a great standing wrong suffered
by mankind.   As early as the beginning of the
fourteenth century, the current language concerning
the birth-state of men, though visibly intended to
be identical with that of Ulpian and his contemporaries has assumed an altogether different form and
meaning.   The preamble to the celebrated ordinance of King Louis Hutin, enfranchising the serfs
of the royal domains, would have sounded strange-
ly to Roman ears.   " Whereas, according to natural law, everybody ought to be born free ; and by
some usages and customs which, from long antiquity, have been introduced and kept until now in our
realm, and peradventure by reason of the misdeeds
of their predecessors, many persons of our common
people have fallen into servitude, therefore, We,"
&c.   This is the enunciation not of a legal rule but
of a political dogma ; and from this time the equality of men is spoken of by the French lawyers just
as if it were a political truth which happened to
have been preserved among the archives of their
science.   Like all other deductions from the hypothesis of a Law Natural, and like the belief
itself in a Law of Nature, it was languidly as-

sented to and suffered to have little influence on opinion and practice until it passed out of the possession of the lawyers into that of the literary men of the eighteenth century and of the public which sat at their feet. With them it became the most distinct tenet of their creed, and was even regarded as a summary of all the others. It is probable, however, that the power which it ultimately acquired over the events of 1789 was not entirely owing to its popularity in France, for in the middle of the century it passed over to America. The American lawyers of the time, and particularly those of Virginia, appear to have possessed a stock of knowledge which differed chiefly from that of their English contemporaries in including much which could only have been derived from the legal literature of continental Europe. A very few glances at the writings of Jefferson will show how strongly his mind was affected by the semi-juridical, semi-popular opinions which were fashionable in France, and we cannot doubt that it was sympathy with the peculiar ideas of the French jurists which led him and the other colonial lawyers who guided the course of events in America to join the specially French assumption that " all men are born equal " with the assumption, more familiar to Englishmen, that all men are born free, in the very first lines of their Declaration of Independence. The passage was one of great importance to the history of the doctrine before us. The American lawyers, in thus

prominently and emphatically affirming the funda·
mental equality of human beings, gave an impulse
to political movements in their own country, and in
a less degree in Great Britain, which is far from
having yet spent itself; but beside this they re·
turned the dogma they had adopted to its home in
France, endowed with vastly greater energy and
enjoying much greater claims on general reception
and respect. Even the more cautious politicians
of the first Constituent Assembly repeated Ulpian's
proposition as if it at once commended itself to the
instincts and intuitions of mankind ; and of all the
" principles of 1789 " it is the one which has been
least strenuously assailed, which has most thor·
oughly leavened modern opinion, and which prom·
ises to modify most deeply the constitution of so·
cieties and the politics of states.

The grandest function of the Law of Nature was
discharged in giving birth to modern International
Law and to the modern Law of War, but this part
of its effects must here be dismissed with considera·
tion very unequal to its importance.

Among the postulates which form the founda·
tion of International Law, or of so much of it as re·
tains the figure which it received from its original
architects, there are two or three of preeminent im·
portance. The first of all is expressed in the posi·
tion that there is a determinable Law of Nature.
Grotius and his successors took the assumption
lirectly from the Romans, but they differed widely

from the Roman jurisconsults and from each othei in their ideas as to the mode of determination. The ambition of almost every Publicist who has flourished since the revival of letters has been to provide new and more manageable definitions of Nature and of her law, and it is indisputable that the conception in passing through the long series of writers on Public Law has gathered round it a large accretion, consisting of fragments of ideas derived from nearly every theory of ethics which has in its turn taken possession of the schools. Yet it is a remarkable proof of the essentially historical character of the conception that, after all the efforts which have been made to evolve the code of nature from the necessary characteristics of the natural state, so much of the result is just what it would have been if men had been satisfied to adopt the dicta of the Roman lawyers without questioning or reviewing them. Setting aside the Conventional or Treaty Law of Nations, it is surprising how large a part of the system is made up of pure Roman law. Wherever there is a doctrine of the jurisconsults affirmed by them to be in harmony with the Jus Gentium, the Publicists have found a reason for borrowing it, however plainly it may bear the marks of a distinctively Roman origin. We may observe too that the derivative theories are afflicted with the weakness of the primary notion. In the majority of the Publicists, the mode of thought is still " mixed." In studying these writers, the great

difficulty is always to discover whether they are
discussing law or morality—whether the state of
international relations they describe is actual or
ideal—whether they lay down that which is, or
that which, in their opinion, ought to be.

The assumption that Natural Law is binding on
states *inter se* is the next in rank of those which
underlie International Law.   A series of assertions
or admissions of this principle may be traced up to
the very infancy of modern juridical science, and at
first sight it seems a direct inference from the teaching of the Romans.   The civil condition of society
being distinguished from the natural by the fact
that in the first there is a distinct author of law,
while in the last there is none, it appears as if the
moment a number of *units* were acknowledged to
obey no common sovereign or political superior
they were thrown back on the ulterior behests of
the Law Natural.   States are such units ; the hypothesis of their independence excludes the notion
of a common lawgiver, and draws with it, therefore,
according to a certain range of ideas, the notion of
subjection to the primeval order of nature.   The
alternative is to consider independent communities
as not related to each other by any law, but this
condition of lawlessness is exactly the vacuum which
the Nature of the jurisconsults abhorred.   There is
certainly apparent reason for thinking that if the
mind of a Roman lawyer rested on any sphere from
which civil law was banished, it would instantly fill

the void with the ordinances of Nature. It is never safe, however, to assume that conclusions, however certain and immediate in our own eyes, were ac tually drawn at any period of history. No passage has ever been adduced from the remains of Roman law which, in my judgment, proves the jurisconsults to have believed natural law to have obligatory force between independent commonwealths; and we cannot but see that to citizens of the Roman empire, who regarded their sovereign's dominions as conterminous with civilization, the equal subjection of states to the Law of Nature, if contemplated at all, must have seemed at most an extreme result of curious speculation. The truth appears to be that modern International Law, undoubted as is its descent from Roman law, is only connected with it by an irregular filiation. The early modern interpreters of the jurisprudence of Rome, misconceiving the meaning of Jus Gentium, assumed without hesi tation that the Romans had bequeathed to them a system of rules for the adjustment of international transactions. This "Law of Nations" was at first an authority which had formidable competitors to strive with, and the condition of Europe was long such as to preclude its universal reception. Gradually, however, the western world arranged itself in a form more favourable to the theory of the civilians; circumstances destroyed the credit of rival doctrines; and at last, at a peculiarly felicitous conjuncture, Ayala and Grotius were able to

obtain for it the enthusiastic assent of Europe, an
assent which has been over and over again renewed
in every variety of solemn engagement. The great
men to whom its triumph is chiefly owing attempted, it need scarcely be said, to place it on an entirely new basis, and it is unquestionable that in the
course of this displacement they altered much of its
structure, though far less of it than is commonly
supposed. Having adopted from the Antonine
jurisconsults the position that the Jus Gentium
and the Jus Naturæ were identical, Grotius, with
his immediate predecessors and his immediate successors, attributed to the Law of Nature an authority which would never perhaps have been claimed
for it, if "Law of Nations" had not in that age
been an ambiguous expression. They laid down
unreservedly that Natural Law is the code of states,
and thus put in operation a process which has continued almost down to our own day, the process of
engrafting on the international system rules which
are supposed to have been evolved from the unassisted contemplation of the conception of Nature.
There is too one consequence of immense practical
importance to mankind which, though not unknown
during the early modern history of Europe, was
never clearly or universally acknowledged till the
doctrines of the Grotian school had prevailed. If
the society of nations is governed by Natural Law
the atoms which compose it must be absolutely
equal. Men under the sceptre of Nature are all

equal, and accordingly commonwealths are equal if the international state be one of nature. The proposition that independent communities, however different in size and power, are all equal in the view of the law of nations, has largely contributed to the happiness of mankind, though it is constantly threatened by the political tendencies of each successive age. It is a doctrine which probably would never have obtained a secure footing at all if International Law had not been entirely derived from the majestic claims of Nature by the Publicists who wrote after the revival of letters.

On the whole, however, it is astonishing, as I have observed before, how small a proportion the additions made to International Law since Grotius's day bear to the ingredients which have been simply taken from the most ancient stratum of the Roman Jus Gentium. Acquisition of territory has always been the great spur of national ambition, and the rules which govern this acquisition, together with the rules which moderate the wars in which it too frequently results, are merely transcribed from the part of the Roman law which treats of the modes of acquiring property *jure gentium.* These modes of acquisition were obtained by the elder jurisconsults, as I have attempted to explain, by abstracting a common ingredient from the usages observed to prevail among the various tribes surrounding Rome ; and, having been classed on account of their origin in the " law common to all nations," they

7

were thought by the later lawyers to fit in on the
score of their simplicity, with the more recent conception of a Law Natural. They thus made their
way into the modern Law of Nations, and the re
sult is that those parts of the international system
which refer to *dominion*, its nature, its limitations,
the modes of acquiring and securing it, are pure
Roman Property Law—so much, that is to say, of
the Roman Law of Property as the Antonine jurisconsults imagined to exhibit a certain congruity
with the natural state. In order that these chapters of International Law may be capable of application, it is necessary that sovereigns should be related to each other like the members of a group of
Roman proprietors. This is another of the postulates which lie at the threshold of the International
Code, and it is also one which could not possibly
have been subscribed to during the first centuries
of modern European history. It is resolvable into
the double proposition that " sovereignty is territorial," *i. e.* that it is always associated with the
proprietorship of a limited portion of the earth's
surface, and that " sovereigns *inter se* are to be
deemed not *paramount*, but *absolute* owners of the
state's territory.

Many contemporary writers on Internationl Law
tacitly assume that the doctrines of their system,
founded on principles of equity and common sense,
were capable of being readily reasoned out in every
stage of modern civilisation. But this assumption,

while it conceals some real defects of the international theory, is altogether untenable so far as
regards a large part of modern history. It is not
true that the authority of the Jus Gentium in the
concerns of nations was always uncontradicted ; on
the contrary, it had to struggle long against the
claims of several competing systems. It is again
not true that the territorial character of sovereignty
was always recognised, for long after the dissolution
of the Roman dominion the minds of men were
under the empire of ideas irreconcileable with such
a conception. An old order of things, and of views
founded on it, had to decay—a new Europe, and
an apparatus of new notions congenial to it, had to
spring up—before two of the chiefest postulates
of International Law could be universally conceded.

It is a consideration well worthy to be kept in
view, that during a large part of what we usually
term modern history no such conception was entertained as that of "*territorial sovereignty.*" Sovereignty was not associated with dominion over a
portion or subdivision of the earth. The world had
lain for so many centuries under the shadow of
Imperial Rome as to have forgotten that distribution of the vast spaces comprised in the empire
which had once parcelled them out into a number
of independent commonwealths, claiming immunity
from extrinsic interference, and pretending to equality of national rights. After the subsidence of the

barbarian irruptions, the notion of sovereignty that
prevailed seems to have been twofold. On the one
hand it assumed the form of what may be called
"*tribe*-sovereignty." The Franks, the Burgundians,
the Vandals, the Lombards, and Visigoths were
masters, of course, of the territories which they
occupied, and to which some of them had given a
geographical appellation ; but they based no claim
of right upon the fact of territorial possession, and
indeed attached no importance to it whatever.
They appear to have retained the traditions which
they brought with them from the forest and the
steppe, and to have still been in their own view a
patriarchal society, a nomad horde, merely encamp-
ed for the time upon the soil which afforded them
sustenance.   Part of Transalpine Gaul, with part of
Germany, had now become the country *de facto* occupied by the Franks—it was France ; but the Mero-
vingian line of chieftains, the descendants of Clovis,
were not Kings of France, they were Kings of the
Franks. Territorial titles were not unknown, but
they seem at first to have come into use only as a
convenient mode of designating the ruler of a *portion* of the tribe's possessions ; the king of a *whole*
tribe was king of his people, not of his people's
lands. The alternative to this peculiar notion of
sovereignty appears to have been—and this is the
important point—the idea of universal dominion.
When a monarch departed from the special relation
of chief to clansmen, and became solicitous, for pur

poses of his own, to invest himself with a novel form of sovereignty, the precedent which suggested itself for his adoption was the domination of the Emperors of Rome. To parody a common quotation, he became " *aut Cæsar aut nullus.*" Either he pretended to the full prerogative of the Byzantine Emperor, or he had no political status. In our own age, when a new dynasty is desirous of obliterating the prescriptive title of a deposed line of sovereigns, it takes its designation from the *people*, instead of the *territory*. Thus we have Emperors and Kings of the French, and a King of the Belgians. At the period of which we have been speaking, under similar circumstances, a different alternative presented itself. The chieftain who would no longer call himself King of the tribe must claim to be Emperor of the world. Thus, when the hereditary Mayors of the Palace had ceased to compromise with the monarchs they had long since virtually dethroned, they soon became unwilling to call themselves merely Kings of the Franks, a title which belonged to the displaced Merovings; but they could not style themselves Kings of France, for such a designation, though apparently not unknown, was not a title of dignity. Accordingly they came forward as aspirants to universal empire. Their motive has been greatly misapprehended. It has been taken for granted by recent French writers that Charlemagne was far before his age, quite as much in the character of his designs as in the energy with

which he prosecuted them. Whether it be true or
not that anybody is at any time before his age, it
is certainly true that Charlemagne, in aiming at an
unlimited dominion, was emphatically taking the
only course which the characteristic idea of his age
permitted him to follow. Of his intellectual emi-
nence there cannot be a question, but it is proved
by his acts and not by his theory.

The speculative universality of sovereignty
long continued to be associated with the Imperial
throne, and indeed was never thoroughly disso-
ciated from it so long as the empire of Germany
lasted. Territorial sovereignty—the view which
connects sovereignty with the possession of a limited portion of the earth's surface—was distinctly
an offshoot, though a tardy one, of *feudalism*.
This might have been expected *à priori*, for it was
feudalism which for the first time linked personal
duties, and by consequence personal rights, to the
ownership of land. Whatever be the proper view
of its origin and legal nature, the best mode of
vividly picturing to ourselves the feudal organisation is to begin with the basis; to consider the
relation of the tenant to the patch of soil which
created and limited his services — and then to
mount up, through narrowing circles of super-
feudation, till we approximate to the apex of the
system. Where that summit exactly was during
the later portion of the dark ages it is not easy to
decide. Probably, wherever the conception of tribe
sovereignty has really decayed, the topmost point

was always assigned to the supposed successor of the Cæsars of the West. But before long, when the actual sphere of imperial authority had immensely contracted, and when the emperors had concentrated the scanty remains of their power upon Germany and North Italy, the highest feudal superiors in all the outlying portions of the former Carlovingian empire found themselves practically without a supreme head. Gradually they habituated themselves to the new situation, and the fact of immunity put at last out of sight the theory of dependence; but there are many symptoms that this change was not quite easily accomplished; and, indeed, to the impression that in the nature of things there must necessarily be a culminating domination somewhere, we may, no doubt, refer the increasing tendency to attribute secular superiority to the See of Rome. The completion of the first stage in the revolution of opinion is marked, of course, by the accession of the Capetian dynasty in France. Before that epoch arrived, several of the holders of the great territorial fiefs into which the Carlovingian empire was now split up, had begun to call themselves Kings, instead of Dukes or Counts; but the important change occurred when the feudal prince of a limited territory surrounding Paris, usurped from the earlier house their dynastic title, *Kings of the French.* Hugues Capet and his descendants were kings in quite a new sense, sovereigns standing in the same relation to the soil of France as the baron to his estate, the

tenant to his freehold ; and the old tribal appella
tion, though long retained in the official Latin
style of the reigning house, passed rapidly, in the
vernacular, into *Kings of France*. The form of
the monarchy in France had visible effects in has
tening changes which were elsewhere proceeding
in the same direction.   The kingship of our Anglo
Saxon regal houses was midway between the chieftainship of a tribe and a territorial supremacy ;
but the superiority of the Norman monarchs, imitated from that of the King of France, was dis
tinctly a territorial sovereignty.   Every subsequent
dominion which was established or consolidated
was formed on the latter model.   Spain, Naples,
and the principalities founded on the ruins of
municipal freedom in Italy, were all under rulers
whose sovereignty was territorial.   Few things, I
may add, are more curious than the gradual lapse
of the *Venetians* from one view to the other.   At
the commencement of its foreign conquests, the republic regarded itself as an antitype of the Roman
commonwealth, governing a number of subject
provinces.   Move a century onwards, and you find
that it wishes to be looked upon as a corporate
sovereign, claiming the rights of a feudal suzerain
over its possessions in Italy and the Ægean.

During the period through which the popular
ideas on the subject of sovereignty were undergoing this remarkable change, the system which
stood in the place of what we now call International Law was heterogeneous in form and incon-

sistent in the principles to which it appealed. Over so much of Europe as was comprised in the Romano-German empire, the connection of the confederate states was regulated by the complex and as yet incomplete mechanism of the Imperial constitution; and, surprising as it may seem to us, it was a favorite notion of German lawyers that the relations of commonwealths, whether inside or outside the empire, ought to be regulated not by the *Jus Gentium*, but by the pure Roman jurisprudence, of which Cæsar was still the centre. This doctrine was less confidently repudiated in the outlying countries than we might have supposed antecedently; but substantially, through the rest of Europe feudal subordinations furnished a substitute for a public law; and when those were undetermined or ambiguous, there lay behind, in theory at least, a supreme regulating force in the authority of the head of the Church. It is certain, however, that both feudal and ecclesiastical influences were rapidly decaying during the fifteenth, and even the fourteenth century; and if we closely examine the current pretexts of wars, and the avowed motives of alliances, it will be seen that, step by step with the displacement of the old principles, the views afterwards harmonized and consolidated by Ayala and Grotius were making considerable progress, though it was silent and but slow. Whether the fusion of all the sources of authority would ultimately have evolved a system of international relations, and whether that system

would have exhibited material differences from the
fabric of Grotius, is not now possible to decide, for
as a matter of fact the Reformation annihilated all
its potential elements except one. Beginning in
Germany, it divided the princes of the empire by
a gulf too broad to be bridged over by the Imperial
supremacy, even if the Imperial superior had stood
neutral. He, however, was forced to take colour
with the church against the reformers; the Pope
was, as a matter of course, in the same predica-
ment; and thus the two authorities to whom belonged the office of mediation between combatants
became themselves the chiefs of one great faction in the schism of the nations. Feudalism,
already enfeebled and discredited as a principle
of public relations, furnished no bond whatever
which was stable enough to countervail the alliances of religion. In a condition, therefore, of
public law which was little less than chaotic, those
views of a state system to which the Roman jurisconsults were supposed to have given their sanction
alone remained standing. The shape, the symmetry, and the prominence which they assumed in the
hands of Grotius are known to every educated
man; but the great marvel of the Treatise " De
Jure Belli et Pacis," was its rapid, complete, and
universal success. The horrors of the Thirty Years'
War, the boundless terror and pity which the un-
bridled license of the soldiery was exciting, must,
no doubt, be taken to explain that success in some
measure, but they do not wholly account for it.

Very little penetration into the ideas of that age is required to convince one that, if the ground plan of the international edifice which was sketched in the great book of Grotius had not appeared to be theoretically perfect, it would have been discarded by jurists and neglected by statesmen and soldiers.

It is obvious that the speculative perfection of the Grotian system is intimately connected with that conception of territorial sovereignty which we have been discussing. The theory of International Law assumes that commonwealths are, relatively to each other, in a state of nature; but the component atoms of a natural society must, by the fundamental assumption, be insulated and independent of each other. If there be a higher power connecting them, however slightly and occasionally, by the claim of common supremacy, the very conception of a common superior introduces the notion of positive law and excludes the idea of a law natural. It follows, therefore, that if the universal suzerainty of an Imperial head had been admitted even in bare theory, the labours of Grotius would have been idle. Nor is this the only point of junction between modern public law and those views of sovereignty of which I have endeavored to describe the development. I have said that there are entire departments of international jurisprudence which consist of the Roman Law of Property. What then is the inference? It is, that if there had been no such change as I have described in the estimate of sovereignty—if sovereignty had not been associated with the proprietorship of a limited portion of the earth, had not, in other words, become territorial—three parts of the Grotian theory would have been incapable of application.

CHAPTER V.

THE necessity of submitting the subject of jurisprudence to scientific treatment has never been entirely
lost sight of in modern times, and the essays which
the consciousness of this necessity has produced have
proceeded from minds of very various calibre, but
there is not much presumption, I think, in asserting
that what has hitherto stood in the place of a sci
ence has for the most part been a set of guesses,
those very guesses of the Roman lawyers which were
examined in the two preceding chapters. A series
of explicit statements, recognising and adopting these
conjectural theories of a natural state, and of a system of principles congenial to it, has been continued
with but brief interruption from the days of their
inventors to our own. They appear in the annota-
tions of the Glossators who founded modern jurisprudence, and in the writings of the scholastic jurists
who succeeded them. They are visible in the dog
mas of the canonists. They are thrust into promi-

nence by those civilians of marvellous erudition, who flourished at the revival of ancient letters. Grotius and his successors invested them not less with brilliancy and plausibility than with practical importance. They may be read in the introductory chapters of our own Blackstone, who has transcribed them textually from Burlamaqui, and wherever the manuals published in the present day for the guidance of the student or the practitioner begin with any discussion of the first principles of law, it always resolves itself into a restatement of the Roman hypothesis. It is however from the disguises with which these conjectures sometimes clothe themselves, quite as much as from their native form, that we gain an adequate idea of the subtlety with which they mix themselves in human thought. The Lockeian theory of the origin of Law in a Social Compact scarcely conceals its Roman derivation, and indeed is only the dress by which the ancient views were rendered more attractive to a particular generation of the moderns; but on the other hand the theory of Hobbes on the same subject was purposely devised to repudiate the reality of a law of nature as conceived by the Romans and their disciples. Yet these two theories, which long divided the reflecting politicians of England into hostile camps, resemble each other strictly in their fundamental assumption of a non-historic, unverifiable, condition of the race. Their authors differed as to the characteristics of the præ-social state, and as to the nature of the abnormal action by which men lifted themselves out of it into that social organisation with which alone we are acquainted, but they agreed in thinking that a great chasm separated man in his primitive condition from man in society and this notion we cannot doubt that they borrowed, consciously or unconsciously, from the Romans. If indeed the phenomena of law be regarded in the way in which these theorists regarded them—that is, as one vast complex whole—it is not surprising that the mind should often evade the task it has set to itself by falling back on some ingenious conjecture which (plausibly interpreted) will seem to reconcile everything, or else that it should sometimes abjure in despair the labour of systematization.

From the theories of jurisprudence which have the same speculative basis as the Roman doctrine two of much celebrity must be excepted. The first of them is that associated with the great name of Montesquieu. Though there are some ambiguous expressions in the early part of the *Esprit des Lois*, which seem to show its writer's unwillingness to break quite openly with the views hitherto popular, the general drift of the book is certainly to indicate a very different conception of its subject from any which had been entertained before. It has often been noticed that, amidst the vast variety of examples which, in its immense width of survey, it sweeps together from supposed systems of jurisprudence, there is an evident anxiety to thrust into especial prominence those manners and institutions which astonish the civilized reader by their uncouthness, strangeness, or indecency. The inference constantly suggested is, that laws are the creatures of climate, local situation, accident, or imposture—the fruit of any causes except those which appear to operate with tolerable constancy. Montesquieu seems, in fact, to have looked on the nature of man as entirely plastic, as passively reproducing the impressions, and submitting implicitly to the impulses, which it receives from without. And here no doubt lies the error which vitiates his system as a system. He greatly underrates the stability of human nature. He pays little or no regard to the inherited qualities of the race, those qualities which each generation receives from its predecessors, and transmits but slightly altered to the generation which follows it. It is quite true, indeed, that no complete account can be given of social phenomena, and consequently of laws, till due allowance has been made for those modifying causes which are noticed in the *Esprit des Lois*; but their number and their force appear to have been overestimated by Montesquieu. Many of the anomalies which he parades have since been shown to rest on false reports or erroneous construction, and of those which remain not a few prove the permanence rather than the variableness of man's nature, since they are relics of older stages of the race which have obstinately defied the influences that have elsewhere had effect. The truth is that the stable part of our mental, moral, and physical constitution is the largest part of it, and the resistance it opposes to change is such that, though the variations of human society in a portion of the world are plain enough, they are neither so rapid nor so extensive that their amount, character, and general direction cannot be ascertained. Approximation to truth may be all that is attainable with our present knowledge, but there is no reason for thinking that this is so remote, or (what is the same thing) that it requires so much future correction, as to be entirely useless and uninstructive.

The other theory which has been adverted to is, the historical theory of Bentham. This theory which is obscurely (and, it might even be said, timidly) propounded in several parts of Bentham's works is quite distinct from that analysis of the conception of law which he commenced in the " Fragment on Government," and which was more recently completed by Mr. John Austin. The resolution of a law into a command of a particular nature, imposed under special conditions, does not affect to do more than protect us against a difficulty—a most formidable one certainly—of language. The whole question remains open as to the motives of societies in imposing these commands on themselves, as to the connexion of these commands with each other, and the nature of their dependence on those which preceded them, and which they have superseded.

8

Bentham suggests the answer that societies modify and have always modified, their laws according to modifications of their views of general expediency. It is difficult to say that this proposition is false, but it certainly appears to be unfruitful. For that which seems expedient to a society, or rather to the governing part of it, when it alters a rule of law is surely the same thing as the object, whatever it may be, which it has in view when it makes the change. Expediency and the greatest good are nothing more than different names for the impulse which prompts the modification; and when we lay down expediency as the rule of change in law or opinion, all we get by the proposition is the substitution of an express term for a term which is necessarily implied when we say that a change takes place.

There is such wide-spread dissatisfaction with existing theories of jurisprudence, and so general a conviction that they do not really solve the questions they pretend to dispose of, as to justify the suspicion that some line of inquiry, necessary to a perfect result, has been incompletely followed or altogether omitted by their authors. And indeed there is one remarkable omission with which all these speculations are chargeable, except perhaps those of Montesquieu. They take no account of what law has actually been at epochs remote from the particular period at which they made their appearance. Their originator carefully observed the institutions of their own age and civilisation, and those of other ages and civilisations with which they had some degree of intellectual sympathy, but, when they turned their attention to archaic states of society which exhibited much superficial difference from their own, they uniformly ceased to observe and began guessing. The mistake which they committed is therefore analogous to the error of one who, in investigating the laws of the material universe, should commence by contemplating the existing physical world as a whole, instead of beginning with the particles which are its simplest ingredients. One does not certainly see why such a scientific solecism should be more defensible in jurisprudence than in any other region of thought. It would seem antecedently that we ought to commence with the simplest social forms in a state as near as possible to their rudimentary condition. In other words, if we followed the course usual in such inquiries, we should penetrate as far up as we could in the history of primitive societies. The phenomena which early societies present us with are not easy at first to understand, but the difficulty of grappling with them bears no proportion to the perplexities which beset us in considering the baffling entanglement of modern social organisation. It is a difficulty arising from their strangeness and uncouthness, not from their number and complexity. One does not readily get over the surprise which they occasion when looked at from a modern point of view; but when that is surmounted they are few enough and simple enough. But, even if they gave more trouble than they do, no pains would be wasted in ascertaining the germs out of which has assuredly been unfolded every form of moral restraint which controls our actions and shapes our conduct at the present moment.

The rudiments of the social state, so far as they are known to us at all, are known through testimony of three sorts—accounts by contemporary observers of civilisation less advanced than their own, the records which particular races have preserved concerning their primitive history, and ancient law. The first kind of evidence is the best we could have expected. As societies do not advance concurrently, but at different rates of progress, there have been epochs at which men trained to habits of methodical observation have really been in a position to watch and describe the infancy of mankind. Tacitus made the most of such an opportunity; but the *Germany*, unlike most celebrated classical books, has not induced others to follow the excellent example set by its author, and the amount of this sort of testimony which we possess is exceedingly small. The lofty contempt which a civilised people entertains for barbarous neighbours has caused a remarkable negligence in observing them, and this carelessness has been aggravated at times by fear, by religious prejudice, and even by the use of these very terms—civilisa-

tion and barbarism—which convey to most persons
the impression of a difference not merely in degree
but in kind.   Even the *Germany* has been suspected by some critics of sacrificing fidelity to poig-
nancy of contrast and picturesqueness of narrative.
Other histories too, which have been handed down
to us among the archives of the people to whose infancy they relate, have been thought distorted by
the pride of race or by the religious sentiment of a
newer age.   It is important then to observe that
these suspicions, whether groundless or rational, do
not attach to a great deal of archaic law.   Much of
the old law which has descended to us was preserved merely because it was old.   Those who
practised and obeyed it did not pretend to understand it ; and in some cases they even ridiculed and
despised it.   They offered no account of it except
that it had come down to them from their ancestors.   If we confine our attention, then, to those
fragments of ancient institutions which cannot reasonably be supposed to have been tampered with,
we are able to gain a clear conception of certain
great characteristics of the society to which they
originally belonged.   Advancing a step further, we
can apply our knowledge to systems of law which,
like the Code of Menu, are as a whole of suspicious
authenticity ; and, using the key we have obtained,
we are in a position to discriminate those portions
of them which are truly archaic from those which
have been affected by the prejudices, interests, or

ignorance of the compiler. It will at least be ac·
knowledged that, if the materials for this process
are sufficient, and if the comparisons be accurately
executed, the methods followed are as little objec·
tionable as those which have led to such surprising
results in comparative philology.

The effect of the evidence derived from com·
parative jurisprudence is to establish that view of
the primeval condition of the human race which is
known as the Patriarchal Theory.   There is no
doubt, of course, that this theory was originally
based on the Scriptural history of the Hebrew
patriarchs in Lower Asia; but, as has been explained already, its connexion with Scripture rather
militated than otherwise against its reception as a
complete theory, since the majority of the inquirers
who till recently addressed themselves with most
earnestness to the colligation of social phenomena,
were either influenced by the strongest prejudice
against Hebrew antiquities or by the strongest desire to construct their system without the assistance of religious records.   Even now there is per·
haps a disposition to undervalue these accounts, or
rather to decline generalising from them, as forming
part of the traditions of a Semitic people.   It is to
be noted, however, that the legal testimony comes
nearly exclusively from the institutions of societies
belonging to the Indo-European stock, the Romans
Hindoos, and Sclavonians, supplying the greater
part of it; and indeed the difficulty, at the present

stage of the inquiry, is to know where to stop, to say of what races of men it is *not* allowable to lay down that the society in which they are united was originally organised on the patriarchal model. The chief lineaments of such a society, as collected from the early chapters in Genesis, I need not attempt to depict with any minuteness, both because they are familiar to most of us from our earliest childhood, and because, from the interest once attaching to the controversy which takes its name from the debate between Locke and Filmer, they fill a whole chapter, though not a very profitable one, in English literature. The points which lie on the surface of the history are these:—The eldest male parent —the eldest ascendant—is absolutely supreme in his household. His dominion extends to life and death, and is as unqualified over his children and their houses as over his slaves; indeed the relations of sonship and serfdom appear to differ in little beyond the higher capacity which the child in blood possesses of becoming one day the head of a family himself. The flocks and herds of the children are the flocks and herds of the father, and the possessions of the parent, which he holds in a representa tive rather than in a proprietary character, are equally divided at his death among his descendants in the first degree, the eldest son sometimes receiving a double share under the name of birthright, but more generally endowed with no hereditary advantage beyond an honorary precedence. A less

obvious inference from the Scriptural accounts is
that they seem to plant us on the traces of the
breach which is first effected in the empire of the
parent. The families of Jacob and Esau separate
and form two nations; but the families of Jacob's
children hold together and become a people. This
looks like the immature germ of a state or commonwealth, and of an order of rights superior to the
claims of family relation.

If I were attempting, for the more special pur
poses of the jurist, to express compendiously the
characteristics of the situation in which mankind
disclose themselves at the dawn of their history, I
should be satisfied to quote a few verses from the
Odyssee of Homer :

τοῖσιν δ᾽ οὔτ᾽ ἀγοραὶ βουληφόροι οὔτε θέμιστες.
.   .   .   Θεμιστεύει δὲ ἕκαστος
παίδων ἠδ᾽ ἀλόχων οὐδ᾽ ἀλλήλων ἀλέγουσιν.

" They have neither assemblies for consultation nor
themistes, but every one exercises jurisdiction over
his wives and his children, and they pay no regard
to one another." These lines are applied to the
Cyclops, and it may not perhaps be an altogether
fanciful idea when I suggest that the Cyclops is
Homer's type of an alien and less advanced civilisation; for the almost physical loathing which a
primitive community feels for men of widely different manners from its own usually expresses itself
by describing them as monsters, such as giants, or

even (which is almost always the case in Oriental mythology) as demons.   However that may be, the verses condense in themselves the sum of the hints which are given us by legal antiquities.   Men are first seen distributed in perfectly insulated groups held together by obedience to the parent.   Law is the parent's word, but it is not yet in the condition of those *themistes* which were analysed in the first chapter of this work.   When we go forward to the state of society in which these early legal conceptions show themselves as formed, we find that they still partake of the mystery and spontaneity which must have seemed to characterise a despotic father's commands, but that at the same time, inasmuch as they proceed from a sovereign, they presuppose a union of family groups in some wider organisation. The next question is, what is the nature of this union and the degree of intimacy which it involves? It is just here that archaic law renders us one of the greatest of its services and fills up a gap which otherwise could only have been bridged by conjecture.   It is full, in all its provinces, of the clearest indications that society in primitive times was not what it is assumed to be at present, a collection of *individuals*.   In fact, and in the view of the men who composed it, it was *an aggregation of families,* The contrast may be most forcibly expressed by saying that the *unit* of an ancient society was the Family, of a modern society the Individual.   We must be prepared to find in ancient law all the con-

sequences of this difference. It is so framed as to
be adjusted to a system of small independent corporations. It is therefore scanty, because it is supplemented by the despotic commands of the heads
of households. It is ceremonious, because the
transactions to which it pays regard resemble international concerns much more than the quick play
of intercourse between individuals. Above all it
has a peculiarity of which the full importance cannot be shown at present. It takes a view of *life*
wholly unlike any which appears in developed
jurisprudence. Corporations *never die*, and accordingly primitive law considers the entities with
which it deals, *i. e.* the patriarchal or family groups,
as perpetual and inextinguishable. This view is
closely allied to the peculiar aspect under which, in
very ancient times, moral attributes present themselves. The moral elevation and moral debasement
of the individual appear to be confounded with, oɪ
postponed to, the merits and offences of the group
to which the individual belongs. If the community
sins, its guilt is much more than the sum of the
offences committed by its members ; the crime is
a corporate act, and extends in its consequences to
many more persons than have shared in its actual
perpetration. If, on the other hand, the individual
is conspicuously guilty, it is his children, his kinsfolk, his tribesmen, or his fellow-citizens, who suffer
with him, and sometimes for him. It thus happens
that the ideas of moral responsibility and retribu

tion often seem to be more clearly realised at very ancient than at more advanced periods, for, as the family group is immortal, and its liability to punishment indefinite, the primitive mind is not perplexed by the questions which become troublesome as soon as the individual is conceived as altogether separate from the group.   One step in the transition from the ancient and simple view of the matter to the theological or metaphysical explanation of later days is marked by the early Greek notion of an inherited curse.   The bequest received by his posterity from the original criminal was not a liability to punishment, but a liability to the commission of fresh offences which drew with them a condign retribution; and thus the responsibility of the family was reconciled with the newer phase of thought which limited the consequences of crime to the person of the actual delinquent.

It would be a very simple explanation of the origin of society if we could base a general conclusion on the hint furnished us by the Scriptural example already adverted to, and could suppose that communities began to exist wherever a family held together instead of separating at the death of its patriarchal chieftain.   In most of the Greek states and in Rome there long remained the vestiges of an ascending series of groups out of which the State was at first constituted.   The Family, House, and Tribe of the Romans may be taken as the type of them, and they are so described to us that we can

scarcely help conceiving them as a system of concen-
tric circles which have gradually expanded from the
same point.   The elementary group is the Family,
connected by common subjection to the highest male
ascendant.   The aggregation of Families forms the
Gens or House.   The aggregation of Houses makes
the Tribe.   The aggregation of Tribes constitutes
the Commonwealth.   Are we at liberty to follow
these indications, and to lay down that the commonwealth is a collection of persons united by
common descent from the progenitor of an original
family?   Of this we may at least be certain, that all
ancient societies regarded themselves as having proceeded from one original stock, and even laboured
under an incapacity for comprehending any reason
except this for their holding together in political
union.   The history of political ideas begins, in fact,
with the assumption that kinship in blood is the sole
possible ground of community in political functions
nor is there any of those subversions of feeling, which
we term emphatically revolutions, so startling and
so complete as the change which is accomplished
when some other principle—such as that, for instance of *local contiguity*—establishes itself for the
first time as the basis of common political action.
It may be affirmed then of early commonwealths
that their citizens considered all the groups in which
they claimed membership to be founded on common
lineage.   What was obviously true of the Family
was believed to be true, first of the House, next of

the Tribe, lastly of the State. And yet we find that along with this belief, or, if we may use the word, this theory, each community preserved records or traditions which distinctly showed that the fundamental assumption was false. Whether we look to the Greek states, or to Rome, or to the Teutonic aristocracies in Ditmarsh which furnished Niebuhr with so many valuable illustrations, or to the Celtic clan associations, or to that strange social organisation of the Sclavonic Russians and Poles which has only lately attracted notice, everywhere we discover traces of passages in their history when men of alien descent were admitted to, and amalgamated with, the original brotherhood. Adverting to Rome singly, we perceive that the primary group, the Family, was being constantly adulterated by the practice of adoption, while stories seem to have been always current respecting the exotic extraction of one of the original Tribes and concerning a large addition to the Houses made by one of the early kings. The composition of the state uniformly assumed to be natural, was nevertheless known to be in great measure artificial. This conflict between belief or theory and notorious fact is at first sight extremely perplexing; but what it really illustrates is the efficiency with which Legal Fictions do their work in the infancy of society. The earl'est and most extensively employed of legal fictions was that which permitted family relations to be created artificially, and there is none to which I conceive man kind to be more deeply indebted. If it had never existed, I do not see how any one of the primitive groups, whatever were their nature, could have ab-sorbed another, or on what terms any two of them could have combined, except those of absolute supe-riority on one side and absolute subjection on the other. No doubt, when with our modern ideas we contemplate the union of independent communities, we can suggest a hundred modes of carrying it out, the simplest of all being that the individuals com-prised in the coalescing groups shall vote or act together according to local propinquity; but the idea that a number of persons should exercise politi-cal rights in common simply because they happened to live within the same topographical limits was ut-terly strange and monstrous to primitive antiquity. The expedient which in those times commanded fa-vour was that the incoming population should *feign themselves* to be descended from the same stock as the people on whom they were engrafted; and it is precisely the good faith of this fiction, and the close-ness with which it seemed to imitate reality, that we cannot now hope to understand. One circum-stance, however, which it is important to recollect, is that the men who formed the various political groups were certainly in the habit of meeting together periodically, for the purpose of acknowl-edging and consecrating their association by com-mon sacrifices. Strangers amalgamated with the brotherhood were doubtless admitted to these sacri-

fices ; and when that was once done, we can believe
that it seemed equally easy, or not more difficult, to
conceive them as sharing in the common lineage.
The conclusion then which is suggested by the evidence is, not that all early societies were formed by
descent from the same ancestor, but that all of them
which had any permanence and solidity either were
so descended or assumed that they were. An indefinite number of causes may have shattered the
primitive groups, but wherever their ingredients
recombined, it was on the model or principle of an
association of kindred. Whatever were the fact, all
thought, language, and law adjusted themselves to
the assumption. But though all this seems to me to
be established with reference to the communities
with whose records we are acquainted, the remainder
of their history sustains the position before laid
down as to the essentially transient and terminable
influence of the most powerful Legal Fictions. At
some point of time—probably as soon as they felt
themselves strong enough to resist extrinsic pressure
—all these states ceased to recruit themselves by
factitious extensions of consanguinity. They necessarily, therefore, became Aristocracies, in all cases
where a fresh population from any cause collected
around them which could put in no claim to community of origin. Their sternness in maintaining
the central principle of a system under which political rights were attainable on no terms whatever
except connexion in blood, real or artificial, taught

their inferiors another principle, which proved to be endowed with a far higher measure of vitality. This was the principle of *local contiguity*, now recognised everywhere as the condition of community in political functions. A new set of political ideas came at once into existence, which, being those of ourselves, our contemporaries, and in great measure of our ancestors, rather obscure our perception of the older theory which they vanquished and dethroned.

The Family then is the type of an archaic society in all the modifications which it was capable of assuming; but the family here spoken of is not exactly the family as understood by a modern. In order to reach the ancient conception we must give to our modern ideas an important extension and an important limitation. We must look on the family as constantly enlarged by the absorption of strangers within its circle, and we must try to regard the fiction of adoption as so closely simulating the reality of kinship that neither law nor opinion makes the slightest difference between a real and an adoptive connexion. On the other hand, the persons theoretically amalgamated into a family by their common descent are practically held together by common obedience to their highest living ascendant, the father, grandfather, or great-grandfather. The patriarchal authority of a chieftain is as necessary an ingredient in the notion of the family group as the fact (or assumed fact) of its having sprung from his loins;

and hence we must understand that if there be any persons who, however truly included in the brother-hood by virtue of their blood-relationship, have nevertheless *de facto* withdrawn themselves from the empire of its ruler, they are always, in the beginnings of law, considered as lost to the family. It is this patriarchal aggregate—the modern family thus cut down on one side and extended on the other—which meets us on the threshold of primitive jurisprudence. Older probably than the State, the Tribe, and the House, it left traces of itself on private law long after the House and the Tribe had been forgotten, and long after consanguinity had ceased to be associated with the composition of States. It will be found to have stamped itself on all the great departments of jurisprudence, and may be detected, I think, as the true source of many of their most important and most durable characteristics. At the outset, the peculiarities of law in its most ancient state lead us irresistibly to the conclusion that it took precisely the same view of the family group which is taken of individual men by the systems of rights and duties now prevalent throughout Europe. There are societies open to our observation at this very moment whose laws and usages can scarcely be explained unless they are supposed never to have emerged from this primitive condition; but in communities more fortunately circumstanced the fabric of jurisprudence fell gradually to pieces and if we carefully observe the disin-

9

tegration we shall perceive that it took place prin cipally in those portions of each system which were most deeply affected by the primitive conception of the family. In one all-important instance, that of the Roman law, the change was effected so slowly that from epoch to epoch we can observe the line and direction which it followed, and can even give some idea of the ultimate result to which it was tending. And, in pursuing this last inquiry, we need not suf- fer ourselves to be stopped by the imaginary barrier which separates the modern from the ancient world. For one effect of that mixture of refined Roman law with primitive barbaric usage, which is known to us by the deceptive name of feudalism, was to revive many features of archaic jurisprudence which had died out of the Roman world, so that the decom- position which had seemed to be over commenced again, and to some extent is still proceeding.

On a few systems of law the family organisa tion of the earliest society has left a plain and broaa mark in the life-long authority of the Father or other ancestor over the person and property of his descendants, an authority which we may conve- niently call by its later Roman name of Patria Po- testas. No feature of the rudimentary associations of mankind is deposed to by a greater amount of evidence than this, and yet none seems to have dis- appeared so generally and so rapidly from the usages of advancing communities. Gaius, writing under the Antonines, describes the institution as distinctively Roman. It is true, that had he glanced across the Rhine or the Danube to those tribes of barbarians which were exciting the curiosity of some among his contemporaries, he would have seen examples of patriarchal power in its crudest form; and in the far East a branch of the same ethnical stock from which the Romans sprang was repeating their Patria Potestas in some of its most technical incidents. But among the races understood to be comprised within the Roman empire, Gaius could find none which exhibited an institution resembling the Roman " Power of the Father," except only the Asiatic Galatæ. There are reasons, indeed, as it seems to me, why the direct authority of the ancestor should, in the greater number of progressive societies, very shortly assume humbler proportions than belonged to it in their earliest state. The implicit obedience of rude men to their parent is doubtless a primary fact, which it would be absurd to explain away altogether by attributing to them any calculation of its advantages; but, at the same time, if it is natural in the sons to obey the father, it is equally natural that they should look to him for superior strength or superior wisdom. Hence, when societies are placed under circumstances which cause an especial value to be attached to bodily and mental vigour, there is an influence at work which tends to confine the Patria Potestas to the cases where its possessor is actually skilful and strong. When we obtain our first glimpse of organised

Hellenic society, it seems as if supereminent wisdom would keep alive the father's power in persons whose bodily strength had decayed; but the relations of Ulysses and Laertes in the *Odyssey* appear to show that, where extraordinary valour and sagacity were united in the son, the father in the decrepitude of age was deposed from the headship of the family. In the mature Greek jurisprudence, the rule advances a few steps on the practice hinted at in the Homeric literature; and though very many traces of stringent family obligation remain, the direct authority of the parent is limited, as in European codes, to the nonage or minority of the children, or, in other words, to the period during which their mental and physical inferiority may always be presumed. The Roman law, however, with its remarkable tendency to innovate on ancient usage only just so far as the exigency of the commonwealth may require, preserves both the primeval institution and the natural limitation to which I conceive it to have been subject. In every relation of life in which the collective community might have occasion to avail itself of his wisdom and strength, for all purposes of counsel or of war, the filius familias, or Son under Power, was as free as his father. It was a maxim of Roman jurisprudence that the Patria Potestas did not extend to the Jus Publicum. Father and son voted together in the city, and fought side by side in the field; indeed, the son, as general, might happen to com mand the father, or, as magistrate, decide on his contracts and punish his delinquencies. But in all the relations created by Private Law, the son lived under a domestic despotism which, considering the severity it retained to the last, and the number of centuries through which it endured, constitutes one of the strangest problems in legal history.

The Patria Potestas of the Romans, which is necessarily our type of the primeval paternal authority, is equally difficult to understand as an institution of civilized life, whether we consider its incidence on the person or its effects on property. It is to be regretted that a chasm which exists in its history cannot be more completely filled. So far as regards the person, the parent, when our information commences, has over his children the *jus vitæ necisque*, the power of life and death, and *à fortiori* of uncontrolled corporal chastisement; he can modify their personal condition at pleasure; he can give a wife to his son; he can give his daughter in marriage; he can divorce his children of either sex; he can transfer them to another family by adoption; and he can sell them. Late in the Imperial period we find vestiges of all these powers, but they are reduced within very narrow limits. The unqualified right of domestic chastisement has become a right of bringing domestic offences under the cognisance of the civil magistrate; the privilege of dictating marriage has declined into a conditional veto; the liberty of selling has been virtually

abolished, and adoption itself, destined to lose almost all its ancient importance in the reformed system of Justinian, can no longer be effected without
the assent of the child transferred to the adoptive
parentage. In short, we are bought very close to
the verge of the ideas which have at length prevailed in the modern world. But between these
widely distant epochs there is an interval of ob-
scurity, and we can only guess at the causes which
permitted the Patria Potestas to last as long as it
did by rendering it more tolerable than it appears.
The active discharge of the most important among
the duties which the son owed to the state must
have tempered the authority of his parent if they
did not annul it. We can readily persuade ourselves that the paternal despotism could not be
brought into play without great scandal against a
man of full age occupying a high civil office. During the earlier history, however, such cases of practical emancipation would be rare compared with
those which must have been created by the constant
wars of the Roman republic. The military tribune
and the private soldier who were in the field three
quarters of a year during the earlier contests, at a
later period the proconsul in charge of a province,
and the legionaries who occupied it, cannot have
had practical reason to regard themselves as the
slaves of a despotic master; and all these avenues
of escape tended constantly to multiply themselves.
Victories led to conquests, conquests to occupations

the mode of occupation by colonies was exchanged
for the system of occupying provinces by standing
armies. Each step in advance was a call for the
expatriation of more Roman citizens and a fresh
draft on the blood of the failing Latin race. We
may infer, I think, that a strong sentiment in favour
of the relaxation of the Patria Potestas had become
fixed by the time that the pacification of the world
commenced on the establishment of the Empire.
The first serious blows at the ancient institution are
attributed to the earlier Cæsars, and some isolated
interferences of Trajan and Hadrian seem to have
prepared the ground for a series of express enactments which, though we cannot always determine
their dates, we know to have limited the father's
powers on the one hand, and on the other to have
multiplied facilities for their voluntary surrender.
The older mode of getting rid of the Potestas, by
effecting a triple sale of the son's person, is evi
dence, I may remark, of a very early feeling against
the unnecessary prolongation of the powers. The
rule which declared that the son should be free
after having been three times sold by his father
seems to have been originally meant to entail penal
consequences on a practice which revolted even the
imperfect morality of the primitive Roman. But
even before the publication of the Twelve Tables it
had been turned, by the ingenuity of the juriscon
sults, into an expedient for destroying the parental

authority wherever the father desired that it should cease.

Many of the causes which helped to mitigate the stringency of the father's power over the persons of his children are doubtless among those which do not lie upon the face of history. We cannot tell how far public opinion may have paralysed an authority which the law conferred, or how far natural affection may have rendered it endurable. But though the powers over the *person* may have been latterly nominal, the whole tenour of the extant Roman jurisprudence suggests that the father's rights over the son's *property* were always exercised without scruple to the full extent to which they were sanctioned by law. There is nothing to astonish us in the latitude of these rights when they first show themselves. The ancient law of Rome forbade the Children under Power to hold property apart from their parent, or (we should rather say) never contemplated the possibility of their claiming a separate ownership. The father was entitled to take the whole of the son's acquisitions, and to enjoy the benefit of his contracts without being entangled in any compensating liability. So much as this we should expect from the constitution of the earliest Roman society, for we can hardly form a notion of the primitive family group unless we suppose that its members brought their earnings of all kinds into the common stock while they were unable to bind it by improvident individual engagements. The true enigma of the Patria Potestas does not reside here, but in the slowness with which these proprietary privileges of the parent were curtailed, and in the circumstance that, before they were seriously diminished, the whole civilised world was brought within their sphere. No innovation of any kind was attempted till the first years of the Empire, when the acquisitions of soldiers on service were withdrawn from the operation of the Patria Potestas, doubtless as part of the reward of the armies which had overthrown the free commonwealth. Three centuries afterwards the same immunity was extended to the earnings of persons who were in the civil employment of the state. Both changes were obviously limited in their application, and they were so contrived in technical form as to interfere as little as possible with the principle of Patria Potestas. A certain qualified and dependent ownership had always been recognised by the Roman law in the perquisites and savings which slaves and sons under power were not compelled to include in the household accounts, and the special name of this permissive property, Peculium, was applied to the acquisitions newly relieved from Patria Potestas, which were called in the case of soldiers Castrense Peculium, and Quasi-castrense Peculium in the case of civil servants. Other modifications of the parental privileges followed, which showed a less studious outward respect for the ancient principle. Shortly after the introduction of the Quasi castrense Peculium, Constantine the Great took away the father's absolute control over property which his children had inherited from their mothers, and reduced it to a *usufruct*, or life-interest. A few more changes of slight importance followed in the Western Empire, but the furthest point reached was in the East, under Justinian, who enacted that unless the acquisitions of the child were derived from the parent's own property, the parent's rights over them should not extend beyond enjoying their produce for the period of his life. Even this, the utmost relaxation of the Roman Patria Potestas, left it far ampler and severer than any analogous institution of the modern world. The earliest modern writers on jurisprudence remark that it was only the fiercer and ruder of the conquerors of the empire, and notably the nations of Sclavonic origin, which exhibited a Patria Potestas at all resembling that which was described in the Pandects and the Code. All the Germanic immigrants seem to have recognised a corporate union of the family under the *mund*, or authority of a patriarchal chief; but his powers are obviously only the relics of a decayed Patria Potestas, and fell far short of those enjoyed by the Roman father. The Franks are particularly mentioned as not having the Roman institution, and accordingly the old French lawyers, even when most busily engaged in filling the interstices of barbarous custom with rules of Roman law, were obliged to protect themselves against the intrusion of the Potestas by the express maxim, *Puyssance de père en France n'a lieu.* The tenacity of the Romans in maintaining this relic of their most ancient condition is in itself remarkable, but it is less remarkable than the diffusion of the Potestas over the whole of a civilisation from which it had once disappeared. While the Castrense Peculium constituted as yet the sole exception to the father's power over property, and while his power over his children's persons was still extensive, the Roman citizenship, and with it the Patria Potestas, were spreading into every corner of the Empire. Every African or Spaniard, every Gaul, Briton, or Jew, who received this honour by gift, purchase, or inheritance, placed himself under the Roman Law of Persons, and, though our authorities intimate that children born before the acquisition of citizenship could not be brought under Power against their will, children born after it and all ulterior descendants were on the ordinary footing of a Roman *filius familias.* It does not fall within the province of this treatise to examine the mechanism of the later Roman society, but I may be permitted to remark that there is little foundation for the opinion which represents the constitution of Antoninus Caracalla conferring Roman citizenship on the whole of his subjects as a measure of small importance. However we may interpret it, it must have enormously enlarged the sphere of the Patria Potestas, and it seems to me that the tightening of family relations which it effected is an agency which ought to be kept in view more than it has been, in accounting for the great moral revolution which was transforming the world.

Before this branch of our subject is dismissed, it should be observed that the Paterfamilias was answerable for the delicts (or *torts*) of his Sons under Power. He was similarly liable for the torts of his slaves; but in both cases he originally possessed the singular privilege of tendering the delinquent's person in full satisfaction of the damage. The responsibility thus incurred on behalf of sons, coupled with the mutual incapacity of Parent and Child under Power to sue one another, has seemed to some jurists to be best explained by the assumption of a " unity of person" between the Paterfamilias and the Filiusfamilias. In the Chapter on Successions I shall attempt to show in what sense, and to what extent, this " unity " can be accepted as a reality. I can only say at present that these responsibilities of the Paterfamilias, and other legal phenomena which will be discussed hereafter, appear to me to point at certain *duties* of the primitive Patriarchal chieftain which balanced his *rights*. I conceive that, if he disposed absolutely of the persons and fortune of his clansmen, this representative ownership was coextensive with a liability to provide for all members of the brotherhood out of the common fund. The difficulty is to throw ourselves out of our habitual associations sufficiently for conceiving the nature of his obligation. It was not a legal duty, for law had not yet penetrated into the precincts of the Family. To call it *moral* is perhaps to anticipate the ideas belonging to a later stage of mental development; but the expression "moral obligation" is significant enough for our purpose, if we understand by it a duty semiconsciously followed and enforced rather by instinct and habit than by definite sanctions.

The Patria Potestas, in its normal shape, has not been, and, as it seems to me, could not have been, a generally durable institution. The proof of its former universality is therefore incomplete so long as we consider it by itself; but the demonstration may be carried much further by examining other departments of ancient law which depend on it ultimately, but not by a thread of connexion visible in all its parts or to all eyes. Let us turn for example to Kinship, or in other words, to the scale on which the proximity of relatives to each other is calculated in archaic jurisprudence. Here again it will be convenient to employ the Roman terms, Agnatic and Cognatic relationship. *Cognatic* relationship is simply the conception of kinship familiar to modern ideas; it is the relationship arising through common descent from the same pair of married persons, whether the descent be traced through males or females. *Agnatic* relationship is something very different: it excludes a number of persons whom we in our day should certainly consider of kin to

ourselves, and it includes many more whom we
should never reckon among our kindred.   It is in
truth the connexion existing between the members
of the Family, conceived as it was in the most ancient times.   The limits of this connexion are far
from conterminous with those of modern relationship.

Cognates then are all those persons who can
trace their blood to a single ancestor and ances-
tress ; or, if we take the strict technical meaning of
the word in Roman law, they are all who trace
their blood to the legitimate marriage of a common
pair.   " Cognation " is therefore a relative term, and
the degree of connexion in blood which it indicates
depends on the particular marriage which is selected
as the commencement of the calculation.   If we begin with the marriage of father and mother, Cognation will only express the relationship of brothers
and sisters ; if we take that of the grandfather and
grandmother, then uncles, aunts, and their descendants will also be included in the notion of Cognation, and following the same process a larger number of Cognates may be continually obtained by
choosing the starting point higher and higher up
in the line of ascent.   All this is easily understood
by a modern ; but who are the Agnates ?   In the
first place, they are all the Cognates who trace
their connexion exclusively through males.   A
table of Cognates is, of course, formed by taking
each lineal ancestor in turn and including all his

descendants of both sexes in the tabular view; if then, in tracing the various branches of such a genealogical table or tree, we stop whenever we come to the name of a female and pursue that particular branch or ramification no further, all who remain after the descendants of women have been excluded are Agnates, and their connexion together is Agnatic Relationship. I dwell a little on the process which is practically followed in separating them from the Cognates, because it explains a memorable legal maxim, " Mulier est finis familiæ"—a woman is the terminus of the family. A female name closes the branch or twig of the genealogy in which it occurs. None of the descendants of a female are included in the primitive notion of family relationship.

If the system of archaic law at which we are looking be one which admits Adoption, we must add to the Agnates thus obtained all persons, male or female, who have been brought into the Family by the artificial extension of its boundaries. But the descendants of such persons will only be Agnates, if they satisfy the conditions which have just been described.

What then is the reason of this arbitrary inclusion and exclusion? Why should a conception of Kinship, so elastic as to include strangers brought into the family by adoption, be nevertheless so narrow as to shut out the descendants of a female member? To solve these questions, we must return

to the Patria Potestas. The foundation of Agnation is not the marriage of Father and Mother, but
the authority of the Father. All persons are Ag-
natically connected together who are under the
same Paternal Power, or who have been under it
or who might have been under it if their lineal ancestor had lived long enough to exercise his empire.
In truth, in the primitive view, Relationship is exactly limited by Patria Potestas. Where the Potestas begins, Kinship begins ; and therefore adoptive relatives are among the kindred. Where the
Potestas ends, Kinship ends ; so that a son emancipated by his father loses all rights of Agnation.
And here we have the reason why the descendants
of females are outside the limits of archaic kinship.
If a woman died unmarried, she could have no legitimate descendants. If she married, her children
fell under the Patria Potestas, not of her Father,
but of her Husband, and thus were lost to her own
family. It is obvious that the organisation of primitive societies would have been confounded, if men
had called themselves relatives of their mother's relatives. The inference would have been that a person might be subject to two distinct Patriæ Potestates ; but distinct Patriæ Potestates implied distinct jurisdictions, so that anybody amenable to
two of them at the same time would have lived
under two different dispensations. As long as the
Family was an imperium in imperio, a community
within the commonwealth, governed by its own in-

stitutions of which the parent was the source, the limitation of relationship to the Agnates was a nec essary security against a conflict of laws in the domestic forum.

The Parental Powers proper are extinguished by the death of the Parent, but Agnation is as it were a mould which retains their imprint after they have ceased to exist.   Hence comes the interest of Agnation for the inquirer into the history of jurisprudence.   The powers themselves are discernible in comparatively few monuments of ancient law, but Agnatic Relationship, which implies their former existence, is discoverable almost everywhere.   There are few indigenous bodies of law belonging to communities of the Indo-European stock, which do not exhibit peculiarities in the most ancient part of their structure which are clearly referable to Agnation.   In Hindoo law, for example, which is saturated with the primitive notions of family dependency, kinship is entirely Agnatic, and I am informed that in Hindoo genealogies the names of women are generally omitted altogether.   The same view of relationship pervades so much of the laws of the races who overran the Roman Empire as appears to have really formed part of their primitive usage, and we may suspect that it would have perpetuated itself even more than it has in modern European jurisprudence, if it had not been for the vast influence of the later Roman law on modern thought.   The Prætors early laid hold on Cogna*

10

tion as the *natural* form of kinship, and spared no pains in purifying their system from the older conception. Their ideas have descended to us, but still traces of Agnation are to be seen in many of the modern rules of succession after death. The exclusion of females and their children from governmental functions, commonly attributed to the usage of the Salian Franks, has certainly an agnatic origin, being descended from the ancient German rule of succession to allodial property. In Agnation too is to be sought the explanation of that extraordinary rule of English Law, only recently repealed, which prohibited brothers of the half-blood from succeeding to one another's lands. In the Customs of Normandy, the rule applies to *uterine* brothers only, that is, to brothers by the same mother but not by the same father; and, limited in this way, it is a strict deduction from the system of Agnation, under which uterine brothers are no relations at all to one another. When it was transplanted to England, the English judges, who had no clue to its principle, interpreted it as a general prohibition against the succession of the half-blood, and extended it to *consanguineous* brothers, that is to sons of the same father by different wives. In all the literature which enshrines the pretended philosophy of law, there is nothing more curious than the pages of elaborate sophistry in which Blackstone attempts to explain and justify the exclusion of the half-blood.

It may be shown, I think, that the Family, as held together by the Patria Potestas, is the nidus out of which the entire Law of Persons has germinated. Of all the chapters of that Law the most important is that which is concerned with the status of Females. It has just been stated that Primitive Jurisprudence, though it does not allow a Woman to communicate any rights of Agnation to her descendants, includes herself nevertheless in the Agnatic bond. Indeed, the relation of a female to the family in which she was born is much stricter, closer, and more durable than that which unites her male kinsmen. We have several times laid down that early law takes notice of Families only; this is the same thing as saying that it only takes notice of persons exercising Patria Potestas, and accordingly the only principle on which it enfranchises a son or grandson at the death of his Parent, is a consideration of the capacity inherent in such son or grandson to become himself the head of a new family and the root of a new set of Parental Powers. But a woman, of course, has no capacity of the kind, and no title accordingly to the liberation which it confers. There is therefore a peculiar contrivance of archaic jurisprudence for retaining her in the bondage of the Family for life. This is the institution known to the oldest Roman law as the Perpetual Tutelage of Women, under which a Female, though relieved from her Parent's authority by his decease, continues subject through life to her nearest male relations, or to her Father's nominees, as her Guardians. Perpetual Guardianship is obviously neither more nor less than an artificial prolongation of the Patria Potestas, when for other purposes it has been dissolved. In India, the system survives in absolute completeness, and its operation is so strict that a Hindoo Mother frequently becomes the ward of her own sons. Even in Europe, the laws of the Scandinavian nations respecting women preserved it until quite recently. The invaders of the Western Empire had it universally among their indigenous usages, and indeed their ideas on the subject of Guardianship, in all its forms, were among the most retrogressive of those which they introduced into the Western world. But from the mature Roman jurisprudence it had entirely disappeared. We should know almost nothing about it, if we had only the compilations of Justinian to consult; but the discovery of the manuscript of Gaius discloses it to us at a most interesting epoch, just when it had fallen into complete discredit and was verging on extinction. The great jurisconsult himself scouts the popular apology offered for it in the mental inferiority of the female sex, and a considerable part of his volume is taken up with descriptions of the numerous expedients, some of them displaying extraordinary ingenuity, which the Roman lawyers had devised for enabling Women to defeat the ancient rules. Led by their theory of Natural Law, the jurisconsults had evidently at this time assumed the equality of the sexes as a principle of their code of equity. The restrictions which they attacked were, it is to be observed, restrictions on the disposition of property, for which the assent of the woman's guardians was still formally required. Control of her person was apparently quite obsolete.

Ancient law subordinates the woman to her blood-relations, while a prime phenomenon of modern jurisprudence has been her subordination to her husband. The history of the change is remarkable. It begins far back in the annals of Rome. Anciently, there were three modes in which marriage might be contracted according to Roman usage, one involving a religious solemnity, the other two the observance of certain secular formalities. By the religious marriage or *Confarreation*; by the higher form of civil marriage, which was called *Coemption*; and by the lower form, which was termed *Usus*, the Husband acquired a number of rights over the person and property of his wife, which were on the whole in excess of such as are conferred on him in any system of modern jurisprudence. But in what capacity did he acquire them? Not as *Husband*, but as *Father*. By the Confarreation, Coemption, and Usus, the woman passed *in manum viri*, that is, in law she became the *Daughter* of her husband. She was included in his Patria Potestas. She incurred all the liabilities springing out of it while it subsisted, and surviving it when it had expired.

All her property became absolutely his, and she was retained in tutelage after his death to the guardian whom he had appointed by will. These three ancient forms of marriage fell, however, gradually into disuse, so that, at the most splendid period of Roman greatness, they had almost entirely given place to a fashion of wedlock—old apparently, but not hitherto considered reputable—which was founded on a modification of the lower form of civil marriage. Without explaining the technical mechanism of the institution now generally popular, I may describe it as amounting in law to little more than a temporary deposit of the woman by her family. The rights of the family remained unimpaired, and the lady continued in the tutelage of guardians whom her parents had appointed and whose privileges of control overrode, in many material respects, the inferior authority of her husband. The consequence was that the situation of the Roman female, whether married or unmarried, became one of great personal and proprietary independence, for the tendency of the later law, as I have already hinted, was to reduce the power of the guardian to a nullity, while the form of marriage in fashion conferred on the husband no compensating superiority. But Christianity tended somewhat from the very first to narrow this remarkable liberty. Led at first by justifiable disrelish for the loose practice of the decaying heathen world, but afterwards hurried on by a passion of

asceticism, the professors of the new faith looked
with disfavour on a marital tie which was in fact
the laxest the Western world has seen. The latest
Roman law, so far as it is touched by the Constitutions of the Christian Emperors, bears some
marks of a reaction against the liberal doctrines of
the great Antonine jurisconsults. And the prevalent state of religious sentiment may explain why
it is that modern jurisprudence, forged in the fur-
nace of barbarian conquest, and formed by the fusion of Roman jurisprudence with patriarchal usage,
has absorbed, among its rudiments, much more than
usual of those rules concerning the position of
women which belong peculiarly to an imperfect
civilisation. During the troubled era which begins
modern history, and while the laws of the Germanic and Sclavonic immigrants remained super-
posed like a separate layer above the Roman jurisprudence of their provincial subjects, the women
of the dominant races are seen everywhere under
various forms of archaic guardianship, and the husband who takes a wife from any family except his
own pays a money-price to her relations for the
tutelage which they surrender to him. When we
move onwards, and the code of the middle ages has
been formed by the amalgamation of the two systems, the law relating to women carries the stamp
of its double origin. The principle of the Roman
jurisprudence is so far triumphant that unmarried
females are generally (though there are local excep-

tions to the rule) relieved from the bondage of the
family ; but the archaic principle of the barbarians
has fixed the position of married women, and the
husband has drawn to himself in his marital character the powers which had once belonged to his
wife's male kindred, the only difference being that
he no longer purchases his privileges. At this
point therefore the modern law of Western and
Southern Europe begins to be distinguished by one
of its chief characteristics, the comparative freedom
it allows to unmarried women and widows, the
heavy disabilities it imposes on wives. It was very
long before the subordination entailed on the other
sex by marriage was sensibly diminished. The
principal and most powerful solvent of the revived
barbarism of Europe was always the codified jurisprudence of Justinian, wherever it was studied with
that passionate enthusiasm which it seldom failed to
awaken. It covertly but most efficaciously undermined the customs which it pretended merely to interpret. But the Chapter of law relating to married women was for the most part read by the light,
not of Roman, but of Canon Law, which in no one
particular departs so widely from the spirit of the
secular jurisprudence as in the view it takes of the
relations created by marriage. This was in part
inevitable, since no society which preserves any
tincture of Christian institution is likely to restore
to married women the personal liberty conferred on
them by the middle Roman law, but the proprie-

tary disabilities of married females stand on quite a
different basis from their personal incapacities, and
it is by the tendency of their doctrines to keep alive
and consolidate the former, that the expositors of
the Canon Law have deeply injured civilisation
There are many vestiges of a struggle between the
secular and ecclesiastical principles, but the Canon
Law nearly everywhere prevailed. In some of the
French provinces, married women, of a rank below
nobility, obtained all the powers of dealing with
property which Roman jurisprudence had allowed,
and this local law has been largely followed by the
Code Napoleon ; but the state of the Scottish law
shows that scrupulous deference to the doctrines of
the Roman jurisconsults did not always extend to
mitigating the disabilities of wives. The systems
however which are least indulgent to married
women are invariably those which have followed
the Canon Law exclusively, or those which, from
the lateness of their contact with European civilisation, have never had their archaisms weeded out.
The Danish and Swedish laws, harsh for many centuries to all females, are still much less favourable
to wives than the generality of Continental codes.
And yet more stringent in the proprietary incapacities it imposes is the English Common Law,
which borrows far the greatest number of its fundamental principles from the jurisprudence of the
Canonists. Indeed, the part of the Common Law
which prescribes the legal situation of married

women may serve to give an Englishman clear notions of the great institution which has been the
principal subject of this chapter. I do not know
how the operation and nature of the ancient Patria
Potestas can be brought so vividly before the mind
as by reflecting on the prerogatives attached to the
husband by the pure English Common Law, and by
recalling the rigorous consistency with which the
view of a complete legal subjection on the part of
the wife is carried by it, where it is untouched by
equity or statutes, through every department of
rights, duties and remedies. The distance between
the eldest and latest Roman law on the subject of
Children under Power may be considered as equivalent to the difference between the Common Law
and the jurisprudence of the Court of Chancery in
the rules which they respectively apply to wives.

   If we were to lose sight of the true origin of
Guardianship in both its forms, and were to employ
the common language on these topics, we should
find ourselves remarking that, while the Tutelage
of Women is an instance in which systems of archaic law push to an extravagant length the fiction
of suspended rights, the rules which they lay down
for the Guardianship of Male Orphans are an ex
ample of a fault in precisely the opposite direction.
Such systems terminate the Tutelage of Males at
an extraordinary early period. Under the ancient
Roman law, which may be taken as their type, the
son who was delivered from Patria Potestas by the

death of his Father or Grandfather remained under
guardianship till an epoch which for general pur
poses may be described as arriving with his fifteenth
year; but the arrival of that epoch placed him at
once in the full enjoyment of personal and proprietary independence.   The period of minority appears therefore to have been as unreasonably short
as the duration of the disabilities of women was
preposterously long.   But, in point of fact, there
was no element either of excess or of shortcoming
in the circumstances which gave their original form
to the two kinds of guardianship.   Neither the one
nor the other of them was based on the slightest
consideration of public or private convenience.   The
guardianship of male orphans was no more designed originally to shield them till the arrival of
years of discretion than the tutelage of women was
intended to protect the other sex against its own
feebleness.   The reason why the death of the father
delivered the son from the bondage of the family
was the son's capacity for becoming himself the
head of a new family and the founder of a new
Patria Potestas; no such capacity was possessed by
the woman, and therefore she was *never* enfranchised.
Accordingly the Guardianship of Male Orphans
was a contrivance for keeping alive the semblance
of subordination to the family of the Parent, up to
the time when the child was supposed capable of
becoming a parent himself.   It was a prolongation
of the Patria Potestas up to the period of bare

physical manhood. It ended with puberty, for the rigour of the theory demanded that it should be so. Inasmuch, however, as it did not profess to con-duct the orphan ward to the age of intellectual maturity or fitness for affairs, it was quite unequal to the purposes of general convenience; and this the Romans seem to have discovered at a very early stage of their social progress. One of the very oldest monuments of Roman legislation is the *Lex Lætoria* or *Plætoria*, which placed all free males who were of full years and rights under the temporary control of a new class of guardians, called *Curatores*, whose sanction was required to validate their acts or contracts. The twenty-sixth year of the young man's age was the limit of this statutory supervision; and it is exclusively with reference to the age of twenty-five that the terms "majority" and "minority" are employed in Roman law. *Pu-pilage* or *wardship* in modern jurisprudence has adjusted itself with tolerable regularity to the sim-ple principle of protection to the immaturity of youth both bodily and mental. It has its natural termination with years of discretion. But for pro-tection against physical weakness and for protection against intellectual incapacity, the Romans looked to two different institutions, distinct both in theory and design. The ideas attendant on both are com bined in the modern idea of guardianship.

The Law of Persons contains but one other chaptei which can be usefully cited for our present

purpose. The legal rules by which systems of mature jurisprudence regulate the connexion of *Master
and Slave*, present no very distinct traces of the
original condition common to ancient societies. But
there are reasons for this exception. There seems
to be something in the institution of Slavery which
has at all times either shocked or perplexed mankind, however little habituated to reflection, and
however slightly advanced in the cultivation of its
moral instincts. The compunction which ancient
communities almost unconsciously experienced appears to have always resulted in the adoption of
some imaginary principle upon which a defence, or
at least a rationale, of slavery could be plausibly
founded. Very early in their history the Greeks
explained the institution as grounded on the intellectual inferiority of certain races and their conse-
quent natural aptitude for the servile condition.
The Romans, in a spirit equally characteristic, derived it from a supposed agreement· between the
victor and the vanquished in which the first stipulated for the perpetual services of his foe ; and the
other gained in consideration the life which he had
legitimately forfeited. Such theories were not only
unsound but plainly unequal to the case for which
they affected to account. Still they exercised powerful influence in many ways. They satisfied the
conscience of the Master. They perpetuated and
probably increased the debasement of the Slave.
And they naturally tended to put out of sight the

relation in which servitude had originally stood to the rest of the domestic system. The relation, though not clearly exhibited, is casually indicated in many parts of the primitive law, and more particularly in the typical system—that of ancient Rome.

Much industry and much learning have been bestowed in the United States of America on the question whether the Slave was in the early stages of society a recognised member of the Family. There is a sense in which an affirmative answer must certainly be given. It is clear, from the testimony both of ancient law and of many primeval histories, that the Slave might under certain conditions be made the Heir, or Universal Successor, of the Master, and this significant faculty, as I shall explain in the Chapter on Succession, implies that the government and representation of the Family might, in a particular state of circumstances, devolve on the bondman. It seems, however, to be assumed in the American arguments on the subject that, if we allow Slavery to have been a primitive Family institution, the acknowledgment is pregnant with an admission of the moral defensibility of Negro-servitude at the present moment. What then is meant by saying that the Slave was originally included in the Family? Not that his situation may not have been the fruit of the coarsest motives which can actuate man. The simple wish to use the bodily powers of another person as a

means of ministering to one's own ease or pleasure
is doubtless the foundation of Slavery, and as old
as human nature. When we speak of the Slave as
anciently included in the Family, we intend to assert nothing as to the motives of those who brought
him into it or kept him there; we merely imply
that the tie which bound him to his master was regarded as one of the same general character with
that which united every other member of the group
to his chieftain. This consequence is, in fact, carried
in the general assertion already made that the
primitive ideas of mankind were unequal to com
prehending any basis of the connexion *inter se* of
individuals, apart from the relations of family. The
Family consisted primarily of those who belonged
to it by consanguinity, and next of those who had
been engrafted on it by adoption; but there was
still a third class of persons who were only joined
to it by common subjection to its head, and these
were the Slaves. The born and the adopted subjects of the chief were raised above the Slave by
the certainty that in the ordinary course of events
they would be relieved from bondage and entitled
to exercise powers of their own; but that the inferiority of the Slave was not such as to place him
outside the pale of the Family, or such as to de-
grade him to the footing of inanimate property, is
clearly proved, I think, by the many traces which
remain of his ancient capacity for inheritance in the
last resort. It would, of course, be unsafe in the

highest degree to hazard conjectures how far the lot of the Slave was mitigated, in the beginnings of society, by having a definite place reserved to him in the empire of the Father. It is, perhaps, more probable that the son was practically assimilated to the Slave, than that the Slave shared any of the tenderness which in later times was shown to the son. But it may be asserted with some confidence of advanced and matured codes that, wherever servitude is sanctioned, the slave has uniformly greater advantages under systems which preserve some memento of his earlier condition than under those which have adopted some other theory of his civil degradation. The point of view from which jurisprudence regards the Slave is always of great importance to him. The Roman law was arrested in its growing tendency to look upon him more and more as an article of property by the theory of the Law of Nature; and hence it is that, wherever servitude is sanctioned by institutions which have been deeply affected by Roman jurisprudence, the servile condition is never intolerably wretched. There is a great deal of evidence that in those American States which have taken the highly Ro manised code of Louisiana as the basis of their ju risprudence, the lot and prospects of the Negro-pop ulation were better in many material respects, until the letter of the fundamental law was overlaid by recent statutory enactments passed under the in- fluence of panic, than under institutions founded on

the English Common Law, which, as recently interpreted, has no true place for the Slave, and can only
therefore regard him as a chattel.

We have now examined all parts of the ancient
Law of Persons which fall within the scope of this
treatise, and the result of the inquiry is, I trust, to
give additional definiteness and precision to our
view of the infancy of jurisprudence. The Civil
laws of States first make their appearance as the
Themistes of a patriarchal sovereign, and we can
now see that these Themistes are probably only
a developed form of the irresponsible commands
which, in a still earlier condition of the race, the
head of each isolated household may have addressed
to his wives, his children, and his slaves. But,
even after the State has been organised, the laws
have still an extremely limited application. Whether they retain their primitive character as Themistes, or whether they advance to the condition of
Customs or Codified Texts, they are binding not on
individuals, but on Families. Ancient jurisprudence, if a perhaps deceptive comparison may be
employed, may be likened to International Law,
filling nothing, as it were, except the interstices between the great groups which are the atoms of so
ciety. In a community so situated, the legislation
of assemblies and the jurisdiction of Courts reach
only to the heads of families, and to every other in
dividual the rule of conduct is the law of his home,
of which his Parent is the legislator. But the

11

sphere of civil law, small at first, tends steadily to enlarge itself. The agents of legal change, Fictions, Equity, and Legislation, are brought in turn to bear on the primeval institutions, and at every point of the progress, a greater number of personal rights and a larger amount of property are removed from the domestic forum to the cognizance of the public tribunals. The ordinances of the government obtain gradually the same efficacy in private concerns as in matters of state, and are no longer liable to be overridden by the behests of a despot enthroned by each hearthstone. We have in the annals of Roman law a nearly complete history of the crumbling away of an archaic system, and of the formation of new institutions from the re-combined materials, institutions some of which descended unimpaired to the modern world, while others, destroyed or corrupted by contact with barbarism in the dark ages, had again to be recovered by mankind. When we leave this jurisprudence at the epoch of its final reconstruction by Justinian, few traces of archaism can be discovered in any part of it except in the single article of the extensive powers still reserved to the living Parent. Everywhere else principles of convenience, or of symmetry, or of simplification —new principles at any rate—have usurped the authority of the jejune considerations which satisfied the conscience of ancient times. Everywhere a new morality has displaced the canons of conduct and the reasons of acquiescence which were in unison with the ancient usages, because in fact they were born of them.

The movement of the progressive societies has been uniform in one respect. Through all its course it has been distinguished by the gradual dissolution of family dependency and the growth of individual obligation in its place. The individual is steadily substituted for the Family, as the unit of which civil laws take account. The advance has been accom plished at varying rates of celerity, and there are societies not absolutely stationary in which the col- lapse of the ancient organisation can only be perceiv- ed by careful study of the phenomena they present. But, whatever its pace, the change has not been subject to reaction or recoil, and apparent retarda- tions will be found to have been occasioned through the absorption of archaic ideas and customs from some entirely foreign source. Nor is it difficult to see what is the tie between man and man which replaces by degrees those forms of reciprocity in rights and duties which have their origin in the Family. It is Contract. Starting, as from one terminus of history, from a condition of society in which all the relations of Persons are summed up in the relations of Fami- ly, we seem to have steadily moved towards a phase of social order in which all these relations arise from the free agreement of individuals. In Western Europe the progress achieved in this direction has been considerable. Thus the status of the Slave has disappeared—it has been superseded by the contractual relation of the servant to his master. The status of the Female under Tutelage, if the tutelage be understood of persons other than her husband, has also ceased to exist; from her coming of age to her marriage all the relations she may form are relations of contract. So too the status of the Son under Power has no true place in the law of modern European societies. If any civil obligation binds together the Parent and the child of full age, it is one to which only contract gives its legal validity. The apparent exceptions are exceptions of that stamp which illustrate the rule. The child before years of discretion, the orphan under guardianship, the adjudged lunatic, have all their capacities and incapacities regulated by the Law of Persons. But why? The reason is differently expressed in the conventional language of different systems, but in substance it is stated to the same effect by all. The great majority of Jurists are constant to the principle that the classes of persons just mentioned are subject to extrinsic control on the single ground that they do not possess the faculty of forming a judgment on their own interests; in other words, that they are wanting in the first essential of an engagement by Contract.

The word Status may be usefully employed to construct a formula expressing the law of progress thus indicated, which, whatever be its value, seems to me to be sufficiently ascertained. All the forms of Status taken notice of in the Law of Persons were derived from, and to some extent are still coloured by, the powers and privileges anciently residing in the Family. If then we employ Status, agreeably with the usage of the best writers, to signify these personal conditions only, and avoid applying the term to such conditions as are the immediate or remote result of agreement, we may say that the movement of the progressive societies has hitherto been a movement *from Status to Contract.*

CHAPTER VI.

IF an attempt were made to demonstrate in England the superiority of the historical method of investigation to the modes of inquiry concerning Jurisprudence which are in fashion among us, no department of Law would better serve as an example than Testaments or Wills. Its capabilities it owes to its great length and great continuity. At the beginning of its history we find ourselves in the very infancy of the social state, surrounded by conceptions which it requires some effort of mind to realise in their ancient form ; while here, at the other extremity of its line of progress, we are in the midst of legal notions which are nothing more than those same conceptions disguised by the phraseology and by the habits of thought which belong to modern times, and exhibiting therefore a difficulty of another kind, the difficulty of believing that ideas which form part of our every-day mental stock can really stand in need of analysis and examination. The growth

of the Law of Wills between these extreme points
can be traced with remarkable distinctness. It was
much less interrupted at the epoch of the birth of
feudalism, than the history of most other branches
of Law. It is, indeed, true that as regards all provinces of jurisprudence, the break caused by the
division between ancient and modern history, or in
other words by the dissolution of the Roman empire,
has been very greatly exaggerated. Indolence has
disinclined many writers to be at the pains of looking for threads of connexion entangled and obscured by the confusions of six troubled centuries,
while other inquirers, not naturally deficient in patience and industry, have been misled by idle pride
in the legal system of their country, and by conse-
quent unwillingness to confess its obligations to the
jurisprudence of Rome. But these unfavourable
influences have had comparatively little effect on the
province of Testamentary Law. The barbarians
were confessedly strangers to any such conception
as that of a Will. The best authorities agree that
there is no trace of it in those parts of their written
codes which comprise the customs practised by them
in their original seats and in their subsequent settlements on the edge of the Roman Empire. But
soon after they became mixed with the population
of the Roman provinces they appropriated from the
Imperial jurisprudence the conception of a Will, at
first in part, and afterwards in all its integrity.
The influence of the Church had much to do with

this rapid assimilation. The ecclesiastical power had very early succeeded to those privileges of custody and registration of Testaments which several of the heathen temples had enjoyed; and even thus early it was almost exclusively to private bequests that the religious foundations owed their temporal possessions. Hence it is that the decrees of the earliest Provincial Councils perpetually contain anathemas against those who deny the sanctity of Wills. Here, in England, Church influence was certainly chief among the causes which by universal acknowledgment have prevented that discontinuity in the history of Testamentary Law which is sometimes believed to exist in the history of other provinces of Jurisprudence. The jurisdiction over one class of Wills was delegated to the Ecclesiastical Courts, which applied to them, though not always intelligently, the principles of Roman jurisprudence; and, though neither the Courts of Common Law nor the Court of Chancery owned any positive obligation to follow the Ecclesiastical tribunals, they could not escape the potent influence of a system of settled rules in course of application by their side. The English law of testamentary succession to personalty has become a modified form of the dispensation under which the inheritances of Roman citizens were administered.

It is not difficult to point out the extreme difference of the conclusions forced on us by the historical treatment of the subject, from those to which

we are conducted when, without the help of history,
we merely strive to analyse our *primâ facie* impres
sions.   I suppose there is nobody who, starting from
the popular or even the legal conception of a Will,
would not imagine that certain qualities are necessarily attached to it.   He would say, for example, that
a Will necessarily takes effect *at death only*,—that it
is *secret*, not known as a matter of course to persons
taking interests under its provisions,—that it is *revo
cable*, i. e. always capable of being superseded by a
new act of testation.   Yet I shall be able to show
that there was a time when none of these characteristics belonged to a Will.   The Testaments from which
our Wills are directly descended at first took effect
immediately on their execution ; they were not secret ; they were not revocable.   Few legal agencies
are, in fact, the fruit of more complex historical
agencies than that by which a man's written intentions control the posthumous disposition of his
goods.   Testaments very slowly and gradually gathered around them the qualities I have mentioned ;
and they did this from causes and under pressure
of events which may be called casual, or which at
any rate have no interest for us at present, except
so far as they have affected the history of law.

At a time when legal theories were more abundant than at present,—theories which, it is true, were
for the most part gratuitous and premature enough,
but which nevertheless rescued jurisprudence from
that worse and more ignoble condition, not unknown

to ourselves, in which nothing like a generalisation is
aspired to, and law is regarded as a mere empirical
pursuit—it was the fashion to explain the ready
and apparently intuitive perception which we have
of certain qualities in a Will, by saying that they
were natural to it, or, as the phrase would run in
full, attached to it by the Law of Nature.   Nobody,
I imagine, would affect to maintain such a doctrine,
when once it was ascertained that all these characteristics had their origin within historical memory ;
at the same time, vestiges of the theory of which
the doctrine is an offshoot, linger in forms of expression which we all of us use and perhaps scarcely know
how to dispense with.   I may illustrate this by mentioning a position common in the legal literature of
the seventeenth century.   The jurists of that period
very commonly assert that the power of Testation
itself is of Natural Law, that it is a right conferred
by the Law of Nature.   Their teaching, though all
persons may not at once see the connexion, is in substance followed by those who affirm that the right
of dictating or controlling the posthumous disposal
of property is a necessary or natural consequence
of the proprietary rights themselves.   And every
student of technical jurisprudence must have come
across the same view, clothed in the language of a
rather different school, which, in its rationale of this
department of law, treats succession *ex testamento* as
the mode of devolution which the property of deceased persons ought primarily to follow, and then

proceeds to account for succession *ab intestato* as the
incidental provision of the lawgiver for the discharge of a function which was only left unperform-
ed through the neglect or misfortune of the deceased
proprietor.   These opinions are only expanded forms
of the more compendious doctrine that Testamentary disposition is an institution of the Law of Nature.   It is certainly never quite safe to pronounce
dogmatically as to the range of association embraced
by modern minds, when they reflect on Nature and
her Law; but I believe that most persons, who affirm that the Testamentary Power is of Natural
Law, may be taken to imply either that, as a matter
of fact, it is universal, or that nations are prompted
to sanction it by an original instinct and impulse.
With respect to the first of these positions, I think
that, when explicitly set forth, it can never be seriously contended for in an age which has seen the
severe restraints imposed on the Testamentary Power by the *Code Napoléon*, and has witnessed the
steady multiplication of systems for which the
French codes have served as a model.   To the second assertion we must object that it is contrary to
the best-ascertained facts in the early history of law,
and I venture to affirm generally that, in all indigenous societies, a condition of jurisprudence in
which Testamentary privileges are *not* allowed, or
rather not contemplated, has preceded that later
stage of legal development in which the mere will
of the proprietor is permitted under more or less of

restriction to override the claims of his kindred in blood.

The conception of a Will or Testament cannot be considered by itself. It is a member, and not the first, of a series of conceptions. In itself a Will is simply the instrument by which the intention of the testator is declared. It must be clear, I think, that before such an instrument takes its turn for discussion, there are several preliminary points to be examined—as for example, what is it, what sort of right or interest, which passes from a dead man on his decease ? to whom and in what form does it pass ? and how came it that the dead were allowed to control the posthumous disposition of their property ? Thrown into technical language, the dependence of the various conceptions which contribute to the notion of a Will is thus expressed. A Will or Testament is an instrument by which the devolution of an inheritance is prescribed. Inheritance is a forn of universal succession. A universal succession is a succession to a *universitas juris*, or university of rights and duties. Inverting this order we have therefore to inquire what is a *universitas juris*; what is a universal succession; what is the form of universal succession which is called an inheritance ? And there are also two further questions, independent to some extent of the points I have mooted, but demanding solution before the subject of Wills can be exhausted. These are, how came an inheri tance to be controlled in any case by the testator's volition, and what is the nature of the instrument by which it came to be controlled?

The first question relates to the *universitas juris;* that is, a university (or bundle) of rights and duties. A *universitas juris* is a collection of rights and duties united by the single circumstance of their having belonged at one time to some one person. It is, as it were, the legal clothing of some given individual. It is not formed by grouping together *any* rights and *any* duties. It can only be constituted by taking all the rights and all the duties of a particular person. The tie which connects a number of rights of property, rights of way, rights to legacies, duties of specific performance, debts, obligations to compensate wrongs—which so connects all these legal privileges and duties together as to constitute them a *universitas juris*, is the *fact* of their having attached to some individual capable of exercising them. Without this *fact* there is no university of rights and duties. The expression *universitas juris* is not classical, but for the notion jurisprudence is exclusively indebted to Roman law; nor is it at all difficult to seize. We must endeavour to collect under one conception the whole set of legal relations in which each one of us stands to the rest of the world. These, whatever be their character and composition, make up together a *universitas juris;* and there is but little danger of mistake in forming the notion, if we are only careful to remember that duties enter into it quite as much as rights. Our duties may overbalance our rights. A man may owe more than he is worth, and therefore if a money value is set on his collective legal relations he may be what is called insolvent. But for all that, the entire group of rights and duties which centres in him is not the less a "juris universitas."

We come next to a "universal succession." A universal succession is a succession to a *universitas juris*. It occurs when one man is invested with the legal clothing of another, becoming at the same moment subject to all his liabilities and entitled to all his rights. In order that the universal succession may be true and perfect, the devolution must take place *uno ictu*, as the jurists phrase it. It is of course possible to conceive one man acquiring the whole of the rights and duties of another at different periods, as for example by successive purchases; or he might acquire them in different capacities, part as heir, part as purchaser, part as legatee. But though the group of rights and duties thus made up should in fact amount to the whole legal personality of a particular individual, the acquisition would not be a universal succession. In order that there may be a true universal succession, the transmission must be such as to pass the whole aggregate of rights and duties at the *same* moment and in virtue of the *same* legal capacity in the recipient. The notion of a universal succession, like that of a juris universitas, is permanent in jurisprudence, though in the English legal system it is obscured by the great variety of

capacities in which rights are acquired, and, above
all, by the distinction between the two great provinces of English property, "realty" and "personalty." The succession of an assignee in bankruptcy
to the entire property of the bankrupt is, however,
a universal succession, though as the assignee only
pays debts to the extent of the assets this is only a
modified form of the primary notion. Were it common among us for persons to take assignments of
all a man's property on condition of paying *all* his
debts, such transfers would exactly resemble the universal successions known to the oldest Roman Law.
When a Roman citizen *adrogated* a son, i. e. took a
man, not already under Patria Potestas, as his adoptive child, he succeeded *universally* to the adoptive
child's estate, i. e. he took all the property and became liable for all the obligations. Several other
forms of universal succession appear in the primitive
Roman Law, but infinitely the most important and
the most durable of all was that one with which we
are more immediately concerned, Hæreditas or Inheritance. Inheritance was a universal succession
occurring at a death. The universal successor was
Hæres or Heir. He stepped at once into all the
rights and all the duties of the dead man. He was
instantly clothed with his entire legal person, and I
need scarcely add that the special character of the
Hæres remained the same, whether he was named
by a Will or whether he took on an Intestacy. The
term Hæres is no more emphatically used of the

Intestate than of the Testamentary Heir, for the manner in which a man became Hæres had nothing to do with the legal character he sustained. The dead man's universal successor, however he became so, whether by Will or by Intestacy, was his Heir. But the heir was not necessarily a single person. A group of persons, considered in law as a single unit, might succeed as *co-heirs* to the Inheritance.

Let me now quote the usual Roman definition of an Inheritance. The reader will be in a position to appreciate the full force of the separate terms. *Hæreditas est successio in universum jus quod defunctus habuit* (" an inheritance is a succession to the entire legal position of a deceased man "). The notion was that though the physical person of the deceased had perished, his legal personality survived and descended unimpaired on his Heir or Co-heirs, in whom his identity (so far as the law was concerned) was continued. Our own law, in constituting the Executor or Administrator the representative of the deceased to the extent of his personal assets, may serve as an illustration of the theory from which it emanated ; but, although it illustrates, it does not explain it. The view of even the later Roman Law required a closeness of correspondence between the position of the deceased and of his Heir which is no feature of an English representation ; and in the primitive jurisprudence everything turned on the continuity of succession. Unless

provision was made in the will for the instant devolution of the testator's rights and duties on the
Heir or Co-heirs, the testament lost all its effect.

In modern Testamentary jurisprudence, as in the
later Roman law, the object of first importance is
the execution of the testator's intentions. In the
ancient law of Rome the subject of corresponding
carefulness was the bestowal of the Universal Succession. One of these rules seems to our eyes a
principle dictated by common sense, while the other
looks very much like an idle crotchet. Yet that
without the second of them the first would never
have come into being is as certain as any proposition of the kind can be.

In order to solve this apparent paradox, and to
bring into greater clearness the train of ideas which
I have been endeavouring to indicate, I must borrow the results of the inquiry which was attempted
in the earlier portion of the preceding chapter.
We saw one peculiarity invariably distinguishing
the infancy of society. Men are regarded and
treated, not as individuals, but always as members
of a particular group. Everybody is first a citizen,
and then, as a citizen, he is a member of his order
—of an aristocracy or a democracy, of an order of
patricians or plebeians ; or in those societies which
an unhappy fate has afflicted with a special perversion in their course of development, of a caste.
Next, he is a member of a gens, house, or clan; and
lastly, he is a member of his *family*. This last was

12

the narrowest and most personal relation in which he stood; nor, paradoxical as it may seem, was he ever regarded as *himself*, as a distinct individual. His individuality was swallowed up in his family. I repeat the definition of a primitive society given before. It has for its units, not individuals, but groups of men united by the reality or the fiction of blood-relationship.

It is in the peculiarities of an undeveloped society that we seize the first trace of a universal succession. Contrasted with the organisation of a modern state, the commonwealths of primitive times may be fairly described as consisting of a number of little despotic governments, each perfectly distinct from the rest, each absolutely controlled by the prerogative of a single monarch. But though the Patriarch, for we must not yet call him the Pater-familias, had rights thus extensive, it is impossible to doubt that he lay under an equal amplitude of obligations. If he governed the family, it was for its behoof. If he was lord of its possessions, he held them as trustee for his children and kindred. He had no privilege or position distinct from that conferred on him by his relation to the petty commonwealth which he governed. The Family, in fact, was a Corporation; and he was its representative or, we might almost say, its Public officer. He enjoyed rights and stood under duties, but the rights and duties were, in the contemplation of his fellow-citizens and in the eye of the law,

quite as much those of the collective body as his
own.   Let us consider for a moment, the effect
which would be produced by the death of such a
representative.   In the eye of the law, in the view
of the civil magistrate, the demise of the domestic
authority would be a perfectly immaterial event.
The person representing the collective body of the
family and primarily responsible to municipal jurisdiction would bear a different name; and that
would be all.   The rights and obligations which
attached to the deceased head of the house would
attach, without breach of continuity, to his successor; for, in point of fact, they would be the rights
and obligations of the family, and the family had
the distinctive characteristic of a corporation—that
it never died.   Creditors would have the same
remedies against the new chieftain as against the
old, for the liability being that of the still existing
family would be absolutely unchanged.   All rights
available to the family would be as available after
the demise of the headship as before it—except that
the Corporation would be obliged—if indeed language so precise and technical can be properly used
of these early times—would be obliged to *sue* under
slightly modified name.

The history of jurisprudence must be followed
in its whole course, if we are to understand how
gradually and tardily society dissolved itself into
the component atoms of which it is now constituted
—by what insensible gradations the relation of man

to man substituted itself for the relation of the individual to his family and of families to each other. The point now to be attended to is that even when the revolution had apparently quite accomplished itself, even when the magistrate had in great measure assumed the place of the Pater-familias, and the civil tribunal substituted itself for the domestic forum, nevertheless the whole scheme of rights and duties administered by the judicial authorities remained shaped by the influence of the obsolete privileges and coloured in every part by their reflection. There seems little question that the devolution of the Universitas Juris, so strenuously insisted upon by the Roman Law as the first condition of a testamentary or intestate succession, was a feature of the older form of society which men's minds had been unable to dissociate from the new, though with that newer phase it had no true or proper connection. It seems, in truth, that the prolongation of a man's legal existence in his heir, or in a group of co-heirs, is neither more nor less than a characteristic of *the family* transferred by a fiction to *the individual*. Succession in corporations is necessarily universal, and the family was a corporation. Corporations never die. The decease of individual members makes no difference to the collective existence of the aggregate body, and does not in any way affect its legal incidents, its faculties or liabilities. Now in the idea of a Roman universal succession all these qualities of a corporation seem to have been transferred to the individual citizen. His physical death is allowed to exercise no effect on the legal position which he filled, apparently on the principle that that position is to be adjusted as closely as possible to the analogies of a family, which in its corporate character was not of course liable to physical extinction.

I observe that not a few continental jurists have much difficulty in comprehending the nature of the connection between the conceptions blended in a universal succession, and there is perhaps no topic in the philosophy of jurisprudence on which their speculations, as a general rule, possess so little value. But the student of English law ought to be in no danger of stumbling at the analysis of the idea which we are examining. Much light is cast upon it by a fiction in our own system with which all lawyers are familiar. English lawyers classify corporations as Corporations aggregate and Corporations sole. A Corporation aggregate is a true corporation, but a Corporation sole is an individual, being a member of a series of individuals, who is invested by a fiction with the qualities of a Corporation. I need hardly cite the King or the Parson of a Parish as instances of Corporations sole. The capacity or office is here considered apart from the particular person who from time to time may occupy it, and, this capacity being perpetual, the series of individuals who fill it are clothed with the leading attribute of Corporations—Perpetuity.

Now in the older theory of Roman Law the indi
vidual bore to the family precisely the same relation
which in the rationale of English jurisprudence a
Corporation sole bears to a Corporation aggregate.
The derivation and association of ideas are exactly
the same. In fact, if we say to ourselves that for
purposes of Roman Testamentary Jurisprudence
each individual citizen was a Corporation sole, we
shall not only realize the full conception of an inheritance, but have constantly at command the clue
to the assumption in which it originated. It is an
axiom with us that the King never dies, being
a Corporation sole. His capacities are instantly
filled by his successor, and the continuity of dominion is not deemed to have been interrupted. With
the Romans it seemed an equally simple and natural
process, to eliminate the fact of death from the devolution of rights and obligations. The testator lived
on in his heir or in the group of his co-heirs. He
was in law the same person with them, and if any
one in his testamentary dispositions had even con-
structively violated the principle which united his
actual and his posthumous existence, the law rejected the defective instrument, and gave the inheritance to the kindred in blood, whose capacity to
fulfil the conditions of heirship was conferred on
them by the law itself, and not by any document
which by possibility might be erroneously framed.

When a Roman citizen died intestate or leaving
no valid Will, his descendants or kindred became

his heirs according to a scale which will be presently described. The person or class of persons who
succeeded did not simply *represent* the deceased,
but, in conformity with the theory just delineated,
they *continued* his civil life, his legal existence.
The same results followed when the order of succession was determined by a Will, but the theory
of the identity between the dead man and his heirs
was certainly much older than any form of Testament or phase of Testamentary jurisprudence. This
indeed is the proper moment for suggesting a doubt
which will press on us with greater force the further
we plumb the depths of this subject—whether *wills*
would ever have come into being at all if it had not
been for these remarkable ideas connected with universal succession. Testamentary law is the application of a principle which may be explained on a variety of philosophical hypotheses as plausible as
they are gratuitous; it is interwoven with every
part of modern society, and it is defensible on the
broadest grounds of general expediency. But the
warning can never be too often repeated, that the
grand source of mistake in questions of jurisprudence is the impression that those reasons which
actuate us at the present moment, in the maintenance of an existing institution, have necessarily
anything in common with the sentiment in which
the institution originated. It is certain that, in the
old Roman Law of Inheritance, the notion of a will
or testament is inextricably mixed up, I might

almost say confounded, with the theory of a man's posthumous existence in the person of his heir.

The conception of a universal succession, firmly as it has taken root in jurisprudence, has not occurred spontaneously to the framers of every body of laws. Wherever it is now found, it may be shown to have descended from Roman law; and with it have come down a host of legal rules on the subject of Testaments and Testamentary gifts, which modern practitioners apply without discerning their relation to the parent theory. But, in the pure Roman jurisprudence, the principle that a man lives on in his Heir—the elimination, if we may so speak, of the fact of death—is too obviously for mistake the centre round which the whole Law of Testamentary and Intestate succession is circling. The unflinching sternness of the Roman law in enforcing compliance with the governing theory would in itself suggest that the theory grew out of something in the primitive constitution of Roman society; but we may push the proof a good way beyond the presumption. It happens that several technical expressions, dating from the earliest institutions of Wills at Rome, have been accidentally preserved to us. We have in Gaius the formula of investiture by which the universal successor was created. We have the ancient name by which the person afterwards called Heir was at first designated. We have further the text of the celebrated clause in the Twelve Tables by which the Testamentary

power was expressly recognised, and the clauses
regulating Intestate Succession have also been preserved.   All these archaic phrases have one salient
peculiarity.   They indicate that what passed from
the Testator to the Heir was the *Family*, that is
the aggregate of rights and duties contained in the
Patria Potestas and growing out of it.   The material property is in three instances not mentioned
at all; in two others, it is visibly named as an
adjunct or appendage of the Family.   The original
Will or Testament was therefore an instrument, or
(for it was probably not at first in writing) a proceeding by which the devolution of the *Family* was
regulated.   It was a mode of declaring who was to
have the chieftainship, in succession to the Testator.
When Wills are understood to have this for their
original object, we see at once how it is that they
came to be connected with one of the most curious
relics of ancient religion and law, the *sacra*, or
Family Rites.   These *sacra* were the Roman form
of an institution which shows itself wherever society
has not wholly shaken itself free from its primitive
clothing.   They are the sacrifices and ceremonies
by which the brotherhood of the family is commemorated, the pledge and the witness of its perpetuity.
Whatever be their nature,—whether it be true or
not that in all cases they are the worship of some
mythical ancestor,—they are everywhere employed
to attest the sacredness of the family relation; and
therefore they acquire prominent significance and

importance, whenever the continuous existence of
the Family is endangered by a change in the person
of its chief.   Accordingly, we hear most about them
in connection with demises of domestic sovereignty.
Among the Hindoos, the right to inherit a dead
man's property is exactly co-extensive with the duty
of performing his obsequies.   If the rites are not
properly performed or not performed by the proper
person, no relation is considered as established between the deceased and anybody surviving him ;
the Law of Succession does not apply, and nobody
can inherit the property.   Every great event in the
life of a Hindoo seems to be regarded as leading up
to and bearing upon these solemnities.   If he mar-
ries, it is to have children who may celebrate them
after his death ; if he has no children, he lies under
the strongest obligation to adopt them from another
family, " with a view," writes the Hindoo doctor,
" to the funeral cake, the water, and the solemn
sacrifice."   The sphere preserved to the Roman
sacra in the time of Cicero, was not less in extent.
It embraced Inheritances and Adoptions.   No
Adoption was allowed to take place without due
provision for the *sacra* of the family from which the
adoptive son was transferred, and no Testament was
allowed to distribute an Inheritance without a strict
apportionment of the expenses of these ceremonies
among the different co-heirs.   The differences between the Roman law at this epoch, when we obtain
our last glimpse of the *sacra*, and the existing Hin-

doo system, are most instructive. Among the Hindoos, the religious element in law has acquired a
complete predominance. Family sacrifices have become the keystone of all the Law of Persons and
much of the Law of Things. They have even received a monstrous extension, for it is a plausible
opinion that the self-immolation of the widow at
her husband's funeral, a practice continued to historical times by the Hindoos, and commemorated in
the traditions of several Indo-European races, was
an addition grafted on the primitive *sacra* under the
influence of the impression, which always accom-
panies the idea of sacrifice, that human blood is the
most precious of all oblations. With the Romans,
on the contrary, the legal obligation and the religious duty have ceased to be blended. The necessity of solemnising the *sacra* forms no part of the
theory of civil law, but they are under the separate
jurisdiction of the College of Pontiffs. The letters
of Cicero to Atticus, which are full of allusions
to them, leave no doubt that they constituted an in-
tolerable burden on Inheritances; but the point of
development at which law breaks away from religion has been passed, and we are prepared for their
entire disappearance from the later jurisprudence.

In Hindoo law there is no such thing as a true
Will. The place filled by Wills is occupied by
Adoptions. We can now see the relation of the
Testamentary Power to the Faculty of Adoption,
and the reason why the exercise of either of them

could call up a peculiar solicitude for the perform
ance of the *sacra*. Both a Will and an Adoption
threaten a distortion of the ordinary course of Family descent, but they are obviously contrivances for
preventing the descent being wholly interrupted
when there is no succession of kindred to carry it
on. Of the two expedients Adoption, the factitious
creation of blood-relationship, is the only one which
has suggested itself to the greater part of archaic
societies. The Hindoos have indeed advanced one
point on what was doubtless the antique practice,
by allowing the widow to adopt when the father
has neglected to do so, and there are in the local
customs of Bengal some faint traces of the Testamentary powers. But to the Romans belongs pre-
eminently the credit of inventing the Will, the institution which, next to the Contract, has exercised
the greatest influence in transforming human society. We must be careful not to attribute to it in
its earliest shape the functions which have attended
it in more recent times. It was at first not a mode
of distributing a dead man's goods, but one among
several ways of transferring the representation of
the household to a new chief. The goods descend
no doubt to the Heir, but that is only because the
government of the family carries with it in its devolution the power of disposing of the common stock.
We are very far as yet from that stage in the history of Wills, in which they become powerful instruments in modifying society through the stimulu

they give to the circulation of property and the plasticity they produce in proprietary rights. No such consequences as these appear in fact to have been associated with the Testamentary power even by the latest Roman lawyers. It will be found that Wills were never looked upon in the Roman community as a contrivance for parting Property and the Family, or for creating a variety of miscellaneous interests, but rather as a means of making a better provision for the members of a household than could be secured through the rules of Intestate succession. We may suspect indeed that the associations of a Roman with the practice of will-making were extremely different from those familiar to us nowadays. The habit of regarding Adoption and Testation as modes of continuing the Family cannot but have had something to do with the singular laxity of Roman notions as to the inheritance of sovereignty. It is impossible not to see that the succession of the early Roman Emperors to each other was considered reasonably regular, and that, in spite of all that had occurred, no absurdity attached to the pretension of such Princes as Theodosius or Justinian to style themselves Cæsar and Augustus.

When the phenomena of primitive societies emerge into light, it seems impossible to dispute a proposition which the jurists of the seventeenth century considered doubtful, that Intestate Inheritance is a more ancient institution than Testamentary Succession. As soon as this is settled, a question of much interest suggests itself, how and under what conditions were the directions of a will first allowed to regulate the devolution of authority over the household, and consequently the posthumous distribution of property. The difficulty of deciding the point arises from the rarity of Testamentary power in archaic communities. It is doubtful whether a true power of testation was known to any original society except the Roman. Rudimentary forms of it occur here and there, but most of them are not exempt from the suspicion of a Roman origin. The Athenian Will was, no doubt, indigenous, but then, as will appear presently, it was only an inchoate Testament. As to the Wills which are sanctioned by the bodies of law which have descended to us as the codes of the barbarian conquerors of imperial Rome, they are almost certainly Roman. The most penetrating German criticism has recently been directed to these *leges Barbarorum*, the great object of investigation being to detach those portions of each system which formed the customs of the tribe in its original home from the adventitious ingredients which were borrowed from the laws of the Romans. In the course of this process, one result has invariably disclosed itself, that the ancient nucleus of the code contains no trace of a Will. Whatever testamentary law exists, has been taken from Roman jurisprudence. Similarly, the rudimentary Testament which (as I am informed) the Rabbinical Jewish law provides for, has been attributed to contact with the Romans. The only form of testament, not belonging to a Roman or Hellenic society, which can reasonably be supposed indigenous, is that recognised by the usages of the province of Bengal; and the testament of Bengal is only a rudimentary Will.

The evidence, however, such as it is, seems to point to the conclusion that Testaments are at first only allowed to take effect on failure of the persons entitled to have the inheritance by right of blood genuine or fictitious. Thus, when Athenian citizens were empowered for the first time by the Laws of Solon to execute Testaments, they were forbidden to disinherit their direct male descendants. So, too, the Will of Bengal is only permitted to govern the succession so far as it is consistent with certain overriding claims of the family. Again, the original institutions of the Jews having provided nowhere for the privileges of Testatorship, the later Rabbinical jurisprudence, which pretends to suply the *casus omissi* of the Mosaic law, allows the power of Testation to attach when all the kindred entitled under the Mosaic system to succeed have failed or are undiscoverable. The limitations by which the ancient German codes hedge in the testamentary jurisprudence which has been incorporated with them are also significant, and point in the same direction. It is the peculiarity of most of these German laws, in the only shape

in which we know them, that, besides the *allod* or
domain of each household, they recognise several
subordinate kinds or orders of property, each of
which probably represents a separate transfusion
of Roman principles into the primitive body of
Teutonic usage. The primitive German or allodial
property is strictly reserved to the kindred. Not
only is it incapable of being disposed of by testament, but it is scarcely capable of being alienated
by conveyance *inter vivos*. The ancient German
law, like the Hindoo jurisprudence, makes the male
children co-proprietors with their father, and the
endowment of the family cannot be parted with except by the consent of all its members. But the
other sorts of property, of more modern origin and
lower dignity than the allodial possessions, are
much more easily alienated than they, and follow
much more lenient rules of devolution. Women
and the descendants of women succeed to them, obviously on the principle that they lie outside the
sacred precinct of the Agnatic brotherhood. Now,
it is on these last descriptions of property, and on
these only, that the Testaments borrowed from
Rome were at first allowed to operate.

These few indications may serve to lend additional plausibility to that which in itself appears to
be the most probable explanation of an ascertained
fact in the early history of Roman wills. We have
it stated on abundant authority that Testaments
during the primitive period of the Roman State,

were executed in the Comitia Calata, that is, in the Comitia Curiata, or Parliament of the Patrician Burghers of Rome, when assembled for Private Business. This mode of execution has been the source of the assertion, handed down by one generation of civilians to another, that every Will at one era of Roman history was a solemn legislative enactment. But there is no necessity whatever for resorting to an explanation which has the defect of attributing far too much precision to the proceedings of the ancient assembly. The proper key to the story concerning the execution of Wills in the Comitia Calata must no doubt be sought in the oldest Roman Law of *intestate* succession. The canons of primitive Roman jurisprudence regulating the inheritance of relations from each other were, so long as they remained unmodified by the Edictal Law of the Prætor, to the following effect :—First, the *sui* or direct descendants who had never been emancipated succeeded. On the failure of the *sui*, the Nearest Agnate came into their place, that is, the nearest person or class of the kindred who was or might have been under the same Patria Potestas with the deceased. The third and last degree came next, in which the inheritance devolved on the *gentiles*, that is, on the collective members of the dead man's *gens* or *House*. The House, I have explained already, was a fictitious extension of the family, consisting of all Roman Patrician citizens who bore the same name, and who on the ground of bearing

13

the same name, were supposed to be descended from a common ancestor. Now the Patrician Assembly called the Comitia Curiata was a Legislature in which Gentes or Houses were exclusively represented. It was a representative assembly of the Roman people, constituted on the assumption that the constituent unit of the state was the Gens. This being so, the inference seems inevitable, that the cognisance of Wills by the Comitia was connected with the rights of the Gentiles, and was intended to secure them in their privilege of ultimate inheritance. The whole apparent anomaly is removed, if we suppose that a Testament could only be made when the testator had no *gentiles* discoverable, or when they waived their claims, and that every Testament was submitted to the General Assembly of the Roman Gentes, in order that those aggrieved by its dispositions might put their veto upon it if they pleased, or by allowing it to pass might be presumed to have renounced their reversion. It is possible that on the eve of the publication of the Twelve Tables this vetoing power may have been greatly curtailed or only occasionally and capriciously exercised. It is much easier, however, to indicate the meaning and origin of the jurisdiction confided to the Comitia Calata, than to trace its gradual development or progressive decay.

The Testament to which the pedigree of all modern Wills may be traced is not, however, the Testament executed in the Calata Comitia, but another Testament designed to compete with it and destined to supersede it. The historical importance of this early Roman Will, and the light it casts on much of ancient thought, will excuse me for describing it at some length.

When the Testamentary power first discloses itself to us in legal history, there are signs that, like almost all the great Roman institutions, it was the subject of contention between the Patricians and the Plebeians. The effect of the political maxim, *Plebs Gentem non habet,* " a Plebeian cannot be a member of a house," was entirely to exclude the Plebeians from the Comitia Curiata. Some critics have accordingly supposed that a Plebeian could not have his Will read or recited to the Patrician Assembly, and was thus deprived of Testamentary privileges altogether. Others have been satisfied to point out the hardships of having to submit a proposed Will to the unfriendly jurisdiction of an assembly in which the Testator was not represented. Whatever be the true view, a form of Testament came into use, which has all the characteristics of a contrivance intended to evade some distasteful obligation. The Will in question was a conveyance *inter vivos*, a complete and irrevocable alienation of the Testator's family and substance to the person whom he meant to be his heir. The strict rules of Roman law must always have permitted such an alienation, but when the transaction was intended to have a posthumous effect, there may have been disputes whether it was valid for Testamentary purposes without the formal assent of the Patrician Parliament. If a difference of opinion existed on the point between the two classes of the Roman population, it was extinguished, with many other sources of heartburning, by the great Decemviral compromise. The text of the Twelve Tables is still extant which says, "*Pater familias uti de pecuniâ tutelâve rei suæ legâssit, ita jus esto*"—a law which can hardly have had any other object than the legalisation of the Plebeian Will.

It is well known to scholars that, centuries after the Patrician Assembly had ceased to be the legislature of the Roman State, it still continued to hold formal sittings for the convenience of private business. Consequently, at a period long subsequent to the publication of the Decemviral Law, there is reason to believe that the Comitia Calata still assembled for the validation of Testaments. Its probable functions may be best indicated by saying that it was a Court of Registration, with the understanding, however, that the Wills exhibited were not *enrolled*, but simply recited to the members, who were supposed to take note of their tenor and to commit them to memory. It is very likely that this form of Testament was never reduced to writing at all, but at all events if the Will had been originally written, the office of the Comitia was certainly confined to hearing it read aloud, the document being retained afterwards in the custody of the

Testator, or deposited under the safeguard of some religious corporation. This publicity may have been one of the incidents of the Testament executed in the Comitia Calata which brought it into popular disfavour. In the early years of the Empire the Comitia still held its meetings, but they seem to have lapsed into the merest form, and few Wills, or none, were probably presented at the periodical sitting.

It is the ancient Plebeian Will—the alternative of the Testament just described—which in its remote effects has deeply modified the civilisation of the modern world. It acquired at Rome all the popularity which the Testament submitted to the Calata Comitia appears to have lost. The key to all its characteristics lies in its descent from the *mancipium*, or ancient Roman conveyance, a proceeding to which we may unhesitatingly assign the parentage of two great institutions without which modern society can scarcely be supposed capable of holding together, the Contract and the Will. The *mancipium*, or, as the word would exhibit itself in later Latinity, the Mancipation, carries us back by its incidents to the infancy of civil society. As it sprang from times long anterior, if not to the invention, at all events to the popularisation, of the art of writing, gestures, symbolical acts, and solemn phrases take the place of documentary forms, and a lengthy and intricate ceremonial is intended to call the attention of the parties to the importance

of the transaction, and to impress it on the memory
of the witnesses.   The imperfection, too, of oral, as
compared with written, testimony necessitates the
multiplication of the witnesses and assistants beyond what in later times would be reasonable or
intelligible limits.

The Roman Mancipation required the presence
first of all the parties, the vendor and vendee,
or we should perhaps rather say, if we are to use
modern legal language, the grantor and grantee.
There were also no less than *five* witnesses; and
an anomalous personage, the Libripens, who brought
with him a pair of scales to weigh the uncoined
copper money of ancient Rome.   The Testament
we are considering—the Testament *per œs et libram*,
" with the copper and the scales," as it long continued to be technically called—was an ordinary Mancipation with no change in the form and hardly
any in words.   The Testator was the grantor; the
five witnesses and the libripens were present; and
the place of grantee was taken by a person known
technically as the *familiæ emptor*, the Purchaser
of the Family.   The ordinary ceremony of a Mancipation was then proceeded with.   Certain formal
gestures were made and sentences pronounced.
The *Emptor familiæ* simulated the payment of a
price by striking the scales with a piece of money,
and finally the Testator ratified what had been done
in a set form of words called the " Nuncupatio " or
publication of the transaction, a phrase which, I

need scarcely remind the lawyer, has had a long history in Testamentary jurisprudence. It is neces- sary to attend particularly to the character of the person called *familiæ emptor.* There is no doubt that at first he was the Heir himself. The Testator conveyed to him outright his whole " familia," that is, all the rights he enjoyed over and through the family; his property, his slaves, and all his an- cestral privileges, together, on the other hand, with all his duties and obligations.

With these data before us, we are able to note several remarkable points in which the Mancipatory Testament, as it may be called, differed in its primi- tive form from a modern will. As it amounted to a conveyance *out-and-out* of the Testator's estate, it was not *revocable.* There could be no new exercise of a power which had been exhausted.

Again, it was not secret. The Familiæ Emptor, being himself the Heir, knew exactly what his rights were, and was aware that he was irreversibly entitled to the inheritance; a knowledge which the violences inseparable from the best-ordered ancient society rendered extremely dangerous. But per- haps the most surprising consequence of this rela- tion of Testaments to Conveyances was the imme- diate vesting of the inheritance in the Heir. This has seemed so incredible to not a few civilians, that they have spoken of the Testator's estate as vesting conditionally on the Testator's death, or as granted to him from a time uncertain, i. e. the death of the

grantor. But down to the latest period of Roman
jurisprudence there were a certain class of transactions which never admitted of being directly modified by a condition, or of being limited to or from a
point of time. In technical language they did not
admit *conditio* or *dies*. Mancipation was one of
them, and therefore, strange as it may seem, we are
forced to conclude that the primitive Roman Will
took effect at once, even though the Testator survived his act of Testation. It is indeed likely that
Roman citizens originally made their Wills only in
the article of death, and that a provision for the
continuance of the Family effected by a man in the
flower of life would take the form rather of an
Adoption than of a Will. Still we must believe
that, if the Testator did recover, he could only continue to govern his household by the sufferance of
his Heir.

Two or three remarks should be made before I
explain how these inconveniences were remedied,
and how Testaments came to be invested with the
characteristics now universally associated with them.
The Testament was not necessarily written : at
first, it seems to have been invariably oral, and even
in later times, the instrument declaratory of the bequests was only incidentally connected with the Will
and formed no essential part of it. It bore in fact
exactly the same relation to the Testament, which
the deed leading the uses bore to the Fines and Recoveries of old English law, or which the charter of

feoffment bore to the feoffment itself. Previously, indeed, to the Twelve Tables, no writing would have been of the slightest use, for the Testator had no power of giving legacies, and the only persons who could be advantaged by a will were the Heir or Co-Heirs. But the extreme generality of the clause in the Twelve Tables soon produced the doctrine that the Heir must take the inheritance burdened by any directions which the Testator might give him, or in other words, take it subject to legacies. Written testamentary instruments assumed thereupon a new value, as a security against the fraudulent refusal of the heir to satisfy the legatees; but to the last it was at the Testator's pleasure to rely exclusively on the testimony of the witnesses, and to declare by word of mouth the legacies which the *familiæ emptor* was commissioned to pay.

The terms of the expression *Emptor familiæ* demand notice. " Emptor " indicates that the Will was literally a sale, and the word " familiæ, " when compared with the phraseology in the Testamentary clause in the Twelve Tables, leads us to some instructive conclusions. " Familia, " in classical Latinity, means always a man's slaves. Here, however, and generally in the language of ancient Roman law, it includes all persons under his Potestas, and the Testator's material property or substance is understood to pass as an adjunct or appendage of his household. Turning to the law of the Twelve Tables, it will be seen that it speaks of *tutela rei suæ* " the guardian-

ship of his substance," a form of expression which
is the exact reverse of the phrase just examined.
There does not therefore appear to be any mode of
escaping from the conclusion, that even at an era so
comparatively recent as that of the Decemviral compromise, terms denoting " household " and " property " were blended in the current phraseology. If a
man's household had been spoken of as his property
we might have explained the expression as pointing
to the extent of the Patria Potestas, but, as the inter-
change is reciprocal, we must allow that the form of
speech carries us back to that primeval period in
which property is owned by the family, and the family is governed by the citizen, so that the members
of the community do not own their property *and*
their family, but rather own their property *through*
their family.

At an epoch not easy to settle with precision, the
Roman Prætors fell into the habit of acting upon
Testaments solemnized in closer conformity with the
spirit than the letter of the law. Casual dispensations became insensibly the established practice till
at length a wholly new form of Will was matured
and regularly engrafted on the Edictal Jurisprudence. The new or *Prætorian* Testament derived
the whole of its impregnability from the *Jus Hono-
rarium* or Equity of Rome. The Prætor of some
particular year must have inserted a clause in his
Inaugural Proclamation declaratory of his intention
to sustain all Testaments which should have been

executed with such and such solemnities; and, the
reform having been found advantageous, the article
relating to it must have been again introduced by
the Prætor's successor, and repeated by the next in
office, till at length it formed a recognised portion
of that body of jurisprudence which from these successive incorporations was styled the Perpetual or
Continuous Edict.   On examining the conditions of
a valid Prætorian Will they will be plainly seen to
have been determined by the requirements of the
Mancipatory Testament, the innovating Prætor having obviously prescribed to himself the retention of
the old formalities just so far as they were warrants
of genuineness or securities against fraud.   At the
execution of the Mancipatory Testament seven persons had been present besides the Testator.   Seven
witnesses were accordingly essential to the Prætorian
Will: two of them corresponding to the *libripens*
and *familiæ emptor*, who were now stripped of their
symbolical character, and were merely present for
the purpose of supplying their testimony.   No em-
blematic ceremony was gone through; the Will was
merely recited; but then it is probable (though
not absolutely certain) that a written instrument was
necessary to perpetuate the evidence of the Testator's dispositions.   At all events, whenever a writing was read or exhibited as a person's last Will, we
know certainly that the Prætorian Court would not
sustain it by special intervention, unless each of
the seven witnesses had severally affixed his seal to

the outside. This is the first appearance of *seal-ing* in the history of jurisprudence, considered as a mode of authentication. The use of seals, however, as mere fastenings, is doubtless of much higher antiquity; and it appears to have been known to the Hebrews. We may observe, that the seals of Roman Wills, and other documents of importance, did not only serve as the index of the presence or assent of the signatary, but were also literally fastenings which had to be broken before the writing could be inspected.

The Edictal Law would therefore enforce the dispositions of a Testator, when, instead of being symbolised through the forms of mancipation, they were simply evidenced by the seals of seven witnesses. But it may be laid down as a general proposition, that the principal qualities of Roman property were incommunicable except through processes which were supposed to be coëval with th origin of the Civil Law. The Prætor therefore could not confer an *Inheritance* on anybody. He could not place the Heir or Co-heirs in that very relation in which the Testator had himself stood to his own rights and obligations. All he could do was to confer on the person designated as Heir the practical enjoyment of the property bequeathed, and to give the force of legal acquittances to his payments of the Testator's debts. When he exerted his powers to these ends, the Prætor was technically said to communicate the *Bonorum Possessio*. The

Heir specially inducted under these circumstances or *Bonorum Possessor*, had every proprietary priv ilege of the Heir by the Civil Law. He took the profits and he could alienate, but then, for all his remedies for redress against wrong, he must go, as we should phrase it, not to the Common Law, but to the Equity side of the Prætorian Court. No great chance of error would be incurred by describ ing him as having an *equitable* estate in the inher itance; but then, to secure ourselves against being deluded by the analogy, we must always recollect that in one year the *Bonorum Possessio* was ope rated upon by a principle of Roman Law known as Usucapion, and the Possessor became Quiritarian owner of all the property comprised in the inher itance.

We know too little of the older law of Civil Process to be able to strike the balance of advan tage and disadvantage between the different classes of remedies supplied by the Prætorian Tribunal. It is certain, however, that, in spite of its many defects, the Mancipatory Testament by which the *universi tas juris* devolved at once and unimpaired was never entirely superseded by the new Will; and at a pe riod less bigoted to antiquarian forms, and perhaps not quite alive to their significance, all the ingenuity of the Jurisconsults seems to have been expended on the improvement of the more venerable instru ment. At the era of Gaius, which is that of the Antonine Cæsars, the great blemishes of the Manci-

patory Will had been removed. Originally, as we
have seen, the essential character of the formalities
had required that the Heir himself should be the
Purchaser of the Family, and the consequence was
that he not only instantly acquired a vested interest
in the Testator's Property, but was formally made
aware of his rights. But the age of Gaius permitted some unconcerned person to officiate as Purchaser of the Family. The Heir, therefore, was not
necessarily informed of the succession to which he
was destined; and Wills thenceforward acquired the
property of *secrecy*. The substitution of a stranger
for the actual Heir in the functions of "Familiæ
Emptor" had other ulterior consequences. As soon
as it was legalised, a Roman Testament came to consist of two parts or stages,—a Conveyance, which
was a pure form, and a Nuncupatio, or Publication.
In this latter passage of the proceeding, the Testator either orally declared to the assistants the wishes
which were to be executed after his death, or produced a written document in which his wishes were
embodied. It was not probably till attention had
been quite drawn off from the imaginary Conveyance, and concentrated on the Nuncupation as the
essential part of the transaction, that Wills were
allowed to become *revocable*.

I have thus carried the pedigree of Wills some
way down in legal history. The root of it is the
old Testament " with the copper and the scales,"
founded on a Mancipation or Conveyance. This

ancient Will has, however, manifold defects, which are remedied, though only indirectly, by the Prætorian law. Meantime the ingenuity of the Jurisconsults effects, in the Common-Law Will or Mancipatory Testament, the very improvements which the Prætor may have concurrently carried out in Equity. These last ameliorations depend, however, on more legal dexterity, and we see accordingly that the Testamentary Law of the day of Gaius or Ulpian is only transitional. What changes next ensued we know not; but at length just before the reconstruction of the jurisprudence by Justinian, we find the subjects of the Eastern Roman Empire employing a form of Will of which the pedigree is traceable to the Prætorian Testament on one side, and to the Testament "with the copper and the scales," on the other. Like the Testament of the Prætor, it required no Mancipation, and was invalid unless sealed by seven witnesses. Like the Mancipatory Will, it passed the Inheritance and not merely a *Bonorum Posses-sio*. Several, however, of its most important features were annexed by positive enactments, and it is out of regard to this threefold derivation from the Prætorian Edict, from the Civil Law, and from the Imperial Constitutions, that Justinian speaks of the Law of Wills in his own days as *Jus Tripertitum*. The New Testament thus described is the one generally known as the Roman Will. But it was the Will of the Eastern Empire only; and the researches of Savigny have shown that in Western Europe the old Mancipatory Testament, with all its apparatus of conveyance, copper, and scales, continued to be the form in use far down in the Middle Ages.

CHAPTER VII.

ANCIENT AND MODERN IDEAS RESPECTING WILLS AND SUCCESSIONS.

ALTHOUGH there is much in the modern European Law of Wills which is intimately connected with the oldest rules of Testamentary disposition practised among men, there are nevertheless some important differences between ancient and modern ideas on the subject of Wills and Successions. Some of the points of difference I shall endeavor to illustrate in this chapter.

At a period, removed several centuries from the era of the Twelve Tables, we find a variety of rules engrafted on the Roman Civil Law with the view of limiting the disinherison of children ; we have the jurisdiction of the Prætor very actively exerted in the same interest ; and we are also presented with a new remedy, very anomalous in character and of uncertain origin, called the Querela Inofficiosi Testamenti, " the Plaint of an Unduteous Will," directed to the reinstatement of the issue in inheritances from

14

which they had been unjustifiably excluded by a father's Testament. Comparing this condition of the law with the text of the Twelve Tables which concedes in terms the utmost liberty of Testation, several writers have been tempted to interweave a good deal of dramatic incident into their history of the Law Testamentary. They tell us of the boundless license of disinherison in which the heads of families instantly began to indulge, of the scandal and injury to public morals which the new practices engendered, and of the applause of all good men which hailed the courage of the Prætor in arresting the progress of paternal depravity. This story, which is not without some foundation for the principal fact it relates, is often so told as to disclose very serious misconceptions of the principles of legal history. The Law of the Twelve Tables is to be explained by the character of the age in which it was enacted. It does not license a tendency which a later era thought itself bound to counteract, but it proceeds on the assumption that no such tendency exists, or, perhaps we should say, in ignorance of the possibility of its existence. There is no likelihood that Roman citizens began immediately to avail themselves freely of the power to disinherit. It is against all reason and sound appreciation of history to suppose that the yoke of family bondage, still patiently submitted to, as we know, where its pressure galled most cruelly, would be cast off in the very particular in which its incidence in our own

day is not otherwise than welcome. The Law of
the Twelve Tables permitted the execution of Testa
ments in the only case in which it was thought possible that they could be executed, viz.: on failure of
children and proximate kindred. It did not forbid
the disinherison of direct descendants, inasmuch as
it did not legislate against a contingency which no
Roman lawgiver of that era could have contemplated. No doubt, as the offices of family affection
progressively lost the aspect of primary personal
duties, the disinherison of children was occasionally
attempted. But the interference of the Prætor, so
far from being called for by the universality of the
abuse, was doubtless first prompted by the fact that
such instances of unnatural caprice were few and
exceptional, and at conflict with the current morality.

The indications furnished by this part of Roman
Testamentary Law are of a very different kind. It
is remarkable that a Will never seems to have been
regarded by the Romans as a means of *disinheriting*
a Family, or of effecting the unequal distribution of
a patrimony. The rules of law preventing its being
turned to such a purpose, increase in number and
stringency as the jurisprudence unfolds itself; and
these rules correspond doubtless with the abiding
sentiment of Roman society, as distinguished from
occasional variations of feeling in individuals. It
would rather seem as if the Testamentary Power
were chiefly valued for the assistance it gave in

making provision for a Family, and in dividing the
inheritance more evenly and fairly than the Law of
Intestate Succession would have divided it.   If this
be the true reading of the general sentiment on the
point, it explains to some extent the singular horror
of Intestacy which always characterised the Roman
No evil seems to have been considered a heavier
visitation than the forfeiture of Testamentary privileges ; no curse appears to have been bitterer than
that which imprecated on an enemy that he might
die without a Will.   The feeling has no counterpart,
or none that is easily recognisable, in the forms of
opinion which exist at the present day.   All men at
all times will doubtless prefer chalking out the desti-
nation of their substance to having that office performed for them by the law ; but the Roman passion
for Testacy is distinguished from the mere desire to
indulge caprice by its intensity ; and it has, of course,
nothing whatever in common with that pride of
family, exclusively the creation of feudalism, which
accumulates one description of property in the hands
of a single representative.   It is probable, *à priori*,
that it was something in the rules of Intestate Succession which caused this vehement preference for
the distribution of property under a Testament over
its distribution by law.   The difficulty, however, is,
that on glancing at the Roman law of Intestate
Succession, in the form which it wore for many
centuries before Justinian shaped it into that scheme
of inheritance which has been almost universally

adopted by modern lawgivers, it by no means strikes one as remarkably unreasonable or inequitable. On the contrary, the distribution it prescribes is so fair and rational, and differs so little from that with which modern society has been generally contented, that no reason suggests itself why it should have been regarded with extraordinary distaste, especially under a jurisprudence which pared down to a narrow compass the testamentary privileges of persons who had children to provide for. We should rather have expected that, as in France at this moment, the heads of families would generally save themselves the trouble of executing a Will, and allow the Law to do as it pleased with their assets. I think, however, if we look a little closely at the pre-Justinianean scale of Intestate Succession, we shall discover the key to the mystery. The texture of the law consists of two distinct parts. One department of rules comes from the Jus Civile, the Common Law of Rome; the other from the Edict of the Prætor The Civil Law, as I have already stated for another purpose, calls to the inheritance only three orders of successors in their turn; the unemancipated children, the nearest class of Agnatic kindred, and the Gentiles. Between these three orders, the Prætor interpolates various classes of relatives, of whom the Civil Law took no notice whatever. Ultimately, the combination of the Edict and of the Civil Law forms a table of succession not materially different from that which has descended to the generality of modern codes.

The point for recollection is, that there must anciently have been a time at which the rules of the Civil Law determined the scheme of Intestate Succession exclusively, and at which the arrangements of the Edict were non-existent, or not consistently carried out. We cannot doubt that, in its infancy, the Prætorian jurisprudence had to contend with formidable obstructions, and it is more than probable that, long after popular sentiment and legal opinion had acquiesced in it, the modifications which it periodically introduced were governed by no certain principles, and fluctuated with the varying bias of successive magistrates. The rules of Intestate Succession, which the Romans must at this period have practised, account, I think—and more than account—for that vehement distaste for an Intestacy to which Roman society during so many ages remained constant. The order of succession was this : on the death of a citizen, having no will or no valid will, his Unemancipated children became his Heirs. His *emancipated* sons had no share in the inheritance. If he left no direct descendants living at his death, the nearest grade of the Agnatic kindred succeeded, but no part of the inheritance was given to any relative united (however closely) with the dead man through female descents. All the other branches of the family were excluded, and the inheritance escheated to the *Gentiles*, or entire body of Roman citizens bearing the same name with the deceased. So that on failing to execute an operative Testament, a Roman of the era under examination left his emancipated children absolutely without provision, while, on the assumption that he died childless, there was imminent risk that his possessions would escape from the family altogether, and devolve on a number of persons with whom he was merely connected by the sacerdotal fiction that assumed all members of the same *gens* to be descended from a common ancestor.   The prospect of such an issue is in itself a nearly sufficient explanation of the popular sentiment; but, in point of fact, we shall only half understand it, if we forget that the state of things I have been describing is likely to have existed at the very moment when Roman society was in the first stage of its transition from its primitive organisation in detached families.   The empire of the father had indeed received one of the earliest blows directed at it through the recognition of Emancipation as a legitimate usage, but the law, still considering the Patria Potestas to be the root of family connection, persevered in looking on the emancipated children as strangers to the rights of Kinship and aliens from the blood.   We cannot, however, for a moment suppose that the limitations of the family imposed by legal pedantry had their counterpart in the natural affection of parents.   Family attachments must still have retained that nearly inconceivable sanctity and intensity which belonged to them under the Patri-

archal system; and so little are they likely to have
been extinguished by the act of emancipation, that
the probabilities are altogether the other way. It
may be unhesitatingly taken for granted that enfran-
chisement from the father's power was a demonstration, rather than a severance, of affection—a mark
of grace and favour accorded to the best-beloved
and most esteemed of the children. If sons thus
honoured above the rest were absolutely deprived
of their heritage by an Intestacy, the reluctance to
incur it requires no farther explanation. We might
have assumed à priori that the passion for Testacy,
was generated by some moral injustice entailed by
the rules of Intestate succession; and here we find
them at variance with the very instinct by which
early society was cemented together. It is possible
to put all that has been urged in a very succinct form.
Every dominant sentiment of the primitive Romans
was entwined with the relations of the family. But
what was the Family? The Law defined it one way
—natural affection another. In the conflict between
the two, the feeling we would analyse grew up,
taking the form of an enthusiasm for the institution
by which the dictates of affection were permitted to
determine the fortunes of its objects.

I regard, therefore, the Roman horror of Intestacy as a monument of a very early conflict between
ancient law and slowly changing ancient sentiment
on the subject of the Family. Some passages in the
Roman Statute-Law, and one statute in particular

which limited the capacity for inheritance possessed
by women, must have contributed to keep alive the
feeling; and it is the general belief that the system
of creating Fidei-Commissa, or bequests in trust, was
devised to evade the disabilities imposed by those
statutes.   But the feeling itself, in its remarkable
intensity, seems to point back to some deeper antagonism between law and opinion; nor is it at all
wonderful that the improvements of jurisprudence
by the Praetor should not have extinguished it.
Everybody conversant with the philosophy of opinion is aware that a sentiment by no means dies out,
of necessity, with the passing away of the circumstances which produced it.   It may long survive
them; nay, it may afterwards attain to a pitch and
climax of intensity which it never attained during
their actual continuance.

The view of a Will which regards it as conferring the power of diverting property from the Family, or of distributing it in such uneven proportions
as the fancy or good sense of the Testator may dic-
tate, is not older than that later portion of the Middle Ages in which Feudalism had completely consolidated itself.   When modern jurisprudence first
shows itself in the rough, Wills are rarely allowed
to dispose with absolute freedom of a dead man's
assets.   Wherever at this period the descent of
property was regulated by Will—and over the
greater part of Europe moveable or personal property was the subject of Testamentary disposition

—the exercise of the Testamentary power was seldom allowed to interfere with the right of the widow
to a definite share, and of the children to certain
fixed proportions, of the devolving inheritance.
The shares of the children, as their amount shows,
were determined by the authority of Roman law.
The provision for the widow was attributable to the
exertions of the Church, which never relaxed its
solicitude for the interest of wives surviving their
husbands—winning, perhaps one of the most ardu-
ous of its triumphs when, after exacting for two or
three centuries an express promise from the husband at marriage to endow his wife, it at length succeeded in engrafting the principle of Dower on the
Customary Law of all Western Europe. Curiously
enough, the dower of lands proved a more stable
institution than the analogous and more ancient reservation of certain shares of the personal property
to the widow and children. A few local customs in
France maintained the right down to the Revolution, and there are traces of similar usages in England; but on the whole the doctrine prevailed that
moveables might be freely disposed of by Will,
and, even when the claims of the widow continued
to be respected, the privileges of the children were
obliterated from jurisprudence. We need not hesitate to attribute the change to the influence of Primogeniture. As the Feudal law of land practically
disinherited all the children in favour of one, the
equal distribution even of those sorts of property

which might have been equally divided ceased to
be viewed as a duty. Testaments were the principal instruments employed in producing inequality,
and in this condition of things originated the shade
of difference which shows itself between the ancient
and modern conception of a Will. But, though the
liberty of bequest, enjoyed through Testaments, was
thus an accidental fruit of Feudalism, there is no
broader distinction than that which exists between
a system of free Testamentary disposition and a system, like that of the Feudal land-law, under which
property descends compulsorily in prescribed lines
of devolution. This truth appears to have been lost
sight of by the authors of the French Codes. In
the social fabric which they determined to destroy,
they saw Primogeniture resting chiefly on Family
settlements, but they also perceived that Testaments
were frequently employed to give the eldest son
precisely the same preference which was reserved to
him under the strictest of entails. In order, therefore, to make sure of their work, they not only rendered it impossible to prefer the eldest son to the
rest in marriage-arrangements, but they almost ex-
pelled Testamentary succession from the law, lest it
should be used to defeat their fundamental principle
of an equal distribution of property among children
at the parent's death. The result is that they have
established a system of small perpetual entails, which
is infinitely nearer akin to the system of feudal
Europe than would be a perfect liberty of bequest.

The land-law of England, " the Herculaneum of
Feudalism," is certainly much more closely allied to
the land-law of the Middle Ages than that of any
Continental country, and Wills with us are frequently
used to aid or imitate that preference of the eldest
son and his line which is a nearly universal feature
in marriage settlements of real property. But nevertheless feeling and opinion in this country have
been profoundly affected by the practice of free
Testamentary disposition ; and it appears to me that
the state of sentiment in a great part of French society, on the subject of the conservation of property in families, is much liker that which prevailed
through Europe two or three centuries ago than are
the current opinions of Englishmen.

The mention of Primogeniture introduces one of
the most difficult problems of historical jurisprudence. Though I have not paused to explain my
expressions, it may have been noticed that I have
frequently spoken of a number of " co-heirs " as
placed by the Roman Law of Succession on the
same footing with a single Heir. In point of fact,
we know of no period of Roman jurisprudence at
which the place of the Heir, or Universal Successor,
might not have been taken by a group of co-heirs.
This group succeeded as a single unit, and the assets
were afterwards divided among them in a separate
legal proceeding. When the Succession was *ab intestato*, and the group consisted of the children of
the deceased, they each took an equal share of the

property; nor, though males had at one time some advantages over females, is there the faintest trace of Primogeniture. The mode of distribution is the same throughout archaic jurisprudence. It certainly seems that, when civil society begins and families cease to hold together through a series of generations, the idea which spontaneously suggests itself is to divide the domain equally among the members of each successive generation, and to reserve no privilege to the eldest son or stock. Some peculiarly significant hints as to the close relation of this phenomenon to primitive thought are furnished by systems yet more archaic than the Roman. Among the Hindoos, the instant a son is born, he acquires a vested right in his father's property, which cannot be sold without recognition of his joint-ownership. On the son's attaining full age, he can sometimes compel a partition of the estate even against the consent of the parent; and should the parent acquiesce, one son can always have a partition even against the will of the others On such partition taking place, the father has no advantage over his children, except that he has two of the shares instead of one. The ancient law of the German tribes was exceedingly similar. The *allod* or domain of the family was the joint-property of the father and his sons. It does not, however, appear to have been habitually divided even at the death of the parent, and in the same way the possessions of a Hindoo, however divisible theoretically, are so rarely dis tributed in fact, that many generations constantly succeed each other without a partition taking place, and thus the Family in India has a perpetual ten- dency to expand into the Village Community, under conditions which I shall hereafter attempt to eluci- date. All this points very clearly to the absolutely equal division of assets among the male children at death as the practice most usual with society at the period when family-dependency is in the first stages of disintegration. Here then emerges the historical difficulty of Primogeniture. The more clearly we perceive that, when the Feudal institutions were in process of formation, there was no source in the world whence they could derive their elements but the Roman law of the provincials on the one hand and the archaic customs of the barbarians on the other, the more are we perplexed at first sight by our knowledge that neither Roman nor barbarian was accustomed to give any preference to the eldest son or his line in the succession to property.

Primogeniture did not belong to the Customs which the barbarians practised on their first estab- lishment within the Roman Empire. It is known to have had its origin in the *benefices* or beneficiary gifts of the invading chieftains. These benefices, which were occasionally conferred by the earlier im migrant kings, but were distributed on a great scale by Charlemagne, were grants of Roman provincial land to be holden by the beneficiary on condition of military service. The *allodial* proprietors do not

seem to have followed their sovereign on distant or
difficult enterprises, and all the grander expeditions
of the Frankish chiefs and of Charlemagne were accomplished with forces composed of soldiers either
personally dependent on the royal house or com
pelled to serve it by the tenure of their land.   The
benefices, however, were not at first in any sense
hereditary.   They were held at the pleasure of the
grantor, or at most for the life of the grantee; but
still, from the very outset, no effort seems to have
been spared by the beneficiaries to enlarge their
tenure, and to continue their lands in their family af
ter death.   Through the feebleness of Charlemagne's
successors these attempts were universally successful, and the Benefice gradually transformed itself
into the hereditary Fief. But, though the fiefs were
hereditary, they did not necessarily descend to the
eldest son.   The rules of succession which they followed were entirely determined by the terms agreed
upon between the grantor and the beneficiary, or
imposed by one of them on the weakness of the
other. The original tenures were therefore extremely various; not indeed so capriciously various as is
sometimes asserted, for all which have hitherto been
described present some combination of the modes of
succession familiar to Romans and to barbarians, but
still exceedingly miscellaneous.   In some of them,
the eldest son and his stock undoubtedly succeeded
to the fief before the others, but such successions,
so far from being universal, do not even appear to

have been general. Precisely the same phenomena
recur during that more recent transmutation of European society which entirely substituted the feudal
form of property for the domainial (or Roman) and
the allodial (or German.) The allods were wholly
absorbed by the fiefs. The greater allodial proprietors transformed themselves into feudal lords by
conditional alienations of portions of their land to
dependants ; the smaller sought an escape from the
oppressions of that terrible time by surrendering
their property to some powerful chieftain, and receiving it back at his hands on condition of service in
his wars. Meantime, that vast mass of the population of Western Europe whose condition was servile
or semi-servile—the Roman and German personal
slaves, the Roman *coloni* and the German *lidi*—were
concurrently absorbed by the feudal organisation, a
few of them assuming a menial relation to the lords,
but the greater part receiving land on terms which in
those centuries were considered degrading. The tenures created during this era of universal infeudation
were as various as the conditions which the tenants
made with their new chiefs or were forced to accept
from them. As in the case of benefices, the succession to some, but by no means to all, of the estates
followed the rule of Primogeniture. No sooner,
however, has the feudal system prevailed throughout the West, than it becomes evident that Primogeniture has some great advantage over every other
mode of succession. It spread over Europe with re-

markable rapidity, the principal instrument of diffusion being Family Settlements, the Pactes de Fam-
ille of France and Haus-Gesetze of Germany, which
universally stipulated that lands held by knightly
service should descend to the eldest son. Ultimately
the law resigned itself to follow inveterate practice,
and we find that in all the bodies of Customary Law,
which were gradually built up, the eldest son and
stock are preferred in the succession to estates of
which the tenure is free and military. As to lands
held by servile tenures (and originally all tenures
were servile which bound the tenant to pay money
or bestow manual labor), the system of succession
prescribed by custom differed greatly in different
countries and different provinces. The more general rule was that such lands were divided equally
at death among all the children, but still in some
instances the eldest son was preferred, in some the
youngest. But Primogeniture usually governed the
inheritance of that class of estates, in some respects
the most important of all, which were held by tenures that, like the English Socage, were of later origin than the rest, and were neither altogether free
nor altogether servile.

The diffusion of Primogeniture is usually accounted for by assigning what are called Feudal reasons for it. It is asserted that the feudal superior
had a better security for the military service he required when the fief descended to a single per son,
instead of being distributed among a number or the

15

decease of the last holder. Without denying that
this consideration may partially explain the favour
gradually acquired by Primogeniture, I must point
out that Primogeniture became a custom of Europe
much more through its popularity with the tenants
than through any advantage it conferred on the
lords. For its origin, moreover, the reason given
does not account at all. Nothing in law springs entirely from a sense of convenience. There are always
certain ideas existing antecedently on which the
sense of convenience works, and of which it can do
no more than form some new combination; and to
find these ideas in the present case is exactly the
problem.

A valuable hint is furnished to us from a quarter
fruitful of such indications. Although in India the
possessions of a parent are divisible at his death, and
may be divisible during his life, among all his male
children in equal shares, and though this principle
of the equal distribution of *property* extends to every
part of the Hindoo institutions, yet wherever *public
office* or *political power* devolves at the decease of
the last Incumbent, the succession is nearly universally according to the rules of Primogeniture. Sov-
ereignties descend therefore to the eldest son, and
where the affairs of the Village Community, the
corporate unit of Hindoo society, are confided to a
single manager, it is generally the eldest son who
takes up the administration at his parent's death.
All offices, indeed, in India, tend to become heredi-

tary, and, when their nature permits it, to vest in
the eldest member of the oldest stock.   Comparing
these Indian successions with some of the ruder social
organisations which have survived in Europe almost
to our own day, the conclusion suggests itself that,
when Patriarchal power is not only *domestic* but
political, it is not distributed among all the issue at
the parent's death, but is the birthright of the eldest
son.   The chieftainship of a Highland clan, for example, followed the order of Primogeniture.   There
seems, in truth, to be a form of family-dependency
still more archaic than any of those which we know
from the primitive records of organised civil societies.
The Agnatic Union of the kindred in ancient Roman
law, and a multitude of similar indications, point to
a period at which all the ramifying branches of the
family tree held together in one organic whole; and
it is no presumptuous conjecture, that, when the
corporation thus formed by the kindred was in itself
an independent society, it was governed by the eldest
male of the oldest line.   It is true that we have no
actual knowledge of any such society.   Even in the
most elementary communities, family-organisations,
as we know them, are at most *imperia in imperio*.
But the position of some of them, of the Celtic clans
in particular, was sufficiently near independence
within historical times to force on us the conviction
that they were once separate *imperia*, and that Primogeniture regulated the succession to the chieftainship.   It is, however, necessary to be on our guard

against modern associations with the term of law We are speaking of a family-connection still closer and more stringent than any with which we are made acquainted by Hindoo society or ancient Roman law. If the Roman Paterfamilias was visibly steward of the family possessions, if the Hindoo father is only joint-sharer with his sons, still more emphatically must the true patriarchal chieftain be merely the administrator of a common fund.

The examples of succession by Primogeniture which were found among the Benefices may, therefore, have been imitated from a system of family-government known to the invading races, though not in general use. Some rude tribes may have still practised it, or, what is still more probable, society may have been so slightly removed from its more archaic condition that the minds of some men spontaneously recurred to it, when they were called upon to settle the rules of inheritance for a new form of property. But there is still the question, Why did Primogeniture gradually supersede every other principle of succession? The answer, I think, is, that European society decidedly retrograded during the dissolution of the Carlovingian empire. It sank a point or two back even from the miserably low degree which it had marked during the early barbarian monarchies. The great characteristic of the period was the feebleness, or rather the abeyance, of kingly and therefore of civil authority; and hence it seems as if, civil society no longer cohering, men universally flung themselves back on a social organisation older than the beginnings of civil communities. The lord with his vassals, during the ninth and tenth centuries, may be considered as a patriarchal house-hold, recruited, not as in the primitive times by Adoption, but by Infeudation; and to such a confederacy, succession by Primogeniture was a source of strength and durability. So long as the land was kept together on which the entire organisation rested, it was powerful for defence and attack; to divide the land was to divide the little society, and voluntarily to invite aggression in an era of univer-sal violence. We may be perfectly certain that into this preference for Primogeniture there entered no idea of disinheriting the bulk of the children in favour of one. Everybody would have suffered by the division of the fief. Everybody was a gainer by its consolidation. The Family grew stronger by the concentration of power in the same hands; nor is it likely that the lord who was invested with the inheritance had any advantage over his brethren and kinsfolk in occupations, interests, or indulgences. It would be a singular anachronism to estimate the privileges succeeded to by the heir of a fief, by the situation in which the eldest son is placed under an English strict settlement.

I have said that I regard the early feudal con-federacies as descended from an archaic form of the Family, and as wearing a strong resemblance to it. But then in the ancient world, and in the societies

which have not passed through the crucible of feu
dalism, the Primogeniture which seems to have prevailed never transformed itself into the Primogeniture of the later feudal Europe.   When the group
of kinsmen ceased to be governed through a series
of generations by a hereditary chief, the domain
which had been managed for all appears to have
been equally divided among all.   Why did this not
occur in the feudal world ?   If during the confusions
of the first feudal period the eldest son held the
land for the behoof of the whole family, why was it
that when feudal Europe had consolidated itself, and
regular communities were again established, the
whole family did not resume that capacity for equal
inheritance which had belonged to Roman and German alike ?   The key which unlocks this difficulty
has rarely been seized by the writers who occupy
themselves in tracing the genealogy of Feudalism.
They perceive the materials of the feudal institutions, but they miss the cement.   The ideas and
social forms which contributed to the formation of
the system were unquestionably barbarian and archaic, but, as soon as Courts and lawyers were called
in to interpret and define it, the principles of interpretation which they applied to it were those of the
latest Roman jurisprudence, and were therefore excessively refined and matured.   In a patriarchally
governed society, the eldest son may succeed to the
government of the Agnatic group, and to the absolute disposal of its property.   But he is not there-

fore a true proprietor. He has correlative duties not involved in the conception of proprietorship, but quite undefined and quite incapable of definition. The later Roman jurisprudence, however, like our own law, looked upon uncontrolled power over property as equivalent to ownership, and did not, and, in fact, could not, take notice of liabilities of such a kind, that the very conception of them belonged to a period anterior to regular law. The contact of the refined and the barbarous notion had inevitably for its effect the conversion of the eldest son into legal proprietor of the inheritance. The clerical and secular lawyers so defined his position from the first; but it was only by insensible degrees that the younger brother, from participating on equal terms in all the dangers and enjoyments of his kinsman, sank into the priest, the soldier of fortune, or the hanger-on of the mansion. The legal revolution was identical with that which occurred on a smaller scale, and in quite recent times, through the greater part of the Highlands of Scotland. When called in to determine the legal powers of the chieftain over the domains which gave sustenance to the clan, Scottish jurisprudence had long since passed the point at which it could take notice of the vague limitations on completeness of dominion imposed by the claims of the clansmen, and it was inevitable therefore, that it should convert the patrimony of many into the estate of one.

For the sake of simplicity, I have called the

mode of succession Primogeniture whenever a single
son or descendant succeeds to the authority over a
household or society. It is remarkable, however,
that in the few very ancient examples which remain
to us of this sort of succession, it is not always the
eldest son, in the sense familiar to us, who takes up
the representation. The form of Primogeniture
which has spread over Western Europe has also been
perpetuated among the Hindoos, and there is every
reason to believe that it is the normal form. Under
it, not only the eldest son, but the eldest line is
always preferred. If the eldest son fails, his eldest
son has precedence not only over brothers but over
uncles; and, if he too fails, the same rule is followed
in the next generation. But when the succession is
not merely to *civil* but to *political* power, a difficulty may present itself which will appear of
greater magnitude according as the cohesion of society is less perfect. The chieftain who last exercised authority may have outlived his eldest son,
and the grandson who is primarily entitled to succeed may be too young and immature to undertake
the actual guidance of the community, and the administration of its affairs. In such an event, the
expedient which suggests itself to the more settled
societies is to place the infant heir under guardianship till he reaches the age of fitness for government.
The guardianship is generally that of the male
Agnates; but it is remarkable that the contingency
supposed is one of the rare cases in which ancient

societies have consented to the exercise of power by
women, doubtless out of respect to the overshadowing claims of the mother.   In India, the widow of
a Hindoo sovereign governs in the name of her infant son, and we cannot but remember that the custom regulating succession to the throne of France
—which, whatever be its origin, is doubtless of the
highest antiquity—preferred the queen-mother to
all other claimants for the Regency, at the same
time that it rigorously excluded all females from the
throne.   There is, however, another mode of obvia-
ting the inconvenience attending the devolution of
sovereignty on an infant heir, and it is one which
would doubtless occur spontaneously to rudely organised communities.   This is to set aside the infant
heir altogether, and confer the chieftainship on the
eldest surviving male of the first generation.   The
Celtic clan-associations, among the many phenomena
which they have preserved of an age in which civil
and political society were not yet even rudimentarily
separated, have brought down this rule of succession
to historical times.   With them, it seems to have
existed in the form of a positive canon, that, failing
the eldest son, his next brother succeeds in priority
to all grandsons, whatever be their age at the moment
when the sovereignty devolves.   Some writers have
explained the principle by assuming that the Celtic
customs took the last chieftain as a sort of root or
stock, and then gave the succession to the descendant who should be least remote from him; the uncle

thus being preferred to the grandson as being nearer to the common root. No objection can be taken to this statement if it be merely intended as a description of the system of succession; but it would be a serious error to conceive the men who first adopted the rule as applying a course of reasoning which evidently dates from the time when feudal schemes of succession began to be debated among lawyers. The true origin of the preference of the uncle to the grandson is doubtless a simple calculation on the part of rude men in a rude society that it is better to be governed by a grown chieftain than by a child, and that the younger son is more likely to have come to maturity than any of the eldest son's descendants. At the same time, we have some evidence that the form of Primogeniture with which we are best acquainted is the primary form, in the tradition that the assent of the clan was asked when an infant heir was passed over in favour of his uncle. There is a tolerably well authenticated instance of this ceremony in the annals of the Scottish Macdonalds; and Irish Celtic antiquities, as interpreted by recent inquirers, are said to disclose many traces of similar practices. The substitution, by means of election, of a "worthier" Agnatic relative for an elder is not unknown, too, in the system of the Indian Village Communities.

Under Mahometan law, which has probably preserved an ancient Arabian custom, inheritances of property are divided equally among sons, the daugh-

ters taking a half share; but if any of the children
die before the division of the inheritance, leaving
issue behind, these grandchildren are entirely excluded by their uncles and aunts.   Consistently with
this principle, the succession, when political authority
devolves, is according to the form of Primogeniture
which appears to have obtained among the Celtic
societies.   In the two great Mahometan families of
the West, the rule is believed to be, that the uncle
succeeds to the throne in preference to the nephew,
though the latter be the son of an elder brother;
but though this rule has been followed quite recently
both in Egypt and in Turkey, I am informed that
there has always been some doubt as to its governing the devolution of the Turkish sovereignty.   The
policy of the Sultans has in fact generally prevented
cases for its application from occurring, and it is possible that their wholesale massacres of their younger
brothers may have been perpetrated quite as much
in the interest of their children as for the sake of
making away with dangerous competitors for the
throne.   It is evident, however, that in polygamous
societies the form of Primogeniture will always tend
to vary.   Many considerations may constitute a
claim on the succession, the rank of the mother, for
example, or her degree in the affections of the father.
Accordingly, some of the Indian Mahometan sovereigns, without pretending to any distinct testamentary power, claim the right of nominating the

son who is to succeed. The *blessing* mentioned in
the Scriptural history of Isaac and his sons has sometimes been spoken of as a will, but it seems rather
to have been a mode of naming an eldest son.

CHAPTER VIII.

THE Roman Institutional Treatises, after giving their definition of the various forms and modifications of ownership, proceed to discuss the Natural Modes of Acquiring Property. Those who are unfamiliar with the history of jurisprudence are not likely to look upon these "natural modes" of acquisition as possessing, at first sight, either much speculative or much practical interest. The wild animal which is snared or killed by the hunter, the soil which is added to our field by the imperceptible deposits of a river, the tree which strikes its roots into our ground, are each said by the Roman lawyers to be acquired by us *naturally*. The older jurisconsults had doubtless observed that such acquisitions were universally sanctioned by the usages of the little societies around them, and thus the lawyers of a later age, finding them classed in the ancient Jus Gentium, and perceiving them to be of the simplest description, allotted them a place among the ordinances of

Nature. The dignity with which they were invested
has gone on increasing in modern times till it is quite
out of proportion to their original importance.
Theory has made them its favourite food, and has
enabled them to exercise the most serious influence
on practice.

It will be necessary for us to attend to one only
among these "natural modes of acquisition," Occu-
patio or Occupancy. Occupancy is the advisedly
taking possession of that which at the moment is the
property of no man, with the view (adds the technical definition) of acquiring property in it for your-
self. The objects which the Roman lawyers called
res nullius—things which have not or have never
had an owner—can only be ascertained by enumer-
ating them. Among things which *never had* an
owner are wild animals, fishes, wild fowl, jewels
disinterred for the first time, and land newly discovered or never before cultivated. Among things
which *have not* an owner are moveables which have
been abandoned, lands which have been deserted,
and (an anomalous but most formidable item) the
property of an enemy. In all these objects the full
rights of dominion were acquired by the *Occupant*,
who first took possession of them with the intention
of keeping them as his own—an intention which, in
certain cases, had to be manifested by specific acts
It is not difficult, I think, to understand the universality which caused the practice of Occupancy to be
placed by one generation of Roman lawyers in the

Law common to all Nations, and the simplicity which occasioned its being attributed by another to the Law of Nature. But for its fortunes in modern legal history we are less prepared by *à priori* considerations. The Roman principle of Occupancy, and the rules into which the jurisconsults expanded it, are the source of all modern International Law on the subject of Capture in War and of the acquisition of sovereign rights in newly discovered countries. They have also supplied a theory of the Origin of Property, which is at once the popular theory, and the theory which, in one form or another, is acquiesced in by the great majority of speculative jurists.

I have said that the Roman principle of Occupancy has determined the tenor of that chapter of International Law which is concerned with Capture in War. The Law of Warlike Capture derives its rules from the assumption that communities are remitted to a state of nature by the outbreak of hostilities, and that, in the artificial natural condition thus produced, the institution of private property falls into abeyance so far as concerns the belligerents. As the later writers on the Law of Nature have always been anxious to maintain that private property was in some sense sanctioned by the system which they were expounding, the hypothesis that an enemy's property is *res nullius* has seemed to them perverse and shocking, and they were careful to stigmatise it as a mere fiction of jurisprudence. But, as soon as the Law of Nature is traced to its source

in the Jus Gentium, we see at once how the goods
of an enemy came to be looked upon as nobody's
property, and therefore as capable of being acquired
by the first occupant. The idea would occur spontaneously to persons practising the ancient forms of
Warfare, when victory dissolved the organisation of
the conquering army and dismissed the soldiers to
indiscriminate plunder. It is probable, however, that
originally it was only moveable property which was
thus permitted to be acquired by the Captor. We
know on independent authority that a very different
rule prevailed in ancient Italy as to the acquisition
of ownership in the soil of a conquered country, and
we may therefore suspect that the application of the
principle of occupancy to land (always a matter of
difficulty) dates from the period when the Jus Gentium was becoming the Code of Nature, and that it
is the result of a generalisation effected by the jurisconsults of the golden age. Their dogmas on the
point are preserved in the Pandects of Justinian, and
amount to an unqualified assertion that enemy's property of every sort is *res nullius* to the other bellig-
erent, and that Occupancy, by which the Captor
makes it his own, is an institution of Natural Law
The rules which International jurisprudence derives
from these positions have sometimes been stigma-
tised as needlessly indulgent to the ferocity and cu-
pidity of combatants, but the charge has been made,
I think, by persons who are unacquainted with the
history of wars, and who are consequently ignorant

how great an exploit it is to command obedience for a rule of any kind. The Roman principle of Occupancy, when it was admitted into the modern law of Capture in War, drew with it a number of subordinate canons, limiting and giving precision to its operation, and if the contests which have been waged since the treatise of Grotius became an authority, are compared with those of an earlier date, it will be seen that, as soon as the Roman maxims were received, Warfare instantly assumed a more tolerable complexion. If the Roman law of Occupancy is to be taxed with having had pernicious influence on any part of the modern Law of Nations, there is another chapter in it which may be said, with some reason, to have been injuriously affected. In applying to the discovery of new countries the same principles which the Romans had applied to the finding of a jewel, the Publicists forced into their service a doctrine altogether unequal to the task expected from it. Elevated into extreme importance by the discoveries of the great navigators of the 15th and 16th centuries, it raised more disputes than it solved. The greatest uncertainty was very shortly found to exist on the very two points on which certainty was most required, the extent of the territory which was acquired for his sovereign by the discoverer, and the nature of the acts which were necessary to complete the *apprehensio* or assumption of sovereign possession. Moreover, the principle itself, conferring as it did such enormous advantages as the consequence of

16

a piece of good luck, was instinctively mutinied against by some of the most adventurous nations in Europe, the Dutch, the English, and the Portuguese. Our own countrymen, without expressly denying the rule of International Law, never did, in practice, admit the claim of the Spaniards to engross the whole of America south of the Gulf of Mexico, or that of the King of France to monopolise the valleys of the Ohio and the Mississippi. From the accession of Elizabeth to the accession of Charles the Second, it cannot be said that there was at any time thorough peace in the American waters, and the encroachments of the New England Colonists on the territory of the French King continued for almost a century longer. Bentham was so struck with the confusion attending the application of the legal principle, that he went out of his way to eulogise the famous Bull of Pope Alexander the Sixth, dividing the undiscovered countries of the world between the Spaniards and the Portuguese by a line drawn one hundred leagues West of the Azores; and, grotesque as his praises may appear at first sight, it may be doubted whether the arrangement of Pope Alexander is absurder in principle than the rule of Public law, which gave half a continent to the monarch whose servants had fulfilled the conditions required by Roman jurisprudence for the acquisition of property in a valuable object which could be covered by the hand.

To all who pursue the inquiries which are the

subject of this volume, Occupancy is pre-eminently
interesting on the score of the service it has been
made to perform for speculative jurisprudence, in
furnishing a supposed explanation of the origin of
private property. It was once universally believed
that the proceeding implied in Occupancy was identical with the process by which the earth and its
fruits, which were at first in common, became the
allowed property of individuals. The course of
thought which led to this assumption is not difficult
to understand, if we seize the shade of difference
which separates the ancient from the modern conception of Natural Law. The Roman lawyers had
laid down that Occupancy was one of the Natural
modes of acquiring property, and they undoubtedly
believed that, were mankind living under the institutions of Nature, Occupancy would be one of their
practices. How far they persuaded themselves that
such a condition of the race had ever existed, is a
point, as I have already stated, which their language
leaves in much uncertainty; but they certainly do
seem to have made the conjecture, which has at all
times possessed much plausibility, that the institution
of property was not so old as the existence of mankind. Modern jurisprudence, accepting all their dogmas without reservation, went far beyond them in
the eager curiosity with which it dwelt on the supposed state of Nature. Since then it had received the
position that the earth and its fruits were once *res
nullius*, and since its peculiar view of Nature led it

to assume without hesitation that the human race had actually practised the Occupancy of *res nullius* long before the organisation of civil societies, the inference immediately suggested itself that Occupancy was the process by which the "no man's goods" of the primitive world became the private property of individuals in the world of history. It would be wearisome to enumerate the jurists who have subscribed to this theory in one shape or another, and it is the less necessary to attempt it because Blackstone, who is always a faithful index of the average opinions of his day, has summed them up in his 2d book and 1st chapter.

"The earth," he writes, "and all things therein were the general property of mankind from the immediate gift of the Creator. Not that the communion of goods seems ever to have been applicable, even in the earliest ages, to aught but the substance of the thing; nor could be extended to the use of it. For, by the law of nature and reason, he who first began to use it acquired therein a kind of transient property that lasted so long as he was using it, and no longer; or to speak with greater precision, the right of possession continued for the same time only that the act of possession lasted. Thus the ground was in common, and no part was the permanent property of any man in particular; yet whoever was in the occupation of any determined spot of it, for rest, for shade, or the like, acquired for the time a sort of ownership, from which it would have

been unjust and contrary to the law of nature to
have driven him by force, but the instant that he
quitted the use of occupation of it, another might
seize it without injustice." He then proceeds to
argue that " when mankind increased in number, it
became necessary to entertain conceptions of more
permanent dominion, and to appropriate to individuals not the immediate use only, but the very
substance of the thing to be used."

Some ambiguities of expression in this passage
lead to the suspicion that Blackstone did not quite
understand the meaning of the proposition which
he found in his authorities, that property in the
earth's surface was first acquired, under the law of
Nature, by the *occupant;* but the limitation which
designedly or through misapprehension he has imposed on the theory brings it into a form which it
has not infrequently assumed. Many writers more
famous than Blackstone for precision of language
have laid down that, in the beginning of things,
Occupancy first gave a right against the world to an
exclusive but temporary enjoyment, and that afterwards this right, while it remained exclusive, became
perpetual. Their object in so stating their theory
was to reconcile the doctrine that in the state of
Nature *res nullius* became property through Occupancy, with the inference which they drew from the
Scriptural history that the Patriarchs did not at first
permanently appropriate the soil which had been
grazed over by their flocks and herds.

The only criticism which could be directly applied to the theory of Blackstone would consist in
inquiring whether the circumstances which make up
his picture of a primitive society are more or less
probable than other incidents which could be imagined with equal readiness. Pursuing this method
of examination, we might fairly ask whether the
man who had *occupied* (Blackstone evidently uses
this word with its ordinary English meaning) a particular spot of ground for rest or shade would be
permitted to retain it without disturbance. The
chances surely are that his right to possession would
be exactly coextensive with his power to keep it,
and that he would be constantly liable to disturbance
by the first comer who coveted the spot and thought
himself strong enough to drive away the possessor.
But the truth is that all such cavil at these positions
is perfectly idle from the very baselessness of the
positions themselves. What mankind did in the
primitive state may not be a hopeless subject of inquiry, but of their motives for doing it it is impossible to know anything. These sketches of the
plight of human beings in the first ages of the world
are effected by first supposing mankind to be di-
vested of a great part of the circumstances by which
they are now surrounded, and by then assuming
that, in the condition thus imagined, they would preserve the same sentiments and prejudices by which
they are now actuated,—although, in fact, these
sentiments may have been created and engendered

by those very circumstances of which, by the hypothesis, they are to be stripped.

There is an aphorism of Savigny which has been sometimes thought to countenance a view of the origin of property somewhat similar to the theories epitomised by Blackstone. The great German jurist has laid down that all Property is founded on Adverse Possession ripened by Prescription. It is only with respect to Roman law that Savigny makes this statement, and before it can be fully appreciated much labour must be expended in explaining and defining the expressions employed. His meaning will, however, be indicated with sufficient accuracy if we consider him to assert that, how far soever we carry our inquiry into the ideas of property received among the Romans, however closely we approach in tracing them to the infancy of law, we can get no farther than a conception of ownership involving the three elements in the canon—Possession, Adverseness of Possession, that is, a holding not permissive or subordinate, but exclusive against the world, and Prescription, or a period of time during which the Adverse Possession has uninterruptedly continued. It is exceedingly probable that this maxim might be enunciated with more generality than was allowed to it by its author, and that no sound or safe conclusion can be looked for from investigations into any system of laws which are pushed farther back than the point at which these combined ideas constitute the notion of proprietary right. Meantime,

so far from bearing out the popular theory of the
origin of property, Savigny's canon is particularly
valuable as directing our attention to its weakest
point.　In the view of Blackstone and those whom
he follows, it was the mode of assuming the exclusive
enjoyment which mysteriously affected the minds of
the fathers of our race.　But the mystery does not
reside here.　It is not wonderful that property began
in adverse possession.　It is not surprising that the
first proprietor should have been the strong man
armed who kept his goods in peace.　But why it
was that lapse of time created a sentiment of respect
for his possession—which is the exact source of the
universal reverence of mankind for that which has
for a long period *de facto* existed—are questions
really deserving the profoundest examination, but
lying far beyond the boundary of our present inquiries.

Before pointing out the quarter in which we may
hope to glean some information, scanty and uncertain at best, concerning the early history of proprietary right, I venture to state my opinion that the
popular impression in reference to the part played
by Occupancy in the first stages of civilisation directly reverses the truth.　Occupancy is the advised
assumption of physical possession; and the notion
that an act of this description confers a title to " res
nullius," so far from being characteristic of very
early societies, is in all probability the growth of
a refined jurisprudence and of a settled condition of

the laws.   It is only when the rights of property
have gained a sanction from long practical inviola
bility, and when the vast majority of the objects of
enjoyment have been subjected to private ownership,
that mere possession is allowed to invest the first
possessor with dominion over commodities in which
no prior proprietorship has been asserted.   The sentiment in which this doctrine originated is absolutely
irreconcilable with that infrequency and uncertainty
of proprietary rights which distinguish the beginnings of civilisation.   Its true basis seems to be, not
an instinctive bias towards the institution of Property, but a presumption, arising out of the long continuance of that institution, that *everything ought
to have an owner*.   When possession is taken of a
" res nullius," that is, of an object which *is* not, or
has *never* been, reduced to dominion, the possessor
is permitted to become proprietor from a feeling
that all valuable things are naturally the subjects of
an exclusive enjoyment, and that in the given case
there is no one to invest with the right of property
except the Occupant.   The Occupant, in short, becomes the owner, because all things are presumed to
be somebody's property and because no one can be
pointed out as having a better right than he to the
proprietorship of this particular thing.

Even were there no other objection to the descriptions of mankind in their natural state which
we have been discussing, there is one particular in
which they are fatally at variance with the authentic

evidence possessed by us. It will be observed, that
the acts and motives which these theories suppose
are the acts and motives of Individuals. It is each
Individual who for himself subscribes the Social
Compact. It is some shifting sandbank in which
the grains are Individual men, that according to the
theory of Hobbes is hardened into the social rock
by the wholesome discipline of force. It is an Individual who, in the picture drawn by Blackstone, " is
in the occupation of a determined spot of ground
for rest, for shade, or the like." The vice is one
which necessarily afflicts all the theories descended
from the Natural Law of the Romans, which differed
principally from their Civil Law in the account
which it took of Individuals, and which has rendered precisely its greatest service to civilisation in
enfranchising the individual from the authority of
archaic society. But Ancient Law, it must again be
repeated, knows next to nothing of Individuals. It
is concerned not with Individuals, but with Families,
not with single human beings, but groups. Even
when the law of the State has succeeded in permea-
ting the small circles of kindred into which it had
originally no means of penetrating, the view it takes
of Individuals is curiously different from that taken
by jurisprudence in its maturest stage. The life of
each citizen is not regarded as limited by birth and
death ; it is but a continuation of the existence of
his forefathers, and it will be prolonged in the existence of his descendants.

The Roman distinction between the Law of Persons and the Law of Things, which though extremely
convenient is entirely artificial, has evidently done
much to divert inquiry on the subject before us from
the true direction. The lessons learned in discussing
the Jus Personarum have been forgotten where the
Jus Rerum is reached, and Property, Contract, and
Delict, have been considered as if no hints concerning their original nature were to be gained from the
facts ascertained respecting the original condition
of Persons. The futility of this method would be
manifest if a system of pure archaic law could be
brought before us, and if the experiment could be
tried of applying to it the Roman classifications.
It would soon be seen that the separation of the
Law of Persons from that of Things has no meaning
in the infancy of law, that the rules belonging to the
two departments are inextricably mingled together,
and that the distinctions of the later jurists are appropriate only to the later jurisprudence. From
what has been said in the earlier portions of this
treatise, it will be gathered that there is a strong *à
priori* improbability of our obtaining any clue to
the early history of property, if we confine our notice to the proprietary rights of individuals. It is
more than likely that joint-ownersh p, and not separate ownership, is the really archaic institution, and
that the forms of property which will afford us instruction will be those which are associated with
the rights of families and of groups of kindred.

The Roman jurisprudence will not here assist in enlightening us, for it is exactly the Roman jurispru dence which, transformed by the theory of Natural Law, has bequeathed to the moderns the impression that individual ownership is the normal state of proprietary right, and that ownership in common by groups of men is only the exception to a general rule. There is, however, one community which will always be carefully examined by the inquirer who is in quest of any lost institution of primeval society. How far soever any such institution may have under-gone change among the branch of the Indo-European family which has been settled for ages in India, it will seldom be found to have entirely cast aside the shell in which it was originally reared. It happens that, among the Hindoos, we do find a form of ownership which ought at once to rivet our atten-tion from its exactly fitting in with the ideas which our studies in the Law of Persons would lead us to entertain respecting the original condition of prop-erty. The Village Community of India is at once an organised patriarchal society and an assemblage of co-proprietors. The personal relations to each other of the men who compose it are indistinguish-ably confounded with their proprietary rights, and to the attempts of English functionaries to separate the two may be assigned some of the most formi-dable miscarriages of Anglo-Indian administration. The Village Community is known to be of immense antiquity. In whatever direction research has been pushed into Indian history, general or local, it has always found the Community in existence at the farthest point of its progress. A great number of intelligent and observant writers, most of whom had no theory of any sort to support concerning its na ture and origin, agree in considering it the least destructible institution of a society which never willingly surrenders any one of its usages to innova- tion. Conquests and revolutions seem to have swept over it without disturbing or displacing it, and the most beneficent systems of government in India have always been those which have recognised it as the basis of administration.

The mature Roman law, and modern jurispru· dence following in its wake, look upon co-ownership as an exceptional and momentary condition of the rights of property. This view is clearly indicated in the maxim which obtains universally in Western Europe, *Nemo in communione potest invitus detineri* (" No one can be kept in co-proprietorship against his will "). But in India this order of ideas is re- versed, and it may be said that separate proprietor- ship is always on its way to become proprietorship in common. The process has been adverted to al- ready. As soon as a son is born, he acquires a vested interest in his father's substance, and on attaining years of discretion he is even, in certain contingen- cies, permitted by the letter of the law to call for a partition of the family estate. As a fact, however, a division rarely takes place even at the death of

the father, and the property constantly remains undivided for several generations, though every member of every generation has a legal right to an
undivided share in it. The domain thus held in
common is sometimes administered by an elected
manager, but more generally, and in some provinces
always, it is managed by the eldest agnate, by the
eldest representative of the eldest line of the stock.
Such an assemblage of joint proprietors, a body of
kindred holding a domain in common, is the simplest
form of an Indian Village Community, but the
Community is more than a brotherhood of relatives
and more than an association of partners. It is an
organised society, and besides providing for the
management of the common fund, it seldom fails to
provide, by a complete staff of functionaries, for internal government, for police, for the administration
of justice, and for the apportionment of taxes and
public duties.

The process which I have described as that under
which a Village Community is formed, may be regarded as typical. Yet it is not to be supposed that
every Village Community in India drew together
in so simple a manner. Although, in the North of
India, the archives, as I am informed, almost invariably show that the Community was founded by a
single assemblage of blood-relations, they also supply
information that men of alien extraction have always, from time to time, been engrafted on it, and
a mere purchaser of a share may generally, under

certain conditions, be admitted to the brotherhood.
In the South of the Peninsula there are often Communities which appear to have sprung not from one
but from two or more families; and there are some
whose composition is known to be entirely artificial,
indeed, the occasional aggregation of men of different castes in the same society is fatal to the hypothesis of a common descent.   Yet in all these brotherhoods either the tradition is preserved, or the
assumption made, of an original common parentage.
Mountstuart Elphinstone, who writes more particularly of the Southern Village Communities, observes
of them (*History of India*, i. 126): "The popular
notion is that the Village landholders are all descended from one or more individuals who settled
the Village; and that the only exceptions are
formed by persons who have derived their rights
by purchase or otherwise from members of the
original stock.   The supposition is confirmed by the
fact that, to this day, there are only single families
of landholders in small villages and not many in
large ones; but each has branched out into so many
members that it is not uncommon for the whole
agricultural labour to be done by the landholders,
without the aid either of tenants or of labourers.
The rights of the landholders are theirs collectively,
and, though they almost always have a more or less
perfect partition of them, they never have an entire
separation.   A landholder, for instance, can sell or
mortgage his rights; but he must first have the con-

sent of the Village, and the purchaser steps exactly
into his place and takes up all his obligations. If a
family becomes extinct, its share returns to the
common stock."

Some considerations which have been offered in
the fifth chapter of this volume will assist the reader,
I trust, in appreciating the significance of Elphinstone's language. No institution of the primitive
world is likely to have been preserved to our day,
unless it has acquired an elasticity foreign to its
original nature through some vivifying legal fiction.
The Village Community then is not necessarily an
assemblage of blood-relations, but it is *either* such an
assemblage *or* a body of co-proprietors formed on
the model of an association of kinsmen. The type
with which it should be compared is evidently not
the Roman Family, but the Roman Gens or House.
The Gens was also a group on the model of the
family; it was the family extended by a variety of
fictions of which the exact nature was lost in antiquity. In historical times, its leading characteristics were the very two which Elphinstone remarks
in the Village Community. There was always the
assumption of a common origin, an assumption sometimes notoriously at variance with fact; and, to repeat the historian's words, "if a family became
extinct, its share returned to the common stock." In
old Roman law, unclaimed inheritances escheated to
the Gentiles. It is further suspected by all who
have examined their history that the Communities,

like the Gentes, have been very generally adulterated by the admission of strangers, but the exact mode
of absorption cannot now be ascertained. At present,
they are recruited, as Elphinstone tells us, by the
admission of purchasers, with the consent of the
brotherhood. The acquisition of the adopted mem
ber is, however, of the nature of a universal succession; together with the share he has bought, he
succeeds to the liabilities which the vendor had
incurred towards the aggregate group. He is an
Emptor Familiæ, and inherits the legal clothing of
the person whose place he begins to fill. The consent of the whole brotherhood required for his admission may remind us of the consent which the
Comitia Curiata, the Parliament of that larger brotherhood of self-styled kinsmen, the ancient Roman
commonwealth, so strenuously insisted on as essential
to the legalisation of an Adoption or the confirmation
of a Will.

The tokens of an extreme antiquity are discov
erable in almost every single feature of the Indian
Village Communities. We have so many independent reasons for suspecting that the infancy of law
is distinguished by the prevalence of co-ownership,
by the intermixture of personal with proprietary
rights, and by the confusion of public with private
duties, that we should be justified in deducing many
important conclusions from our observation of these
proprietary brotherhoods, even if no similarly com-
pounded societies could be detected in any other

17

part of the world.   It happens, however, that much
earnest curiosity has been very recently attracted to
a similar set of phenomena in those parts of Europe
which have been most slightly affected by the feudal
transformation of property, and which in many im
portant particulars have as close an affinity with the
Eastern as with the Western world.   The researches
of M. de Haxthausen, M. Tengoborski, and others,
have shown us that the Russian villages are not fortuitous assemblages of men, nor are they unions
founded on contract ; they are naturally organised
communities like those of India.   It is true that these
villages are always in theory the patrimony of some
noble proprietor, and the peasants have within historical times been converted into the predial, and to
a great extent into the personal, serfs of the seignior.
But the pressure of this superior ownership has
never crushed the ancient organisation of the village,
and it is probable that the enactment of the Czar of
Russia, who is supposed to have introduced serfdom,
was really intended to prevent the peasants from
abandoning that co-operation without which the old
social order could not long be maintained.   In the
assumption of an agnatic connection between the
villagers, in the blending of personal rights with
privileges of ownership, and in a variety of spontaneous provisions for internal administration, the
Russian village appears to be a nearly exact repeti-
tion of the Indian Community ; but there is one
important difference which we note with the greatest

interest. The co-owners of an Indian village, though
their property is blended, have their rights distinct,
and this separation of rights is complete and continues indefinitely. The severance of rights is also
theoretically complete in a Russian village, but there
it is only temporary. After the expiration of a
given, but not in all cases of the same, period, separate ownerships are extinguished, the land of the
village is thrown into a mass, and then it is re-dis-
tributed among the families composing the community, according to their number. This repartition
having been effected, the rights of families and of
individuals are again allowed to branch out into
various lines, which they continue to follow till
another period of division comes round. An even
more curious variation from this type of ownership
occurs in some of those countries which long formed
a debateable land between the Turkish Empire and
the possessions of the House of Austria. In Servia,
in Croatia, and the Austrian Sclavonia, the villages
are also brotherhoods of persons who are at once co-
owners and kinsmen; but there the internal arrangements of the community differ from those adverted
to in the last two examples. The substance of the
common property is in this case neither divided in
practice nor considered in theory as divisible, but the
entire land is cultivated by the combined labour of
all the villagers, and the produce is annually distributed among the households, sometimes according to
their supposed wants, sometimes according to rules

which give to particular persons a fixed share of the usufruct. All these practices are traced by the jurists of the East of Europe to a principle which is asserted to be found in the earliest Sclavonian laws, the principle that the property of families cannot be divided for a perpetuity.

The great interest of these phenomena in an inquiry like the present arises from the light they throw on the development of distinct proprietary rights *inside* the groups by which property seems to have been originally held. We have the strongest reason for thinking that property once belonged not to individuals nor even to isolated families, but to larger societies composed on the patriarchal model ; but the mode of transition from ancient to modern ownerships, obscure at best, would have been infinitely obscurer if several distinguishable forms of Village Communities had not been discovered and examined. It is worth while to attend to the varieties of internal arrangement within the patriarchal groups which are, or were till recently, observable among races of Indo-European blood. The chiefs of the ruder Highland clans used, it is said, to dole out 'ood to the heads of the households under their jurisdiction at the very shortest intervals, and sometimes day by day. A periodical distribution is also made to the Sclavonian villagers of the Austrian and Turkish provinces by the elders of their body, but then it is a distribution once for all of the total produce of the year. In the Russian villages, however, the substance of the property ceases to be looked upon as indivisible, and separate proprietary claims are allowed freely to grow up, but then the progress of separation is peremptorily arrested after it has continued a certain time.   In India, not only is there no indivisibility of the common fund, but separate proprietorship in parts of it may be indefinitely prolonged and may branch out into any number of derivative ownerships, the *de facto* partition of the stock being, however, checked by inveterate usage, and by the rule against the admission of strangers without the consent of the brotherhood.   It is not of course intended to insist that these different forms of the Village Community represent distinct stages in a process of transmutation which has been everywhere accomplished in the same manner.   But, though the evidence does not warrant our going so far as this, it renders less presumptuous the conjecture that private property, in the shape in which we know it, was chiefly formed by the gradual disentanglement of the separate rights of individuals from the blended rights of a community.   Our studies in the Law of Persons seemed to show us the Family expanding into the Agnatic group of kinsmen, then the Agnatic group dissolving into separate households; lastly, the household supplanted by the individual; and it is now suggested that each step in the change corresponds to an analogous alteration in the nature of Ownership.   If there be any truth in the suggestion, it is to be observed that it materially affects the problem which theorists on the origin of Property have generally proposed to themselves The question—perhaps an insoluble one—which they have mostly agitated is, what were the motives which first induced men to respect each other's pos- sessions? It may still be put, without much hope of finding an answer to it, in the form of an inquiry into the reasons which led one composite group to keep aloof from the domain of another. But, if it be true that far the most important passage in the history of Private Property is its gradual separation from the co-ownership of kinsmen, then the great point of inquiry is identical with that which lies on the threshold of all historical law—what were the motives which originally prompted men to hold to- gether in the family union? To such a question, Jurisprudence, unassisted by other sciences, is not competent to give a reply. The fact can only be noted.

The undivided state of property in ancient socie- ties is consistent with a peculiar sharpness of divis- ion, which shows itself as soon as any single share is completely separated from the patrimony of the group. This phenomenon springs, doubtless, from the circumstance that the property is supposed to become the domain of a new group, so that any dealing with it, in its divided state, is a transaction between two highly complex bodies. I have already compared Ancient Law to Modern International Law, in re- spect of the size of the corporate associations, whose

rights and duties it settles. As the contracts and
conveyances known to ancient law are contracts and
conveyances to which not single individuals, but organised companies of men, are parties, they are in
the highest degree ceremonious; they require a variety of symbolical acts and words intended to impress the business on the memory of all who take
part in it; and they demand the presence of an inordinate number of witnesses. From these peculiarities, and others allied to them, springs the universally unmalleable character of the ancient forms of
property. Sometimes the patrimony of the family
is absolutely inalienable, as was the case with the
Sclavonians, and still oftener, though alienations may
not be entirely illegitimate, they are virtually im-
practicable, as among most of the Germanic tribes,
from the necessity of having the consent of a large
number of persons to the transfer. Where these impediments do not exist, or can be surmounted, the act
of conveyance itself is generally burdened with a perfect load of ceremony, in which not one iota can be
safely neglected. Ancient law uniformly refuses to
dispense with a single gesture, however grotesque;
with a single syllable, however its meaning may have
been forgotten; with a single witness, however super-
fluous may be his testimony. The entire solemnities must be scrupulously completed by persons le-
gally entitled to take part in it, or else the conveyance is null, and the seller is re-established in the

rights of which he had vainly attempted to divest himself.

These various obstacles to the free circulation of the objects of use and enjoyment, begin of course to make themselves felt as soon as society has acquired even a slight degree of activity, and the expedients by which advancing communities endeavour to overcome them form the staple of the history of Property. Of such expedients there is one which takes precedence of the rest from its antiquity and universality. The idea seems to have spontaneously suggested itself to a great number of early societies, to classify property into kinds. One kind or sort of property is placed on a lower footing of dignity than the others, but at the same time is relieved from the fetters which antiquity has imposed on them. Subsequently, the superior convenience of the rules governing the transfer and descent of the lower order of property becomes generally recognised, and by a gradual course of innovation the plasticity of the less dignified class of valuable objects is communicated to the classes which stand conventionally higher. The history of Roman Property Law is the history of the assimilation of Res Mancipi to Res Nec Mancipi. The history of Property on the European Continent is the history of the subversion of the feudalised law of land by the Romanised law of moveables; and though the history of ownership in England is not nearly completed, it is visibly the law of personalty which threatens to absorb and annihilate the law of realty.

The only *natural* classification of the objects of enjoyment, the only classification which corresponds with an essential difference in the subject matter, is that which divides them into Moveables and Immoveables. Familiar as is this classification to jurisprudence, it was very slowly developed by Roman law, from which we inherit it, and was only finally adopted by it in its latest stage. The classifications of Ancient Law have sometimes a superficial resemblance to this. They occasionally divide property into categories, and place immoveables in one of them; but then it is found that they either class along with immoveables a number of objects which have no sort of relation with them, or else divorce them from various rights to which they have a close affinity. Thus, the Res Mancipi of Roman Law included not only land but slaves, horses, and oxen. Scottish law ranks with land a certain class of securities, and Hindoo law associates it with slaves. English law, on the other hand, parts leases of land for years from other interests in the soil, and joins them to personalty under the name of chattels real. Moreover, the classifications of Ancient Law are classifications implying superiority and inferiority; while the distinction between moveables and immoveables, so long at least as it was confined to Roman jurisprudence, carried with it no suggestion whatever of a difference in dignity. The Res Mancipi, however,

did certainly at first enjoy a precedence over the Res
Nec Mancipi, as did heritable property in Scotland,
and realty in England, over the personalty to which
they were opposed. The lawyers of all systems have
spared no pains in striving to refer these classifications to some intelligible principle ; but the reasons
of the severance must ever be vainly sought for in
the philosophy of law ; they belong not to its philosophy, but to its history. The explanation which appears to cover the greatest number of instances is
that the objects of enjoyment honoured above the
rest were forms of property known first and earliest
to each particular community, and dignified therefore emphatically with the designation of *Property*.
On the other hand, the articles not enumerated
among the favoured objects seem to have been placed
on a lower standing, because the knowledge of their
value was posterior to the epoch at which the cata-
logue of superior property was settled. They were
at first unknown, rare, limited in their uses, or else
regarded as mere appendages to the privileged objects. Thus, though the Roman Res Mancipi included a number of moveable articles of great value,
still the most costly jewels were never allowed to
take rank as Res Mancipi, because they were unknown to the early Romans. In the same way chattels real in England are said to have been degraded
to the footing of personalty, from the infrequency
and valuelessness of such estates under the feudal
land-law. But the grand point of interest is, the con-

tinued degradation of these commodities when their importance had increased and their number had multiplied. Why were they not successively included among the favoured objects of enjoyment? One reason is found in the stubbornness with which Ancient Law adheres to its classifications. It is a characteristic both of uneducated minds and of early societies, that they are little able to conceive a general rule apart from the particular applications of it with which they are practically familiar. They cannot dissociate a general term or maxim from the special examples which meet them in daily experience; and in this way the designation covering the best-known forms of property is denied to articles which exactly resemble them in being objects of enjoyment and subjects of right. But to these influences, which exert peculiar force in a subject-matter so stable as that of law, are afterwards added others more consistent with progress in enlightenment and in the conceptions of general expediency. Courts and lawyers become at last alive to the inconvenience of the embarrassing formalities required for the transfer, recovery, or devolution of the favoured commodities, and grow unwilling to fetter the newer descriptions of property with the technical trammels which characterised the infancy of law. Hence arises a disposition to keep these last on a lower grade in the arrangements of Jurisprudence, and to permit their transfer by simpler processes than those which, in archaic conveyances, serve as stumbling-blocks to

good faith and stepping-stones to fraud. We are
perhaps in some danger of underrating the inconveniences of the ancient modes of transfer. Our instruments of conveyance are written, so that their language, well pondered by the professional drafts-
man, is rarely defective in accuracy. But an ancient
conveyance was not written, but *acted*. Gestures and
words took the place of written technical phraseology, and any formula mispronounced, or symbolical
act omitted, would have vitiated the proceeding as fatally as a material mistake in stating the uses or setting out the remainders would, two hundred years
ago, have vitiated an English deed. Indeed, the mischiefs of the archaic ceremonial are even thus only
half stated. So long as elaborate conveyances, written or acted, are required for the alienation of *land*
alone, the chances of mistake are not considerable in
the transfer of a description of property which is
seldom got rid of with much precipitation. But the
higher class of property in the ancient world comprised not only land but several of the commonest
and several of the most valuable moveables. When
once the wheels of society had begun to move quickly, there must have been immense inconvenience in
demanding a highly intricate form of transfer for a
horse or an ox, or for the most costly chattel of the
old world—the Slave. Such commodities must have
been constantly and even ordinarily conveyed with
incomplete forms, and held, therefore, under imperfect titles.

The Res Mancipi of old Roman law were, land, —in historical times, land on Italian soil,—slaves and beasts of burden, such as horses and oxen. It is impossible to doubt that the objects which make up the class are the instruments of agricultural labour, the commodities of first consequence to a primitive people. Such commodities were at first, I imagine, called emphatically Things or Property, and the mode of conveyance by which they were transferred was called a Mancipium or Mancipation; but it was not probably till much later that they received the distinctive appellation of Res Mancipi, "Things which require a Mancipation." By their side there may have existed or grown up a class of objects, for which it was not worth while to insist upon the full ceremony of Mancipation. It would be enough if, in transferring these last from owner to owner, a part only of the ordinary formalities were proceeded with, namely, that actual delivery, physical transfer, or *tradition*, which is the most obvious index of a change of proprietorship. Such commodities were the Res Nec Mancipi of the ancient jurisprudence, "things which did not require a Mancipation," little prized probably at first, and not often passed from one group of proprietors to another. While, however, the list of the Res Mancipi was irrevocably closed, that of the Res Nec Mancipi admitted of indefinite expansion; and hence every fresh conquest of man over material nature added an item to the Res Nec Mancipi, or effected an improvement in those already recognised. In sensibly, therefore, they mounted to an equality with the Res Mancipi, and the impression of an intrinsic inferiority being thus dissipated, men began to observe the manifold advantages of the simple formality which accompanied their transfer over the more intricate and more venerable ceremonial. Two of the agents of legal amelioration, Fictions and Equity, were assiduously employed by the Roman lawyers to give the practical effects of a Mancipation to a Tradition; and, though Roman legislators long shrank from enacting that the right of property in a Res Mancipi should be immediately transferred by bare delivery of the article, yet even this step was at last ventured upon by Justinian, in whose jurisprudence the difference between Res Mancipi and Res Nec Mancipi disappears, and Tradition or Delivery becomes the one great conveyance known to the law. The marked preference which the Roman lawyers very early gave to Tradition caused them to assign it a place in their theory which has helped to blind their modern disciples to its true history. It was classed among the "natural" modes of acquisition, both because it was generally practised among the Italian tribes, and because it was a process which attained its object by the simplest mechanism. If the expressions of the jurisconsults be pressed, they undoubtedly imply that Tradition, which belongs to the Law Natural, is more ancient than Mancipation, which is an institution of Civil

Society; and this, I need not say, is the exact reverse of the truth.

The distinction between Res Mancipi and Res Nec Mancipi is the type of a class of distinctions to which civilisation is much indebted, distinctions which run through the whole mass of commodities, placing a few of them in a class by themselves, and relegating the others to a lower category. The inferior kinds of property are first, from disdain and disregard, released from the perplexed ceremonies in which primitive law delights, and then afterwards, in another state of intellectual progress, the simple methods of transfer and recovery which have been allowed to come into use serve as a model which condemns by its convenience and simplicity the cumbrous solemnities inherited from ancient days. But, in some societies, the trammels in which Property is tied up are much too complicated and stringent to be relaxed in so easy a manner. Whenever male children have been born to a Hindoo, the law of India, as I have stated, gives them all an interest in his property, and makes their consent a necessary condition of its alienation. In the same spirit, the general usage of the old Germanic peoples—it is remarkable that the Anglo-Saxon customs seem to have been an exception—forbade alienations without the consent of the male children; and the primitive law of the Sclavonians even prohibited them altogether. It is evident that such impediments as these cannot be overcome by a distinction between kinds

of property, inasmuch as the difficulty extends to
commodities of all sorts; and accordingly, Ancient
Law, when once launched on a course of improvement, encounters them with a distinction of another
character, a distinction classifying property, not according to its nature but according to its origin.   In
India, where there are traces of both systems of
classification, the one which we are considering is
exemplified in the difference which Hindoo law
establishes between Inheritances and Acquisitions.
The inherited property of the father is shared by
the children as soon as they are born; but according
to the custom of most provinces, the acquisitions
made by him during his lifetime are wholly his own,
and can be transferred by him at pleasure.   A similar distinction was not unknown to Roman law, in
which the earliest innovation on the Parental Powers
took the form of a permission given to the son to
keep for himself whatever he might have acquired
in military service.   But the most extensive use
ever made of this mode of classification appears to
have been among the Germans.   I have repeatedly
stated that the *allod*, though not inalienable, was
commonly transferable with the greatest difficulty;
and moreover, it descended exclusively to the agnatic
kindred.   Hence an extraordinary variety of distinctions came to be recognised, all intended to di-
minish the inconveniences inseparable from allodial
property.   The *wehrgeld*, for example, or composi
tion for the homicide of a relative, which occupies

so large a space in German jurisprudence, formed no part of the family domain, and descended according to rules of succession altogether different. Similarly, the *reipus*, or fine leviable on the re-marriage of a widow, did not enter into the *allod* of the person to whom it was paid, and followed a line of devolution in which the privileges of the agnates were neglected. The law, too, as among the Hindoos, distinguished the Acquisitions of the chief of the household from his Inherited property, and permitted him to deal with them under much more liberal conditions. Classifications of the other sort were also admitted, and the familiar distinction drawn between land and moveables; but moveable property was divided into several subordinate categories, to each of which different rules applied. This exuberance of classification, which may strike us as strange in so rude a people as the German conquerors of the Empire, is doubtless to be explained by the presence in their systems of a considerable element of Roman law, absorbed by them during their long sojourn on the confines of the Roman dominion. It is not difficult to trace a great number of the rules governing the transfer and devolution of the commodities which lay outside the *allod*, to their source in Roman jurisprudence, from which they were probably borrowed at widely distant epochs, and in fragmentary importations. How far the obstacles to the free circulation of property were surmounted by such contrivances, we have not the means even of

18

conjecturing, for the distinctions adverted to have
no modern history. As I before explained, the allodial form of property was entirely lost in the feudal,
and when the consolidation of feudalism was once
completed, there was practically but one distinction
left standing of all those which had been known to
the western world—the distinction between land
and goods, immoveables and moveables. Externally
this distinction was the same with that which Roman
law had finally accepted, but the law of the middle
ages differed from that of Rome in distinctly considering immoveable property to be more dignified
than moveable. Yet this one sample is enough to
show the importance of the class of expedients to
which it belongs. In all the countries governed by
systems based on the French codes, that is, through
much the greatest part of the Continent of Europe,
the law of moveables, which was always Roman law,
has superseded and annulled the feudal law of land.
England is the only country of importance in which
this transmutation, though it has gone some way, is
not nearly accomplished. Our own, too, it may be
added, is the only considerable European country in
which the separation of moveables from immoveables has been somewhat disturbed by the same in
fluences which caused the ancient classifications to
depart from the only one which is countenanced by
nature. In the main, the English distinction has
been between land and goods; but a certain class of
goods have gone as heir-looms with the land, and a

certain description of interests in land have from historical causes been ranked with personalty. This is not the only instance in which English jurisprudence, standing apart from the main current of legal modification, has reproduced phenomena of archaic law.

I proceed to notice one or two more contrivances by which the ancient trammels of proprietary right were more or less successfully relaxed, premising that the scheme of this treatise only permits me to mention those which are of great antiquity. On one of them in particular it is necessary to dwell for a moment or two, because persons unacquainted with the early history of law will not be easily persuaded that a principle, of which modern jurisprudence has very slowly and with the greatest difficulty obtained the recognition, was really familiar to the very infancy of legal science. There is no principle in all law which the moderns, in spite of its beneficial character, have been so loath to adopt and to carry to its legitimate consequences as that which was known to the Romans as Usucapion, and which has descended to modern jurisprudence under the name of Prescription. It was a positive rule of the oldest Roman law, a rule older than the Twelve Tables, that commodities which had been uninterruptedly possessed for a certain period became the property of the possessor. The period of possession was exceedingly short—one or two years, according to the nature of the commodities—and in historical times

Usucapion was only allowed to operate when possession had commenced in a particular way; but I think it likely that at a less advanced epoch possession was converted into ownership under conditions even less severe than we read of in our authorities. As I have said before, I am far from asserting that the respect of men for *de facto* possession is a phenomenon which jurisprudence can account for by itself, but it is very necessary to remark that primitive societies, in adopting the principle of Usucapion, were not beset with any of the speculative doubts and hesitations which have impeded its reception among the moderns. Prescriptions were viewed by the modern lawyers, first with repugnance, afterwards with reluctant approval. In several countries, including our own, legislation long declined to advance beyond the rude device of barring all actions based on a wrong which had been suffered earlier than a fixed point of time in the past, generally the first year of some preceding reign; nor was it till the middle ages had finally closed, and James the First had ascended the throne of England, that we obtained a true statute of limitation of a very imperfect kind. This tardiness in copying one of the most famous chapters of Roman law, which was no doubt constantly read by the majority of European lawyers, the modern world owes to the influence of the Canon Law. The ecclesiastical customs out of which the Canon Law grew, concerned as they were with sacred or quasi

sacred interests, very naturally regarded the privileges which they conferred as incapable of being
lost through disuse however prolonged; and in accordance with this view, the spiritual jurisprudence,
when afterwards consolidated, was distinguished by
a marked leaning against Prescriptions.   It was the
fate of the Canon Law, when held up by the clerical
lawyers as a pattern to secular legislation, to have a
peculiar influence on first principles.   It gave to the
bodies of custom which were formed throughout
Europe far fewer express rules than did the Roman
law, but then it seems to have communicated a bias
to professional opinion on a surprising number of
fundamental points, and the tendencies thus produced progressively gained strength as each system
was developed.   One of the dispositions it produced
was a disrelish for Prescriptions; but I do not know
that this prejudice would have operated as powerfully as it has done, if it had not fallen in with the
doctrine of the scholastic jurists of the realist sect,
who taught that, whatever turn actual legislation
might take, a *right*, how long soever neglected, was
in point of fact indestructible.   The remains of this
state of feeling still exist.   Wherever the philosophy of law is earnestly discussed, questions respecting the speculative basis of Prescription are always
hotly disputed; and it is still a point of the greatest
interest in France and Germany, whether a person
who has been out of possession for a series of years
is deprived of his ownership as a penalty for his

neglect, or loses it through the summary interposition of the law in its desire to have a *finis litium*.
But no such scruples troubled the mind of early
Roman society.   Their ancient usages directly took
away the ownership of everybody who had been
out of possession, under certain circumstances, during
one or two years.   What was the exact tenor of the
rule of Usucapion in its earliest shape, it is not easy
to say; but, taken with the limitations which· we
find attending it in the books, it was a most useful
security against the mischiefs of a too cumbrous
system of conveyance.   In order to have the benefit
of Usucapion, it was necessary that the adverse possession should have begun in good faith, that is,
with belief on the part of the possessor that he was
lawfully acquiring the property, and it was further
required that the commodity should have been
transferred to him by some mode of alienation
which, however unequal to conferring a complete
title in the particular case, was at least recognised
by the law.   In the case therefore of a Mancipation,
however slovenly the performance might have been,
yet if it had been carried so far as to involve a Tradition or Delivery, the vice of the title would be
cured by Usucapion in two years at most.   I know
nothing in the practice of the Romans which testifies
so strongly to their legal genius as the use which
they made of the Usucapion.   The difficulties which
beset them were nearly the same with those which
embarrassed and still embarrass the lawyers of

England. Owing to the complexity of their system, which as yet they had neither the courage nor the power to reconstruct, actual right was constantly getting divorced from technical right, the equitable ownership from the legal. But Usucapion, as manipulated by the jurisconsults, supplied a self-acting machinery, by which the defects of titles to property were always in course of being cured, and by which the ownerships that were temporarily separated were again rapidly cemented together with the briefest possible delay. Usucapion did not lose its advantages till the reforms of Justinian. But as soon as law and equity had been completely fused, and when Mancipation ceased to be the Roman conveyance, there was no further necessity for the ancient contrivance, and Usucapion, with its periods of time considerably lengthened, became the Prescription which has at length been adopted by nearly all systems of modern law.

I pass by with brief mention another expedient having the same object with the last, which, though it did not immediately make its appearance in English legal history, was of immemorial antiquity in Roman law; such indeed is its apparent age that some German civilians, not sufficiently aware of the light thrown on the subject by the analogies of English law, have thought it even older than the Mancipation. I speak of the Cessio in Jure, a collusive recovery, in a Court of Law, of property sought to be conveyed. The plaintiff claimed the subject of this proceeding with the ordinary forms of a litigation; the defendant made default; and the commodity was of course adjudged to the plaintiff. I need scarcely remind the English lawyer that this expedient suggested itself to our forefathers, and produced those famous Fines and Recoveries which did so much to undo the harshest trammels of the feudal land-law. The Roman and English contrivances have very much in common, and illustrate each other most instructively, but there is this difference between them, that the object of the English lawyers was to remove complications already introduced into the title, while the Roman jurisconsults sought to prevent them by substituting a mode of transfer necessarily unimpeachable for one which too often miscarried. The device is in fact one which suggests itself as soon as Courts of Law are in steady operation, but are nevertheless still under the empire of primitive notions. In an advanced state of legal opinion, tribunals regard collusive litigation as an abuse of their procedure; but there has always been a time when, if their forms were scrupulously complied with, they never dreamed of looking further.

The influence of Courts of Law and of their procedure upon property has been most extensive, but the subject is too large for the dimensions of this treatise, and would carry us further down the course of legal history than is consistent with its scheme. It is desirable, however, to mention, that to this influence we must attribute the importance of the distinction between Property and Possession —not, indeed, the distinction itself, which (in the language of an eminent English civilian) is the same thing as the distinction between the legal right to act upon a thing and the physical power to do so— but the extraordinary importance which the distinction has obtained in the philosophy of the law. Few educated persons are so little versed in legal literature as not to have heard that the language of the Roman jurisconsults on the subject of Possession long occasioned the greatest possible perplexity, and that the genius of Savigny is supposed to have chiefly proved itself by the solution which he discovered for the enigma. Possession, in fact, when employed by the Roman lawyers, appears to have contracted a shade of meaning not easily accounted for. The word, as appears from its etymology, must have originally denoted physical contact or physical contact resumeable at pleasure ; but as actually used, without any qualifying epithet, it signifies not simply physical detention, but physical detention coupled with the intention to hold the thing detained as one's own. Savigny, following Niebuhr, perceived that for this anomaly there could only be a historical origin. He pointed out that the Patrician burghers of Rome, who had become tenants of the greatest part of the public domain at nominal rents, were, in the view of the old Roman law, mere possessors, but then they were possessors intending to keep their land against all comers. They, in truth, put forward a claim almost identical with that which has recently been advanced in England by the les-sees of Church lands. Admitting that in theory they were the tenants-at-will of the state, they con-tended that time and undisturbed enjoyment had ripened their holding into a species of ownership, and that it would be unjust to eject them for the purpose of redistributing the domain. The asso-ciation of this claim with the Patrician tenancies, permanently influenced the sense of " possession." Meanwhile the only legal remedies of which the tenants could avail themselves, if ejected or threat-ened with disturbance, were the Possessory Inter-dicts, summary processes of Roman law which were either expressly devised by the Prætor for their protection, or else, according to another theory, had in older times been employed for the provisional maintenance of possessions pending the settlement of questions of legal right. It came, therefore, to be understood that everybody who possessed prop-erty *as his own* had the power of demanding the Interdicts, and, by a system of highly artificial pleading, the Interdictal process was moulded into a shape fitted for the trial of conflicting claims to a disputed possession. Then commenced a movement which, as Mr. John Austin pointed out, exactly re-produced itself in English law. Proprietors, *domini*, began to prefer the simpler forms or speedier course of the Interdict to the lagging and intricate formalities of the Real Action, and for the purpose of availing themselves of the possessory remedy fell back upon the possession which was supposed to be involved in their proprietorship. The liberty con ceded to persons who were not true Possessors, but Owners, to vindicate their rights by possessory remedies, though it may have been at first a boon, had ultimately the effect of seriously deteriorating both English and Roman jurisprudence. The Roman law owes to it those subtleties on the subject of Possession which have done so much to discredit it, while English law, after the actions which it appropriated to the recovery of real property had fallen into the most hopeless confusion, got rid at last of the whole tangled mass by a heroic remedy No one can doubt that the virtual abolition of the English real actions which took place nearly thirty years since was a public benefit, but still persons sensitive to the harmonies of jurisprudence will lament that, instead of cleansing, improving, and simplifying the true proprietary actions, we sacrificed them all to the possessory action of ejectment, thus basing our whole system of land recovery upon a legal fiction.

Legal tribunals have also powerfully assisted to shape and modify conceptions of proprietary right by means of the distinction between Law and Equity, which always makes its first appearance as a distinction between jurisdictions. Equitable property in England is simply property held under the

jurisdiction of the Court of Chancery. At Rome
the Prætor's Edict introduced its novel principles in
the guise of a promise that under certain circum
stances a particular action or a particular plea would
be granted; and, accordingly, the property *in bonis,*
or Equitable Property, of Roman law was property
exclusively protected by remedies which had their
source in the Edict. The mechanism by which equitable rights were saved from being overridden by
the claims of the legal owner was somewhat different
in the two systems. With us their independence is
secured by the Injunction of the Court of Chancery.
Since however Law and Equity, while not as yet
consolidated, were administered under the Roman
system by the same Court, nothing like the Injunction was required, and the Magistrate took the simpler course of refusing to grant to the Civil Law
Owner those actions and pleas by which alone he
could obtain the property that belonged in equity
to another. But the practical operation of both
systems was nearly the same. Both, by means of a
distinction in procedure, were able to preserve new
forms of property in a sort of provisional existence,
until the time should come when they were recognised by the whole law. In this way, the Roman
Prætor gave an immediate right of property to the
person who had acquired a Res Mancipi by mere
delivery, without waiting for the ripening of Usucapion. Similarly he in time recognised an ownership
in the Mortgagee, who had at first been a mere

" bailee" or depositary, and in the Emphyteuta, or
tenant of land which was subject to a fixed perpetual rent.   Following a parallel line of progress,
the English Court of Chancery created a special
proprietorship for the Mortgagor, for the Cestui
que Trust, for the Married Woman who had the
advantage of a particular kind of settlement, and
for the Purchaser who had not yet acquired a complete legal ownership.   All these are examples in
which forms of proprietary right, distinctly new,
were recognised and preserved.   But indirectly
Property has been affected in a thousand ways by
equity, both in England and at Rome.   Into whatever corner of jurisprudence its authors pushed the
powerful instrument in their command, they were
sure to meet, and touch, and more or less materially
modify the law of property.   When in the preceding
pages I have spoken of certain ancient legal distinctions and expedients as having powerfully affected
the history of ownership, I must be understood to
mean that the greatest part of their influence has
arisen from the hints and suggestions of improvement infused by them into the mental atmosphere
which was breathed by the fabricators of equitable
systems.

But to describe the influence of Equity on Ownership would be to write its history down to our
own days.   I have alluded to it principally because
several esteemed contemporary writers have thought
that in the Roman severance of Equitable from Le-

gal property we have the clue to that difference in
the conception of Ownership, which apparently distinguishes the law of the middle ages from the law
of the Roman Empire.   The leading characteristic
of the feudal conception is its recognition of a double
proprietorship, the superior ownership of the lord
of the fief coexisting with the inferior property or
estate of the tenant.   Now, this duplication of proprietary right looks, it is urged, extremely like a
generalised form of the Roman distribution of rights
over property into *Quiritarian* or legal, and (to use
a word of late origin) *Bonitarian* or equitable.
Gaius himself observes upon the splitting of *dominion* into two parts as a singularity of Roman law,
and expressly contrasts it with the entire or allodial
ownership to which other nations were accustomed.
Justinian, it is true, reconsolidated dominion into
one, but then it was the partially reformed system
of the Western Empire, and not Justinian's jurisprudence, with which the barbarians were in contact
during so many centuries.   While they remained
poised on the edge of the Empire, it may well be
that they learned this distinction, which afterwards
bore remarkable fruit.   In favour of this theory, it
must at all events be admitted that the element of
Roman law in the various bodies of barbarian custom has been very imperfectly examined.   The erroneous or insufficient theories which have served to
explain Feudalism resemble each other in their tendency to draw off attention from this particular in

gredient in its texture. The older investigators,
who have been mostly followed in this country,
attached an exclusive importance to the circum
stances of the turbulent period during which the
Feudal system grew to maturity; and in later times
a new source of error has been added to those already
existing, in that pride of nationality which has led
German writers to exaggerate the completeness of
the social fabric which their forefathers had built up
before their appearance in the Roman world. One
or two English inquirers who looked in the right
quarter for the foundations of the feudal system,
failed nevertheless to conduct their investigations to
any satisfactory result, either from searching too exclusively for analogies in the compilations of Justinian, or from confining their attention to the compendia of Roman law which are found appended to
some of the extant barbarian codes. But, if Roman
jurisprudence had any influence on the barbarous
societies, it had probably produced the greatest part
of its effects before the legislation of Justinian, and
before the preparation of these compendia. It was
not the reformed and purified jurisprudence of Justinian, but the undigested system which prevailed in
the Western Empire, and which the Eastern *Corpus
Juris* never succeeded in displacing, that I conceive
to have clothed with flesh and muscle the scanty
skeleton of barbarous usage. The change must be
supposed to have taken place before the Germanic
tribes had distinctly appropriated, as conquerors,

any portion of the Roman dominions, and therefore
long before Germanic monarchs had ordered brevia-
ries of Roman law to be drawn up for the use of
their Roman subjects.   The necessity for some such
hypothesis will be felt by everybody who can appreciate the difference between archaic and developed
law.   Rude as are the *Leges Barbarorum* which remain to us, they are not rude enough to satisfy the
theory of their purely barbarous origin; nor have
we any reason for believing that we have received,
in written records, more than a fraction of the fixed
rules which were practised among themselves by the
members of the conquering tribes.   If we can once
persuade ourselves that a considerable element of
debased Roman law already existed in the barbarian
systems, we shall have done something to remove a
grave difficulty.   The German law of the conquerors
and the Roman law of their subjects would not have
combined if they had not possessed more affinity for
each other than refined jurisprudence has usually for
the customs of savages.   It is extremely likely that
the codes of the barbarians, archaic as they seem,
are only a compound of true primitive usage with
half-understood Roman rules, and that it was the
foreign ingredient which enabled them to coalesce
with a Roman jurisprudence that had already rece-
ded somewhat from the comparative finish which it
had acquired under the Western Emperors.

   But, though all this must be allowed, there are
several considerations which render it unlikely that

the feudal form of ownership was directly suggested
by the Roman duplication of domainial rights.   The
distinction between legal and equitable property
strikes one as a subtlety little likely to be appreciated
by barbarians; and, moreover, it can scarcely be understood unless Courts of Law are contemplated in
regular operation.   But the strongest reason against
this theory is the existence in Roman law of a form
of property—a creation of Equity, it is true—which
supplies a much simpler explanation of the transition from one set of ideas to the other.   This is the
Emphyteusis, upon which the Fief of the middle
ages has often been fathered, though without much
knowledge of the exact share which it had in bringing feudal ownership into the world.   The truth is
that the Emphyteusis, not probably as yet known
by its Greek designation, marks one stage in a current of ideas which led ultimately to feudalism.   The
first mention in Roman history of estates larger than
could be farmed by a Paterfamilias, with his household of sons and slaves, occurs when we come to the
holdings of the Roman patricians.   These great proprietors appear to have had no idea of any system
of farming by free tenants.   Their *latifundia* seem
to have been universally cultivated by slave-gangs,
under bailiffs who were themselves slaves or freed
men; and the only organisation attempted appears
to have consisted in dividing the inferior slaves into
small bodies, and making them the *peculium* of the
better and trustier sort, who thus acquired a kind

19

of interest in the efficiency of their labour. This
system was, however, especially disadvantageous to
one class of estated proprietors, the Municipalities.
Functionaries in Italy were changed with the rapidity which often surprises us in the administration
of Rome herself; so that the superintendence of a
large landed domain by an Italian corporation must
have been excessively imperfect. Accordingly, we
are told that with the municipalities began the practice of letting out *agri vectigules*, that is, of leasing
land for a perpetuity to a free tenant, at a fixed
rent, and under certain conditions. The plan was
afterwards extensively imitated by individual proprietors, and the tenant, whose relation to the owner
had originally been determined by his contract, was
subsequently recognised by the Prætor as having
himself a qualified proprietorship, which in time became known as an Emphyteusis. From this point
the history of tenure parts into two branches. In
the course of that long period during which our
records of the Roman Empire are most incomplete,
the slave-gangs of the great Roman families became
transformed into the *coloni*, whose origin and situation constitute one of the obscurest questions in all
history. We may suspect that they were formed
partly by the elevation of the slaves, and partly by
the degradation of the free farmers ; and that they
prove the richer classes of the Roman Empire to
have become aware of the increased value which
landed property obtains when the cultivator has an

interest in the produce of the land. We know that
their servitude was predial; that it wanted many
of the characteristics of absolute slavery, and that
they acquitted their service to the landlord in rendering to him a fixed portion of the annual crop.
We know further that they survived all the muta-
tions of society in the ancient and modern worlds.
Though included in the lower courses of the feudal
structure, they continued in many countries to render to the landlord precisely the same dues which
they had paid to the Roman *dominus*, and from a
particular class among them, the *coloni medietarii*,
who reserved half the produce for the owner, are
descended the *metayer* tenantry, who still conduct
the cultivation of the soil in almost all the South of
Europe. On the other hand, the Emphyteusis, if
we may so interpret the allusions to it in the *Corpus
Juris*, became a favorite and beneficial modification
of property; and it may be conjectured that wherever free farmers existed, it was this tenure which
regulated their interest in the land. The Prætor,
as has been said, treated the Emphyteuta as a true
proprietor. When ejected, he was allowed to rein-
state himself by a Real Action, the distinctive badge
of proprietary right, and he was protected from disturbance by the author of his lease so long as the
canon, or quit-rent, was punctually paid. But at
the same time it must not be supposed that the
ownership of the author of the lease was either ex
tinct or dormant. It was kept alive by a power of

re-entry on non-payment of the rent, a right of pre-
emption in case of sale, and a certain control over
the mode of cultivation.   We have, therefore, in the
Emphyteusis a striking example of the double ownership which characterised feudal property, and one,
moreover, which is much simpler and much more
easily imitated than the juxtaposition of legal and
equitable rights.   The history of the Roman tenure
does not end, however, at this point.   We have
clear evidence that between the great fortresses
which, disposed along the line of the Rhine and
Danube, long secured the frontier of the Empire
against its barbarian neighbours, there extended a
succession of strips of land, the *agri limitrophi*,
which were occupied by veteran soldiers of the Roman army on the terms of an Emphyteusis.   There
was a double ownership.   The Roman State was
landlord of the soil, but the soldiers cultivated it
without disturbance so long as they held themselves
ready to be called out for military service whenever
the state of the border should require it.   In fact, a
sort of garrison-duty, under a system closely resembling that of the military colonies on the Austro-
Turkish border, had taken the place of the quit-rent
which was the service of the ordinary Emphyteuta.
It seems impossible to doubt that this was the precedent copied by the barbarian monarchs who
founded feudalism.   It had been within their view
for some hundred years, and many of the veterans
who guarded the border were, it is to be remem-

bered, themselves of barbarian extraction, who probably spoke the Germanic tongues. Not only does the proximity of so easily followed a model explain whence the Frankish and Lombard Sovereigns got the idea of securing the military service of their followers by granting away portions of their public domain; but it perhaps explains the tendency which immediately showed itself in the Benefices to become hereditary, for an Emphyteusis, though capable of being moulded to the terms of the original contract, nevertheless descended as a general rule to the heirs of the grantee. It is true that the holder of a benefice, and more recently the lord of one of those fiefs into which the benefices were transformed, appears to have owed certain services which were not likely to have been rendered by the military colonist, and were certainly not rendered by the Emphyteuta. The duty of respect and gratitude to the feudal superior, the obligation to assist in endowing his daughter and equipping his son, the liability to his guardianship in minority, and many other similar incidents of tenure, must have been literally borrowed from the relations of Patron and Freedman under Roman law, that is, of quondam-master and quondam-slave. But then it is known that the earliest beneficiaries were the personal companions of the sovereign, and it is indisputable that this position, brilliant as it seems, was at first attended by some shade of servile debasement. The person who ministered to the Sovereign in his Court had given up something of that absolute personal freedom which was the proudest privilege of the allodial proprietor.

CHAPTER IX.

THERE are few general propositions concerning the age to which we belong which seem at first sight likely to be received with readier concurrence than the assertion that the society of our day is mainly distinguished from that of preceding generations by the largeness of the sphere which is occupied in it by Contract. Some of the phenomena on which this proposition rests are among those most frequently singled out for notice, for comment, and for eulogy. Not many of us are so unobservant as not to perceive that in innumerable cases where old law fixed a man's social position irreversibly at his birth, modern law allows him to create it for himself by convention; and indeed several of the few exceptions which remain to this rule are constantly denounced with passionate indignation. The point, for instance, which is really debated in the vigorous controversy still carried on upon the subject of negro servitude, is whether the status of the slave does not

belong to by-gone institutions, and whether the only
relation between employer and labourer which com
mends itself to modern morality be not a relation determined exclusively by contract. The recognition
of this difference between past ages and the present
enters into the very essence of the most famous contemporary speculations. It is certain that the science
of Political Economy, the only department of moral
inquiry which has made any considerable progress in
our day, would fail to correspond with the facts of
life if it were not true that Imperative Law had
abandoned the largest part of the field which it once
occupied, and had left men to settle rules of conduct
for themselves with a liberty never allowed to them
till recently. The bias indeed of most persons trained
in political economy is to consider the general truth
on which their science reposes as entitled to become
universal, and, when they apply it as an art, their efforts are ordinarily directed to enlarging the province
of Contract and to curtailing that of Imperative Law,
except so far as law is necessary to enforce the performance of Contracts. The impulse given by thinkers who are under the influence of these ideas is beginning to be very strongly felt in the Western
world. Legislation has nearly confessed its inability
to keep pace with the activity of man in discovery,
in invention, and in the manipulation of accumulated
wealth ; and the law even of the least advanced
communities tends more and more to become a mere
surface-stratum, having under it an ever-changing as-

semblage of contractual rules with which it rarely interferes except to compel compliance with a few fundamental principles, or unless it be called in to punish the violation of good faith.

Social inquiries, so far as they depend on the consideration of legal phenomena, are in so backward a
condition that we need not be surprised at not finding these truths recognised in the commonplaces
which pass current concerning the progress of society. These commonplaces answer much more to
our prejudices than to our convictions. The strong
disinclination of most men to regard morality as advancing seems to be especially powerful when the
virtues on which Contract depends are in question,
and many of us have an almost instinctive reluctance
to admitting that good faith and trust in our fellows
are more widely diffused than of old, or that there
is anything in contemporary manners which parallels
the loyalty of the antique world. From time to
time, these prepossessions are greatly strengthened
by the spectacle of frauds, unheard of before the period at which they were observed, and astonishing
from their complication as well shocking from criminality. But the very character of these frauds shows
clearly that, before they became possible, the moral
obligations of which they are the breach must have
been more than proportionately developed. It is the
confidence reposed and deserved by the many which
affords facilities for the bad faith of the few, so that,
if colossal examples of dishonesty occur, there is no

surer conclusion than that scrupulous honesty is displayed in the average of the transactions which, in the particular case, have supplied the delinquent with his opportunity. If we insist on reading the history of morality as reflected in jurisprudence, by turning our eyes not on the law of Contract but on the law of Crime, we must be careful that we read it aright. The only form of dishonesty treated of in the most ancient Roman law is Theft. At the moment at which I write, the newest chapter in the English criminal law is one which attempts to prescribe punishment for the frauds of Trustees. The proper inference from this contrast is not that the primitive Romans practised a higher morality than ourselves. We should rather say that, in the interval between their day and ours, morality had advanced from a very rude to a highly refined conception—from viewing the rights of property as exclusively sacred, to looking upon the rights growing out of the mere unilateral reposal of confidence as entitled to the protection of the penal law.

The definite theories of jurists are scarcely nearer the truth in this point than the opinions of the multitude. To begin with the views of the Roman lawyers, we find them inconsistent with the true history of moral and legal progress. One class of contracts, in which the plighted faith of the contracting parties was the only material ingredient, they specifically denominated Contracts *juris gentium*, and though these contracts were undoubtedly the latest born

into the Roman system, the expression employed
implies, if a definite meaning be extracted from
it, that they were more ancient than certain other
forms of engagement treated of in Roman law, in
which the neglect of a mere technical formality was
as fatal to the obligation as misunderstanding or
deceit. But then the antiquity to which they were
referred was vague, shadowy, and only capable of
being understood through the Present; nor was it
until the language of the Roman lawyers became the
language of an age which had lost the key to their
mode of thought that a " Contract of the Law of Nations" came to be distinctly looked upon as a Contract
known to man in a state of Nature. Rousseau adopted
both the judicial and the popular error. In the Dis-
sertation on the effects of Art and Science upon
Morals, the first of his works which attracted attention and the one in which he states most unreservedly the opinions which made him the founder of a sect,
the veracity and good faith attributed to the ancient
Persians are repeatedly pointed out as traits of primitive innocence which have been gradually obliterated by civilisation; and at a later period he found a
basis for all his speculations in the doctrine of an
original Social Contract. The Social Contract or
Compact is the most systematic form which has ever
been assumed by the error we are discussing. It is
a theory which, though nursed into importance by
political passions, derived all its sap from the speculations of lawyers. True it certainly is that the fa-

mous Englishmen, for whom it had first had attraction, valued it chiefly for its political serviceableness, but, as I shall presently attempt to explain, they would never have arrived at it, if politicians had not long conducted their controversies in legal phraseology. Nor were the English authors of the theory blind to that speculative amplitude which recommended it so strongly to the Frenchmen who inherited it from them. Their writings show they perceived that it could be made to account for all social, quite as well as for all political phenomena. They had observed the fact, already striking in their day, that of the positive rules obeyed by men, the greater part were created by Contract, the lesser by imperative Law. But they were ignorant or careless of the historical relation of these two constituents of jurisprudence. It was for the purpose, therefore, of gratifying their speculative tastes by attributing all jurisprudence to a uniform source, as much as with the view of eluding the doctrines which claimed a divine parentage for Imperative Law, that they devised the theory that all Law had its origin in Contract. In another stage of thought, they would have been satisfied to leave their theory in the condition of an ingenious hypothesis or a convenient verbal formula. But that age was under the dominion of legal superstitions. The State of Nature had been talked about till it had ceased to be regarded as paradoxical, and hence it seemed easy to give a fallacious reality and definiteness to the contractual origin of Law by insisting on the Social Compact as a historical fact.

Our own generation has got rid of these erroneous juridical theories, partly by outgrowing the intellectual state to which they belong, and partly by almost ceasing to theorise on such subjects altogether. The favorite occupation of active minds at the present moment, and the one which answers to the speculations of our forefathers on the origin of the social state, is the analysis of society as it exists and moves before our eyes; but, through omitting to call in the assistance of history, this analysis too often degenerates into an idle exercise of curiosity, and is especially apt to incapacitate the inquirer for comprehending states of society which differ considerably from that to which he is accustomed. The mistake of judging the men of other periods by the morality of our own day has its parallel in the mistake of supposing that every wheel or bolt in the modern social machine had its counterpart in more rudimentary societies. Such impressions ramify very widely, and masque themselves very subtly, in historical works written in the modern fashion ; but I find the trace of their presence in the domain of jurisprudence in the praise which is frequently bestowed on the little apologue of Montesquieu concerning the Troglodytes, inserted in the *Lettres Persanes*. The Troglodytes were a people who systematically violated their Contracts, and so perished utterly. If the story bears the moral which its author intended, and is employ-

ed to expose an anti-social heresy by which this century and the last have been threatened, it is most un-
exceptionable ; but if the inference be obtained from
it that society could not possibly hold together without attaching a sacredness to promises and agreements which should be on something like a par with
the respect that is paid to them by a mature civilisation, it involves an error so grave as to be fatal to
all sound understanding of legal history. The fact is
that the Troglodytes have flourished and founded
powerful states with very small attention to the obligations of Contract. The point which before all
others has to be apprehended in the constitution of
primitive societies is that the individual creates for
himself few or no rights, and few or no duties. The
rules which he obeys are derived first from the station into which he is born, and next from the imperative commands addressed to him by the chief of
the household of which he forms a part. Such a system leaves the very smallest room for Contract. The
members of the same family (for so we may interpret
the evidence) are wholly incapable of contracting
with each other, and the family is entitled to disregard the engagements by which any one of its subordinate members has attempted to bind it. Family,
it is true, may contract with family, and chieftain with
chieftain, but the transaction is one of the same nature, and encumbered by as many formalities, as the
alienation of property, and the disregard of one iota
of the performance is fatal to the obligation. The

positive duty resulting from one man's reliance on the word of another is among the slowest conquests of advancing civilisation.

Neither Ancient Law nor any other source of evidence discloses to us society entirely destitute of the conception of Contract. But the conception, when it first shows itself, is obviously rudimentary. No trustworthy primitive record can be read without perceiving that the habit of mind which induces us to make good a promise is as yet imperfectly developed, and that acts of flagrant perfidy are often mentioned without blame and sometimes described with approbation. In the Homeric literature, for instance, the deceitful cunning of Ulysses appears as a virtue of the same rank with the prudence of Nestor, the constancy of Hector, and the gallantry of Achilles. Ancient law is still more suggestive of the distance which separates the crude form of Contract from its maturity. At first, nothing is seen like the interposition of law to compel the performance of a promise. That which the law arms with its sanctions is not a promise, but a promise accompanied with a solemn ceremonial. Not only are the formalities of equal importance with the promise itself, but they are, if anything, of greater importance; for that delicate analysis which mature jurisprudence applies to the conditions of mind under which a particular verbal assent is given appears, in ancient law, to be transferred to the words and gestures of the accompanying performance. No pledge is enforced if a single form be omitted or misplaced, but, on the other hand, if the forms can be shown to have been accurately proceeded with, it is of no avail to plead that the promise was made under duress or deception. The transmutation of this ancient view into the familiar notion of a Contract is plainly seen in the history of jurisprudence. First one or two steps in the ceremonial are dispensed with ; then the others are simplified or permitted to be neglected on certain conditions ; lastly, a few specific contracts are separated from the rest and allowed to be entered into without form, the selected contracts being those on which the activity and energy of social intercourse depend. Slowly, but most distinctly, the mental engagement isolates itself amid the technicalities, and gradually becomes the sole ingredient on which the interest of the jurisconsult is concentrated. Such a mental engagement, signified through external acts, the Romans called a Pact or Convention ; and when the Convention has once been conceived as the nucleus of a Contract, it soon becomes the tendency of advancing jurisprudence to break away the external shell of form and ceremony. Forms are thenceforward only retained so far as they are guarantees of authenticity, and securities for caution and deliberation. The idea of a Contract is fully developed, or, to employ the Roman phrase, Contracts are absorbed in Pacts.

The history of this course of change in Roman law is exceedingly instructive. At the earliest dawn of the jurisprudence, the term in use for a Contract was one which is very familiar to the students of historical Latinity. It was *nexum*, and the parties to the contract were said to be *nexi*, expressions which must be carefully attended to on account of the singular durableness of the metaphor on which they are founded. The notion that persons under a contractual engagement are connected together by a strong *bond* or *chain*, continued till the last to influence the Roman jurisprudence of Contract; and flowing thence it has mixed itself with modern ideas. What then was involved in this nexum or bond? A definition which has descended to us from one of the Latin antiquarians describes *nexum* as *omne quod geritur per æs et libram*, "every transaction with the copper and the balance," and these words have occasioned a good deal of perplexity. The copper and the balance are the well-known accompaniments of the Mancipation, the ancient solemnity described in a former chapter, by which the right of owner-ship in the highest form of Roman Property was transferred from one person to another. Mancipa-tion was a *conveyance*, and hence has arisen the difficulty, for the definition thus cited appears to confound Contracts and Conveyances, which in the philosophy of jurisprudence are not simply kept apart, but are actually opposed to each other. The *jus in re*, right *in rem*, right "availing against all the world," or Proprietary Right, is sharply distin-guished by the analyst of mature jurisprudence from

20

the *jus ad rem*, right *in personam*, right "availing against a single individual or group," or Obligation. Now Conveyances transfer Proprietary Rights, Contracts create Obligations—how then can the two be included under the same name or same general conception? This, like many similar embarrassments, has been occasioned by the error of ascribing to the mental condition of an unformed society a faculty which pre-eminently belongs to an advanced stage of intellectual development, the faculty of distinguishing in speculation ideas which are blended in practice. We have indications not to be mistaken of a state of social affairs in which Conveyances and Contracts were practically confounded; nor did the discrepance of the conceptions become perceptible till men had begun to adopt a distinct practice in contracting and conveying.

It may here be observed that we know enough of ancient Roman law to give some idea of the mode of transformation followed by legal conceptions and by legal phraseology in the infancy of Jurisprudence. The change which they undergo appears to be a change from general to special; or, as we might otherwise express it, the ancient conceptions and the ancient terms are subjected to a process of gradual specialisation. An ancient legal conception corresponds not to one but to several modern conceptions. An ancient technical expression serves to indicate a variety of things which in modern law have separate names allotted to them. If, however, we take up the history of Jurisprudence at the next stage, we find that the subordinate conceptions have gradually disengaged themselves, and that the old general names are giving way to special appellations. The old general conception is not obliterated, but it has ceased to cover more than one or a few of the notions which it first included. So too the old technical name remains, but it discharges only one of the functions which it once performed. We may exemplify this phenomenon in various ways. Patriarchal Power of all sorts appears, for instance, to have been once conceived as identical in character, and it was doubtless distinguished by one name. The Power exercised by the ancestor was the same whether it was exercised over the family or the material property—over flocks, herds, slaves, children, or wife. We cannot be absolutely certain of its old Roman name, but there is very strong reason for believing, from the number of expressions indicating shades of the notion of *power* into which the word *manus* enters, that the ancient general term was *manus*. But, when Roman law has advanced a little, both the name and the idea have become specialised. Power is discriminated, both in word and in conception, according to the object over which it is exerted. Exercised over material commodities or slaves, it has become *dominium*—over children it is *Potestas* —over free persons whose services have been made away to another by their own ancestor, it is *mancipium*—over a wife, it is still *manus*. The old

word, it will be perceived, has not altogether fallen
into desuetude, but is confined to one very special
exercise of the authority it had formerly denoted.
This example will enable us to comprehend the
nature of the historical alliance between Contracts
and Conveyances. There seems to have been one
solemn ceremonial at first for all solemn transactions,
and its name at Rome appears to have been *nexum*.
Precisely the same forms which were in use when
a conveyance of property was effected seem to have
been employed in the making of a contract. But
we have not very far to move onwards before we
come to a period at which the notion of a Contract
has disengaged itself from the notion of a Conveyance. A double change has thus taken place. The
transaction " with the copper and the balance," when
intended to have for its office the transfer of property, is known by the new and special name of
Mancipation. The ancient Nexum still designates
the same ceremony, but only when it is employed
for the special purpose of solemnising a contract.

When two or three legal conceptions are spoken
of as anciently blended in one, it is not intended to
imply that some one of the included notions may
not be older than the others, or, when those others
have been formed, may not greatly predominate over
and take precedence over them. The reason why
one legal conception continues so long to cover several conceptions, and one technical phrase to do
instead of several, is doubtless that practical changes

are accomplished in the law of primitive societies
long before men see occasion to notice or name
them. Though I have said that Patriarchal Power
was not at first distinguished according to the objects over which it was exercised, I feel sure that
Power over Children was the root of the old conception of Power; and I cannot doubt that the
earliest use of the Nexum, and the one primarily
regarded by those who resorted to it, was to give
proper solemnity to the alienation of property. It
is likely that a very slight perversion of the Nexum
from its original functions first gave rise to its employment in Contracts, and that the very slightness
of the change long prevented its being appreciated
or noticed. The old name remained because men
had not become conscious that they wanted a new
one; the old notion clung to the mind because nobody had seen reason to be at the pains of examining it. We have had the process clearly exemplified
in the history of Testaments. A Will was at first
a simple conveyance of Property. It was only the
enormous practical difference that gradually showed
itself between this particular conveyance and all
others which caused it to be regarded separately,
and even as it was, centuries elapsed before the
ameliorators of law cleared away the useless encum-
brance of the nominal mancipation, and consented
to care for nothing in the Will but the expressed
intentions of the Testator. It is unfortunate that
we cannot track the early history of Contracts with

the same absolute confidence as the early history of
Wills, but we are not quite without hints that contracts first showed themselves through the *nexum*
being put to a new use and afterwards obtained
recognition as distinct transactions through the im
portant practical consequences of the experiment.
There is some, but not very violent, conjecture in
the following delineation of the process. Let us
conceive a sale for ready money as the normal type
of the Nexum. The seller brought the property of
which he intended to dispose—a slave, for example
—the purchaser attended with the rough ingots of
copper which served for money—and an indispensable assistant, the *libripens*, presented himself with a
pair of scales. The slave with certain fixed formalities was handed over to the vendee—the copper
was weighed by the *libripens* and passed to the vendor. So long as the business lasted it was a *nexum*,
and the parties were *nexi;* but the moment it was
completed, the *nexum* ended, and the vendor and
purchaser ceased to bear the name derived from
their momentary relation. But now, let us move a
step onward in commercial history. Suppose the
slave transferred, but the money not paid. In *that*
case the *nexum* is finished, so far as the seller is concerned, and when he has once handed over his property, he is no longer *nexus;* but, in regard to the
purchaser, the *nexum* continues. The transaction,
as to his part of it, is incomplete, and he is still considered to be *nexus*. It follows, therefore, that the

same term described the conveyance by which the right of property was transmitted, and the personal obligation of the debtor for the unpaid purchase-money. We may still go forward, and picture to ourselves a proceeding wholly formal, in which *nothing* is handed over and *nothing* paid ; we are brought at once to a transaction indicative of much higher commercial activity, an *executory Contract of Sale.*

If it be true that, both in the popular and in the professional view, a *Contract* was long regarded as an *incomplete Conveyance*, the truth has importance for many reasons. The speculations of the last century concerning mankind in a state of nature, are not unfairly summed up in the doctrine that "in the primitive society property was nothing, and obligation everything;" and it will now be seen that, if the proposition were reversed, it would be nearer the reality. On the other hand, considered historically, the primitive association of Conveyances and Contracts explains something which often strikes the scholar and jurist as singularly enigmatical, I mean the extraordinary and uniform severity of very ancient systems of law to *debtors*, and the extravagant powers which they lodge with *creditors*. When once we understand that the *nexum* was artificially prolonged to give time to the debtor, we can better comprehend his position in the eye of the public and of the law His indebtedness was doubtless regarded as an anomaly, and suspense of payment

in general as an artifice and a distortion of strict
rule. The person who had duly consummated his
part in the transaction must, on the contrary, have
stood in peculiar favour; and nothing would seem
more natural than to arm him with stringent facilities for enforcing the completion of a proceeding
which, of strict right, ought never to have been extended or deferred.

Nexum, therefore, which originally signified a
Conveyance of property, came insensibly to denote
a Contract also, and ultimately so constant became
the association between this word and the notion of
a Contract, that a special term, Mancipium or Man-
cipatio, had to be used for the purpose of designating
the true nexum or transaction in which the property
was really transferred.   Contracts are therefore now
severed from Conveyances, and the first stage in their
history is accomplished, but still they are far enough
from that epoch of their development when the
promise of the contractor has a higher sacredness
than the formalities with which it is coupled. In
attempting to indicate the character of the changes
passed through in this interval, it is necessary to trespass a little on a subject which lies properly beyond
the range of these pages, the analysis of Agreement
effected by the Roman jurisconsults. Of this analysis, the most beautiful monument of their sagacity,
I need not say more than that it is based on the
theoretical separation of the Obligation from the
Convention or Pact.   Bentham and Mr. Austin have

laid down that the " two main essentials of a contract are these : first, a signification by the promising party of his *intention* to do the acts or to observe
the forbearances which he promises to do or to observe.   Secondly, a signification by the promisee that
he *expects* the promising party will fulfil the prof
ferred promise."   This is virtually identical with
the doctrine of the Roman lawyers, but then, in
their view, the result of these " significations " was
not a Contract, but a Convention or Pact.   A Pact
was the utmost product of the engagements of individuals agreeing among themselves, and it distinctly
fell short of a Contract.   Whether it ultimately became a Contract depended on the question whether
the law annexed an Obligation to it.   A Contract
was a Pact (or Convention) *plus* an Obligation.   So
long as the Pact remained unclothed with the Obligation, it was called *nude* or *naked*.

What was an Obligation ?   It is defined by the
Roman lawyers as " Juris vinculum, quo necessitate
adstringimur alicujus solvendæ rei."   This definition
connects the Obligation with the Nexum through
the common metaphor on which they are founded,
and shows us with much clearness the pedigree of a
peculiar conception.   The obligation is the " bond "
or " chain," with which the law joins together persons or groups of persons, in consequence of certain
voluntary acts.   The acts which have the effect of
attracting an Obligation are chiefly those classed
under the heads of Contract and Delict, of Agree-

ment and Wrong; but a variety of other acts have
a similar consequence which are not capable of being comprised in an exact classification. It is to be
remarked, however, that the Pact does not draw to
itself the Obligation in consequence of any moral
necessity; it is the law which annexes it in the plenitude of its power, a point the more necessary to be
noted, because a different doctrine has sometimes
been propounded by modern interpreters of the
Civil Law who had moral or metaphysical theories
of their own to support. The image of a *vinculum
juris* colours and pervades every part of the Roman
law of Contract and Delict. The law bound the
parties together, and the *chain* could only be un-
done by the process called *solutio*, an expression still
figurative, to which our word "payment" is only
occasionally and incidentally equivalent. The consistency with which the figurative image was allowed
to present itself, explains an otherwise puzzling peculiarity of Roman legal phraseology, the fact that
"Obligation" signifies rights as well as duties, the
right, for example, to have a debt paid as well as
the duty of paying it. The Romans kept, in fact,
the entire picture of the "legal chain" before their
eyes, and regarded one end of it no more and no
less than the other.

In the developed Roman law, the Convention, as
soon as it was completed, was, in almost all cases, at
once crowned with the Obligation, and so became a
Contract; and this was the result to which contract-

law was surely tending. But for the purpose of this inquiry, we must attend particularly to the intermediate stage—that in which something more than a perfect agreement was required to attract the Obligation. This epoch is synchronous with the period at which the famous Roman classification of Contracts into four sorts—the Verbal, the Literal, the Real, and the Consensual—had come into use, and during which these four orders of Contract constituted the only descriptions of engagement which the law would enforce. The meaning of the fourfold distribution is readily understood as soon as we apprehend the theory which severed the Obligation from the Convention. Each class of contracts was in fact named from certain formalities which were required over and above the mere agreement of the contracting parties. In the Verbal Contract, as soon as the Convention was effected, a form of words had to be gone through before the vinculum juris was attached to it. In the Literal Contract, an entry in a ledger or table-book had the effect of clothing the Convention with the Obligation, and the same result followed, in the case of the Real Contract, from the delivery of the Res or Thing which was the subject of the preliminary engagement. The Contracting parties came, in short, to an understanding in each case; but, if they went no further, they were not *obliged* to one another, and could not compel performance or ask redress for a breach of faith. But let them comply with certain prescribed formalities, and the

Contract was immediately complete, taking its name
from the particular form which it had suited them
to adopt.   The exceptions to this practice will be
noticed presently.

I have enumerated the four Contracts in their
historical order, which order, however, the Roman
Institutional writers did not invariably follow. There
can be no doubt that the Verbal Contract was the
most ancient of the four, and that it is the eldest
known descendant of the primitive Nexum. Several
species of Verbal Contract were anciently in use, but
the most important of all, and the only one treated
of by our authorities, was effected by means of a
stipulation, that is, a Question and Answer ; a question addressed by the person who exacted the promise,
and an answer given by the person who made it.
This question and answer constituted the additional
ingredient which, as I have just explained, was demanded by the primitive notion over and above th
mere agreement of the persons interested.   They
formed the agency by which the Obligation was annexed.   The old Nexum has now bequeathed to
maturer jurisprudence first of all the conception
of a chain uniting the contracting parties, and this
has become the Obligation.   It has further transmitted the notion of a ceremonial accompanying and
consecrating the engagement, and this ceremonial
has been transmuted into the Stipulation.   The conversion of the solemn conveyance, which was the
prominent feature of the original Nexum, into a

mere question and answer, would be more of a mystery than it is if we had not the analogous history of Roman Testaments to enlighten us. Looking at that history, we can understand how the formal conveyance was first separated from the part of the proceeding which had immediate reference to the business in hand, and how afterwards it was omitted altogether. As then the question and answer of the Stipulation were unquestionably the Nexum in a simplified shape, we are prepared to find that they long partook of the nature of a technical term. It would be a mistake to consider them exclusively recommending themselves to the older Roman lawyers through their usefulness in furnishing persons meditating an agreement with an opportunity for consideration and reflection. It is not to be disputed that they had a value of this kind, which was gradually recognised; but there is proof that their function in respect to Contracts was at first formal and ceremonial in the statement of authorities, that not every question and answer was of old sufficient to constitute a Stipulation, but only a question and answer couched in technical phraseology specially appropriated to the particular occasion.

But although it is essential for the proper appreciation of the history of contract-law that the Stipulation should be understood to have been looked upon as a solemn form before it was recognised as a useful security, it would be wrong on the other hand to shut our eyes to its real usefulness. The Verbal

Contract, though it had lost much of its ancient im
portance, survived to the latest period of Roman
jurisprudence; and we may take it for granted that
no institution of Roman law had so extended a lon‑
gevity unless it served some practical advantage
I observe in an English writer some expressions of
surprise that the Romans even of the earliest times
were content with so meagre a protection against
haste and irreflection.   But on examining the Stipu
lation closely, and remembering that we have to do
with a state of society in which written evidence
was not easily procurable, I think we must admit
that this Question and Answer, had it been expressly
devised to answer the purpose which it served, would
have been justly designated a highly ingenious ex‑
pedient.   It was the *promisee* who, in the character
of stipulator, put all the terms of the contract into
the form of a question, and the answer was given by
the *promisor*.   " Do you promise that you will de‑
liver me such and such a slave, at such and such a
place, on such and such a day ? "   " I do promise."
Now, if we reflect for a moment, we shall see that
this obligation to put the promise interrogatively
inverts the natural position of the parties, and, by
effectually breaking the tenor of the conversation,
prevents the attention from gliding over a dangerous
pledge.   With us, a verbal promise is, generally
speaking, to be gathered exclusively from the words
of the promisor.   In old Roman law, another step
was absolutely required; it was necessary for the

promisee, after the agreement had been made, to sum up all its terms in a solemn interrogation; and it was of this interrogation, of course, and of the assent to it, that proof had to be given at the trial —*not* of the promise, which was not in itself bind ing. How great a difference this seemingly insig nificant peculiarity may make in the phraseology of contract-law is speedily realised by the beginner in Roman jurisprudence, one of whose first stumbling blocks is almost universally created by it. When we in English have occasion, in mentioning a con tract, to connect it for convenience' sake with one of the parties,—for example, if we wished to speak generally of a contractor,—it is always the promis*or* at whom our words are pointing. But the general language of Roman law takes a different turn; it always regards the contract, if we may so speak, from the point of view of the promis*ee*; in speaking of a party to a contract, it is always the Stipulator, the person who asks the question, who is primarily alluded to. But the serviceableness of the stipula tion is most vividly illustrated by referring to the actual examples in the pages of the Latin comic dramatists. If the entire scenes are read down in which these passages occur (ex. gra. Plautus, *Pseu dolus*, Act I. sc. 1; Act IV. sc. 6; *Trinummus*, Act V. sc. 2), it will be perceived how effectually the at tention of the person meditating the promise must have been arrested by the question, and how ample was the opportunity for withdrawal from an im provident undertaking.

In the Literal or Written Contract, the formal act by which an Obligation was superinduced on the Convention, was an entry of the sum due, where it could be specifically ascertained, on the debit side of a ledger. The explanation of this contract turns on a point of Roman domestic manners, the systematic character and exceeding regularity of bookkeeping in ancient times. There are several minor difficulties of old Roman law, as, for example, the nature of the Slave's Peculium, which are only cleared up when we recollect that a Roman household consisted of a number of persons strictly accountable to its head, and that every single item of domestic receipt and expenditure, after being entered in waste books, was transferred at stated periods to a general household ledger. There are some obscurities, however, in the descriptions we have received of the Literal Contract, the fact being that the habit of keeping books ceased to be universal in later times, and the expression " Literal Contract," came to signify a form of engagement entirely different from that originally understood. We are not, therefore, in a position to say, with respect to the primitive Literal Contract, whether the obligation was created by a simple entry on the part of the creditor or whether the consent of the debtor or a correspond ent entry in his own books was necessary to give it legal effect. The essential point is however estab

lished, that, in the case of this Contract, all formalities were dispensed with on a condition being com
plied with. This is another step downwards in the
history of contract-law.

The Contract which stands next in historical
succession, the Real Contract, shows a great advance
in ethical conceptions. Whenever any agreement
had for its object the delivery of a specific thing—
and this is the case with the large majority of simple
engagements—the Obligation was drawn down as
soon as the delivery had actually taken place. Such
a result must have involved a serious innovation on
the oldest ideas of Contract; for doubtless, in the
primitive times, when a contracting party had neglected to clothe his agreement in a stipulation, nothing done in pursuance of the agreement would be
recognised by the law. A person who had paid
over money on loan would be unable to sue for its
repayment unless he had formally *stipulated* for it.
But, in the Real Contract, performance on one side
is allowed to impose a legal duty on the other—
evidently on ethical grounds. For the first time
then moral considerations appear as an ingredient
in Contract-law, and the Real Contract differs from
its two predecessors in being founded on these, rather
than on respect for technical forms or on deference
to Roman domestic habits.

We now reach the fourth class, or Consensual
Contracts, the most interesting and important of all.
Four specified Contracts were distinguished by this

21

name : Mandatum, *i. e.* Commission or Agency; So-
cietas or Partnership ; Emtio Venditio or Sale ; and
Locatio Conductio or Letting and Hiring. A few
pages back, after stating that a Contract consisted
of a Pact or Convention to which an Obligation had
been superadded, I spoke of certain acts or formalities by which the law permitted the Obligation to
be attracted to the Pact. I used this language on
account of the advantage of a general expression,
but it is not strictly correct unless it be understood
to include the negative as well as the positive. For,
in truth, the peculiarity of these Consensual Contracts is that *no* formalities are required to create
them out of the Pact. Much that is indefensible,
and much more that is obscure, has been written
about the Consensual Contracts, and it has even been
asserted that in them the *consent* of the Parties is
more emphatically given than in any other species
of agreement. But the term Consensual merely in
dicates that the Obligation is here annexed at once
to the *Consensus*. The Consensus, or mutual assent
of the parties, is the final and crowning ingredient
in the Convention, and it is the special characteristic
of agreements falling under one of the four heads
of Sale, Partnership, Agency, and Hiring, that, as
soon as the assent of the parties has supplied this
ingredient, there is *at once* a Contract. The Consensus draws with it the Obligation, performing, in
transactions of the sort specified, the exact functions
which are discharged, in the other contracts, by the

Res or Thing, by the *Verba* stipulationis, and by the *Literæ* or written entry in a ledger. Consensual is therefore a term which does not involve the slightest anomaly, but is exactly analogous to Real, Verbal, and Literal.

In the intercourse of life the commonest and most important of all the contracts are unquestionably the four styled Consensual. The larger part of the collective existence of every community is consumed in transactions of buying and selling, of letting and hiring, of alliances between men for purposes of business, of delegation of business from one man to another; and this is no doubt the consideration which led the Romans, as it has led most societies, to relieve these transactions from technical incumbrance, to abstain as much as possible from clogging the most efficient springs of social movement. Such motives were not of course confined to Rome, and the commerce of the Romans with their neighbours must have given them abundant opportunities for observing that the contracts before us tended everywhere to become *Consensual*, obligatory on the mere signification of mutual assent. Hence, following their usual practice, they distinguished these contracts as contracts *Juris Gentium.* Yet I do not think that they were so named at a very early period. The first notions of a Jus Gentium may have been deposited in the minds of the Roman lawyers long before the appointment of a Prætor Peregrinus, but it would only be through

extensive and regular trade that they would be
familiarised with the contractual system of other
Italian communities, and such a trade would scarcely
attain considerable proportions before Italy had
been thoroughly pacified, and the supremacy of
Rome conclusively assured. Although, however,
there is strong probability that the Consensual Contracts were the latest-born into the Roman system,
and though it is likely that the qualification, *Juris
Gentium*, stamps the recency of their origin, yet
this very expression, which attributes them to the
" Law of Nations," has in modern times produced
the notion of their extreme antiquity. For, when
the " Law of Nations " had been converted into the
"Law of Nature," it seemed to be implied that the
Consensual Contracts were the type of the agreements most congenial to the natural state ; and hence
arose the singular belief that the younger the civilisation, the simpler must be its forms of contract.

The Consensual Contracts, it will be observed,
were extremely limited in number. But it cannot
be doubted that they constituted the stage in the
history of Contract-law from which all modern conceptions of contract took their start. The motion
of the will which constitutes agreement was now
completely insulated, and became the subject of separate contemplation ; forms were entirely elimina-
ted from the notion of contract, and external acts
were only regarded as symbols of the internal act
of volition. The Consensual Contracts had, more

over, been classed in the Jus Gentium, and it was
long before this classification drew with it the inference that they were the species of agreement which
represented the engagements approved of by Nature
and included in her code.   This point once reached,
we are prepared for several celebrated doctrines and
distinctions of the Roman lawyers.   One of them is
the distinction between Natural and Civil Obligations.   When a person of full intellectual maturity
had deliberately bound himself by an engagement,
he was said to be under a *natural obligation*, even
though he had omitted some necessary formality, and
even though through some technical impediment he
was devoid of the formal capacity for making a valid
contract.   The law (and this is what the distinction implies) would not enforce the obligation, but
it did not absolutely refuse to recognise it; and *natural obligations* differed in many respects from obligations which were merely null and void, more particularly in the circumstance that they could be
civilly confirmed, if the capacity for contract were
subsequently acquired.   Another very peculiar doctrine of the jurisconsults could not have had its origin earlier than the period at which the Convention
was severed from the technical ingredients of Contract.   They taught that though nothing but a Contract could be the foundation of an *action*, a mere
Pact or Convention could be the basis of a *plea*.   It
followed from this, that though nobody could sue
upon an agreement which he had not taken the pre

caution to mature into a Contract by complying with the proper forms, nevertheless a claim arising out of a valid contract could be rebutted by proving a counter-agreement which had never got beyond the state of a simple convention. An action for the recovery of a debt could be met by showing a mere informal agreement to waive or postpone the payment.

The doctrine just stated indicates the hesitation of the Prætors in making their advances towards the greatest of their innovations. Their theory of Natural law must have led them to look with especial favour on the Consensual Contracts and on those Pacts or Conventions of which the Consensual Contracts were only particular instances ; but they did not at once venture on extending to all Conventions the liberty of the Consensual Contracts. They took advantage of that special superintendence over procedure which had been confided to them since the first beginnings of Roman law, and, while they still declined to permit a suit to be launched which was not based on a formal contract, they gave full play to their new theory of agreement in directing the ulterior stages of the proceeding. But when they had proceeded thus far, it was inevitable that they should proceed farther. The revolution of the ancient law of Contract was consummated when the Prætor of some one year announced in his Edict that he would grant equitable actions upon Pacts which had never been matured at all into Contracts, provided only that the Pacts in question had been founded on a

consideration (*causa*). Pacts of this sort are always
enforced under the advanced Roman jurisprudence
The principle is merely the principle of the Consensual Contract carried to its proper consequence;
and, in fact, if the technical language of the Romans
had been as plastic as their legal theories, these
Pacts enforced by the Prætor would have been
styled new Contracts, new Consensual Contracts.
Legal phraseology is, however, the part of the law
which is the last to alter, and the Pacts equitably
enforced continued to be designated simply Prætorian Pacts.   It will be remarked that unless there
were consideration for the Pact, it would continue
nude so far as the new jurisprudence was concerned;
in order to give it effect, it would be necessary to
convert it by a stipulation into a Verbal Contract.

The extreme importance of this history of Contract, as a safeguard against almost innumerable
delusions, must be my justification for discussing it
at so considerable a length.   It gives a complete
account of the march of ideas from one great land-
mark of jurisprudence to another.   We begin with
the Nexum, in which a Contract and a Conveyance
are blended, and in which the formalities which ac
company the agreement are even more important
than the agreement itself.   From the Nexum we
pass to the Stipulation, which is a simplified form of
the older ceremonial.   The Literal Contract comes
next and here all formalities are waived, if proof
of the agreement can be supplied from the rigid

observances of a Roman household. In the Real Contract a moral duty is for the first time recognised, and persons who have joined or acquiesced in the partial performance of an engagement are forbidden to repudiate it on account of defects in form. Lastly, the Consensual Contracts emerge, in which the mental attitude of the contractors is solely regarded, and external circumstances have no title to notice except as evidence of the inward undertaking. It is of course uncertain how far this progress of Roman ideas from a gross to a refined conception exemplifies the necessary progress of human thought on the subject of Contract. The Contract-law of all other ancient societies but the Roman is either too scanty to furnish information, or else is entirely lost; and modern jurisprudence is so thoroughly leavened with the Roman notions that it furnishes us with no contrasts or parallels from which instruction can be gleaned. From the absence, however, of everything violent, marvellous, or unintelligible in the changes I have described, it may be reasonably believed that the history of Ancient Roman Contracts is, up to a certain point, typical of the history of this class of legal conceptions in other ancient societies. But it s only up to a certain point that the progress of Roman law can be taken to represent the progress of other systems of jurisprudence. The theory of Natural law is exclusively Roman. The notion of the *vinculum juris*, so far as my knowledge extends, is exclusively Roman. The many peculiarities of

the mature Roman law of Contract and Delict which
are traceable to these two ideas, whether singly or
in combination, are therefore among the exclusive
products of one particular society. These later legal
conceptions are important, not because they typify
the necessary results of advancing thought under all
conditions, but because they have exercised perfectly
enormous influence on the intellectual diathesis of
the modern world.

I know nothing more wonderful than the variety
of sciences to which Roman law, Roman Contract-
law more particularly, has contributed modes of
thought, courses of reasoning, and a technical language. Of the subjects which have whetted the
intellectual appetite of the moderns, there is scarcely
one, except Physics, which has not been filtered
through Roman jurisprudence. The science of pure
Metaphysics had, indeed, rather a Greek than a
Roman parentage, but Politics, Moral Philosophy,
and even Theology, found in Roman law not only a
vehicle of expression, but a nidus in which some of
their profoundest inquiries were nourished into maturity. For the purpose of accounting for this phenomenon, it is not absolutely necessary to discuss the
mysterious relation between words and ideas, or to
explain how it is that the human mind has never
grappled with any subject of thought, unless it has
been provided beforehand with a proper store of
language and with an apparatus of appropriate
logical methods. It is enough to remark, that,

when the philosophical interests of the Eastern and
Western worlds were separated, the founders of
Western thought belonged to a society which spoke
Latin and reflected in Latin. But in the Western
provinces the only language which retained sufficient
precision for philosophical purposes was the language of Roman law, which by a singular fortune
had preserved nearly all the purity of the Augustan
age, while vernacular Latin was degenerating into
a dialect of portentous barbarism. And if Roman
jurisprudence supplied the only means of exactness
in speech, still more emphatically did it furnish
the only means of exactness, subtlety, or depth in
thought. For at least three centuries, philosophy
and science were without a home in the West; and
though metaphysics and metaphysical theology were
engrossing the mental energies of multitudes of
Roman subjects, the phraseology employed in these
ardent inquiries was exclusively Greek, and their
theatre was the Eastern half of the Empire. Sometimes, indeed, the conclusions of the Eastern disputants became so important that every man's assent
to them, or dissent from them, had to be recorded,
and then the West was introduced to the results of
Eastern controversy, which it generally acquiesced
in without interest and without resistance. Meanwhile, one department of inquiry, difficult enough
for the most laborious, deep enough for the most
subtle, delicate enough for the most refined, had
never lost its attractions for the educated classes of

the Western provinces. To the cultivated citizen of Africa, of Spain, of Gaul, and of Northern Italy, it was jurisprudence, and jurisprudence only, which stood in the place of poetry and history, of philosophy and science. So far then from there being anything mysterious in the palpably legal complexion of the earliest efforts of Western thought, it would rather be astonishing if it had assumed any other hue. I can only express my surprise at the scantiness of the attention which has been given to the difference between Western ideas and Eastern, between Western theology and Eastern, caused by the presence of a new ingredient. It is precisely because the influence of jurisprudence begins to be powerful that the foundation of Constantinople and the subsequent separation of the Western empire from the Eastern, are epochs in philosophical history. But continental thinkers are doubtless less capable of appreciating the importance of this crisis by the very intimacy with which notions derived from Roman law are mingled up with their every-day ideas. Englishmen, on the other hand, are blind to it through the monstrous ignorance to which they condemn themselves of the most plentiful source of the stream of modern knowledge, of the one intellectual result of the Roman civilisation. At the same time, an Englishman, who will be at the pains to familiarise himself with the classical Roman law, is perhaps, from the very slightness of the interest which his countrymen have hitherto taken in the subject, a better judge than a Frenchman or German of the value of the assertions I have ventured to make, Anybody who knows what Roman jurisprudence is as actually practised by the Romans, and who will observe in what characteristics the earliest Western theology and philosophy differ from the phases of thought which preceded them, may be safely left to pronounce what was the new element which had begun to pervade and govern speculation.

The part of Roman law which has had most extensive influence on foreign subjects of inquiry has been the law of Obligation, or, what comes nearly to the same thing, of Contract and Delict. The Romans themselves were not unaware of the offices which the copious and malleable terminology belonging to this part of their system might be made to discharge, and this is proved by their employment of the peculiar adjunct *quasi* in such expressions as Quasi-Contract and Quasi-Delict. " Quasi," so used, is exclusively a term of classification. It has been usual with English critics to identify the quasi-contracts with *implied* contracts, but this is an error, for implied contracts are true contracts, which quasi-contracts are not. In implied contracts, acts and circumstances are the symbols of the same ingredients which are symbolised, in express contracts, by words; and whether a man employs one set of symbols or the other must be a matter of indifference so far as concerns the theory of agreement. But a Quasi-Contract is not a contract at all. The

commonest sample of the class is the relation sub-
sisting between two persons, one of whom has paid
money to the other through mistake. The law,
consulting the interests of morality, imposes an obligation on the receiver to refund, but the very nature of the transaction indicates that it is not a
contract, inasmuch as the Convention, the most
essential ingredient of Contract, is wanting. This
word " quasi," prefixed to a term of Roman law, implies that the conception to which it serves as an
index is connected with the conception with which
the comparison is instituted by a strong superficial
analogy or resemblance. It does not denote that
the two conceptions are the same, or that they belong to the same genus. On the contrary, it nega-
tives the notion of an identity between them; but
it points out that they are sufficiently similar for one
to be classed as the sequel to the other, and that the
phraseology taken from one department of law may
be transferred to the other, and employed without
violent straining in the statement of rules which
would otherwise be imperfectly expressed.

It has been shrewdly remarked, that the confusion between Implied Contracts, which are true
contracts, and Quasi-Contracts, which are not contracts at all, has much in common with the famous
error which attributed political rights and duties to
an Original Compact between the governed and the
governor. Long before this theory had clothed
itself in definite shape, the phraseology of Roman

contract-law had been largely drawn upon to describe that reciprocity of rights and duties which men had always conceived as existing between sovereigns and subjects. While the world was full of maxims setting forth with the utmost positiveness the claims of kings to implicit obedience—maxims which pretended to have had their origin in the New Testament, but which were really derived from indelible recollections of the Cæsarian despotism—the consciousness of correlative rights possessed by the governed would have been entirely without the means of expression if the Roman law of Obligation had not supplied a language capable of shadowing forth an idea which was as yet imperfectly developed. The antagonism between the privileges of kings and their duties to their subjects was never, I believe, lost sight of since Western history began, but it had interest for few except speculative writers so long as feudalism continued in vigour, for feudalism effectually controlled by express customs the exorbitant theoretical pretensions of most European sovereigns. It is notorious, however, that as soon as the decay of the Feudal System had thrown the mediæval constitutions out of working order, and when the Reformation had discredited the authority of the Pope, the doctrine of the divine right of Kings rose immediately into an importance which had never before attended it. The vogue which it obtained entailed still more constant resort to the phraseology of Roman law, and a controversy which had originally worn a theological aspect assumed more and more the air of a legal disputation. A phenomenon then appeared which has repeatedly shown itself in the history of opinion. Just when the argument for monarchical authority rounded itself into the definite doctrine of Filmer, the phraseology, borrowed from the Law of Contract, which had been used in defence of the rights of subjects, crystallised into the theory of an actual original compact between king and people, a theory which, first in English and afterwards, and more particularly, in French hands, expanded into a comprehensive explanation of all the phenomena of society and law. But the only real connection between political and legal science had consisted in the last giving to the first the benefit of its peculiarly plastic terminology. The Roman jurisprudence of Contract had performed for the relation of sovereign and subject precisely the same service which, in a humbler sphere, it rendered to the relation of persons bound together by an obligation of " quasi-contract." It had furnished a body of words and phrases which approximated with sufficient accuracy to the ideas which then were from time to time forming on the subject of political obligation. The doctrine of an Original Compact can never be put higher than it is placed by Dr. Whewell, when he suggests that, though unsound, " it may be a *convenient* form for the expression of moral truths."

The extensive employment of legal language on

political subjects previously to the invention of the
Original Compact, and the powerful influence which
that assumption has exercised subsequently, amply
account for the plentifulness in political science of
words and conceptions, which were the exclusive
creation of Roman jurisprudence. Of their plentifulness in Moral Philosophy a rather different explanation must be given, inasmuch as ethical writings
have laid Roman law under contribution much more
directly than political speculations, and their authors
have been much more conscious of the extent of
their obligation. In speaking of moral philosophy
as extraordinarily indebted to Roman jurisprudence,
I must be understood to intend moral philosophy
as understood previously to the break in its history
effected by Kant, that is, as the science of the rules
governing human conduct, of their proper interpretation and of the limitations to which they are subject. Since the rise of the Critical Philosophy, moral
science has almost wholly lost its older meaning,
and, except where it is preserved under a debased
form in the casuistry still cultivated by Roman
Catholic theologians, it seems to be regarded nearly
universally as a branch of ontological inquiry. I do
not know that there is a single contemporary English writer, with the exception of Dr. Whewell, who
understands moral philosophy as it was understood
before it was absorbed by metaphysics and before
the groundwork of its rules came to be a more important consideration than the rules themselves. So

long, however, as ethical science had to do with the practical regimen of conduct, it was more or less saturated with Roman law. Like all the great subjects of modern thought, it was originally incorporated with theology. The science of Moral Theology, as it was at first called, and as it is still designated by the Roman Catholic divines, was undoubtedly constructed, to the full knowledge of its authors, by taking principles of conduct from the system of the Church, and by using the language and methods of jurisprudence for their expression and expansion. While this process went on, it was inevitable that jurisprudence, though merely intended to be the vehicle of thought, should communicate its colour to the thought itself. The tinge received through contact with legal conceptions is perfectly perceptible in the earliest ethical literature of the modern world, and it is evident, I think, that the Law of Contract, based as it is on the complete reciprocity and indissoluble connection of rights and duties, has acted as a wholesome corrective to the predispositions of writers who, if left to themselves, might have exclusively viewed a moral obligation as the public duty of a citizen in the Civitas Dei. But the amount of Roman Law in moral theology becomes sensibly smaller at the time of its cultivation by the great Spanish moralists. Moral theology, developed by the juridical method of doctor commenting on doctor, provided itself with a phraseology of its own, and Aristotelian peculiarities of reasoning and expres-

22

sion, imbibed doubtless in great part from the Dis-
putations on Morals in the academical schools, take
the place of that special turn of thought and speech
which can never be mistaken by any person conversant with the Roman law. If the credit of the
Spanish school of moral theologians had continued,
the juridical ingredient in ethical science would have
been insignificant, but the use made of their conclusions by the next generation of Roman Catholic
writers on these subjects almost entirely destroyed
their influence. Moral Theology, degraded into
Casuistry, lost all interest for the leaders of European speculation; and the new science of Moral
Philosophy, which was entirely in the hands of the
Protestants, swerved greatly aside from the path
which the moral theologians had followed. The
effect was vastly to increase the influence of Roman
law on ethical inquiry.

"Shortly * after the Reformation, we find two
great schools of thought dividing this class of subjects between them. The most influential of the
two was at first the sect or school known to us as the
Casuists, all of them in spiritual communion with
the Roman Catholic Church, and nearly all of them
affiliated to one or other of her religious orders. On
the other side were a body of writers connected with
each other by a common intellectual descent from
the great author of the treatise *De Jure Belli et*

---

* The passage quoted is transcribed, with slight alterations, from
a paper contributed by the author to the *Cambridge Essays* for 1856.

Pacis, Hugo Grotius.   Almost all of the latter were
adherents of the Reformation; and though it cannot
be said that they were formally and avowedly at
conflict with the Casuists, the origin and object of
their system were nevertheless essentially different
from those of Casuistry.   It is necessary to call attention to this difference, because it involves the
question of the influence of Roman law on that department of thought with which both systems are
concerned.   The book of Grotius, though it touches
questions of pure Ethics in every page, and though
it is the parent immediate or remote of innumerable volumes of formal morality, is not, as is well
known, a professed treatise on Moral Philosophy; it
is an attempt to determine the Law of Nature, or
Natural Law.   Now, without entering upon the
question, whether the conception of a Law Natural
be not exclusively a creation of the Roman jurisconsults, we may lay down that, even on the admission
of Grotius himself, the dicta of the Roman jurisprudence as to what parts of known positive law must
be taken to be parts of the Law of Nature, are, if
not infallible, to be received at all events with the
profoundest respect.   Hence the system of Grotius
is implicated with Roman law at its very foundation,
and this connection rendered inevitable—what the
legal training of the writer would perhaps have entailed without it—the free employment in every
paragraph of technical phraseology, and of modes
of reasoning, defining, and illustrating, which must

sometimes conceal the sense, and almost always the force and cogency, of the argument from the reader who is unfamiliar with the sources whence they have been derived. On the other hand, Casuistry borrows little from Roman law, and the views of mo rality contended for have nothing whatever in com mon with the undertaking of Grotius. All that philosophy of right and wrong which has become famous, or infamous, under the name of Casuistry, had its origin in the distinction between Mortal and Venial sin. A natural anxiety to escape the awful consequences of determining a particular act to be mortally sinful, and a desire, equally intelligible, to assist the Roman Catholic Church in its conflict with Protestantism by disburthening it of an inconvenient theory, were the motives which impelled the authors of the Casuistical philosophy to the invention of an elaborate system of criteria, intended to remove immoral actions, in as many cases as possible, out of the category of mortal offences, and to stamp them as venial sins. The fate of this experiment is matter of ordinary history. We know that the distinctions of Casuistry, by enabling the priesthood to adjust spiritual control to all the varieties of human character, did really confer on it an influence with princes, statesmen, and generals, unheard of in the ages before the Reformation, and did really contribute largely to that great reaction which checked and narrowed the first successes of Protestantism. But beginning in the attempt, not to establish, but to evade—not to discover a principle, but to escape a postulate—not to settle the nature of right and wrong, but to determine what was not wrong of a particular nature,—Casuistry went on with its dexterous refinements till it ended in so attenuating the moral features of actions, and so belying the moral instincts of our being, that at length the conscience of mankind rose suddenly in revolt against it, and consigned to one common ruin the system and its doctors. The blow, long pending, was finally struck in the *Provincial Letters* of Pascal, and since the appearance of those memorable Papers, no moralist of the smallest influence or credit has ever avowedly conducted his speculations in the footsteps of the Casuists. The whole field of ethical science was thus left at the exclusive command of the writers who followed Grotius; and it still exhibits in an extraordinary degree the traces of that entanglement with Roman law which is sometimes imputed as a fault, and sometimes the highest of its recommendations, to the Grotian theory. Many inquirers since Grotius's day have modified his principles, and many, of course, since the rise of the critical philosophy, have quite deserted them; but even those who have departed most widely from his fundamental assumptions have inherited much of his method of statement, of his train of thought, and of his mode of illustration; and these have little meaning and no point to the person ignorant of Roman jurisprudence."

I have already said that, with the exception of
the physical sciences, there is no walk of knowledge
which has been so slightly affected by Roman law
as Metaphysics. The reason is that discussion on
metaphysical subjects has always been conducted ir
Greek, first in pure Greek, and afterwards in a dia
lect of Latin expressly constructed to give expression
to Greek conceptions. The modern languages have
only been fitted to metaphysical inquiries by adopting this Latin dialect, or by imitating the process
which was originally followed in its formation. The
source of the phraseology which has been always
employed for metaphysical discussion in modern
times was the Latin translations of Aristotle, in
which, whether derived or not from Arabic versions,
the plan of the translator was not to seek for analogous expressions in any part of Latin literature, but
to construct anew from Latin roots a set of phrases
equal to the expression of Greek philosophical ideas.
Over such a process the terminology of Roman law
can have exercised little influence; at most, a few
Latin law terms in a transmuted shape have made
their way into metaphysical language. At the same
time it is worthy of remark that whenever the problems of metaphysics are those which have been most
strongly agitated in Western Europe, the thought,
if not the language, betrays a legal parentage. Few
things in the history of speculation are more im
pressive than the fact that no Greek-speaking people
has ever felt itself seriously perplexed by the great

question of Free-will and Necessity. I do not pretend to offer any summary explanation of this, but it does not seem an irrelevant suggestion that neither the Greeks, nor any society speaking and thinking in their language, ever showed the smallest capacity for producing a philosophy of law. Legal science is a Roman creation, and the problem of Free-will arises when we contemplate a metaphysical conception under a legal aspect. How came it to be a question whether invariable sequence was identical with necessary connection? I can only say that the tendency of Roman law, which became stronger as it advanced, was to look upon legal consequences as united to legal causes by an inexorable necessity, a tendency most markedly exemplified in the definition of Obligation which I have repeatedly cited, " Juris vinculum quo necessitate adstringimur alicujus solvendæ rei."

But the problem of Free-will was theological before it became philosophical, and, if its terms have been affected by jurisprudence, it will be because Jurisprudence has made itself felt in Theology. The great point of inquiry which is here suggested has never been satisfactorily elucidated. What has to be determined, is whether jurisprudence has ever served as the medium through which theological principles have been viewed; whether, by supplying a peculiar language, a peculiar mode of reasoning and a peculiar solution of many of the problems of life, it has ever opened new channels in which theological speculation could flow out and expand itself. For the purpose of giving an answer it is necessary to recol· lect what is already agreed upon by the best writers as to the intellectual food which theology first assi- milated. It is conceded on all sides that the earliest language of the Christian Church was Greek, and that the problems to which it first addressed itself were those for which Greek philosophy in its later forms had prepared the way. Greek metaphysical literature contained the sole stock of words and ideas out of which the human mind could provide itself with the means of engaging in the profound controversies as to the Divine Persons, the Divine Substance, and the Divine Natures. The Latin lan- guage and the meagre Latin philosophy were quite unequal to the undertaking, and accordingly the Western or Latin speaking provinces of the Empire adopted the conclusions of the East without disput- ing or reviewing them. "Latin Christianity," says Dean Milman, "accepted the creed which its narrow and barren vocabulary could hardly express in ade- quate terms. Yet, throughout, the adhesion of Rome and the West was a passive acquiescence in the dog- matic system which had been wrought out by the profounder theology of the Eastern divines, rather than a vigorous and original examination on her part of those mysteries. The Latin Church was the scholar as well as the loyal partizan of Athanasius." But when the separation of East and West became wider, and the Latin-speaking Western Empire began to

live with an intellectual life of its own, its deference
to the East was all at once exchanged for the agita-
tion of a number of questions entirely foreign to
Eastern speculation. "While Greek theology (Milman, *Latin Christianity*, Preface, 5) went on defining with still more exquisite subtlety the Godhead
and the nature of Christ "—" while the interminable
controversy still lengthened out and cast forth sect
after sect from the enfeebled community "—the
Western Church threw itself with passionate ardour
into a new order of disputes, the same which from
those days to this have never lost their interest for
any family of mankind at any time included in the
Latin communion. The nature of Sin and its transmission by inheritance—the debt owed by man and its
vicarious satisfaction—the necessity and sufficiency
of the Atonement—above all the apparent antagonism between Free-will and the Divine Providence—
these were points which the West began to debate
as ardently as ever the East had discussed the articles of its more special creed. Why is it then that
on the two sides of the line which divides the Greek-
speaking from the Latin-speaking provinces there lie
two classes of theological problems so strikingly different from one another? The historians of the
Church have come close upon the solution when they
remark that the new problems were more " practical," less absolutely speculative, than those which
had torn Eastern Christianity asunder, but none of
them, so far as I am aware, has quite reached it. I

affirm without hesitation that the difference between
the two theological systems is accounted for by the
fact that, in passing from the East to the West, theological peculation had passed from a climate of Greek
metaphysics to a climate of Roman law. For some
centuries before these controversies rose into over-
whelming importance, all the intellectual activity of
the Western Romans had been expended on jurisprudence exclusively. They had been occupied in
applying a peculiar set of principles to all combinations in which the circumstances of life are capable
of being arranged. No foreign pursuit or taste called off their attention from this engrossing occupation, and for carrying it on they possessed a vocabulary as accurate as it was copious, a strict method of
reasoning, a stock of general propositions on conduct
more or less verified by experience, and a rigid moral
philosophy. It was impossible that they should not
select from the questions indicated by the Christian
records those which had some affinity with the order of speculations to which they were accustomed,
and that their manner of dealing with them should
borrow something from their forensic habits. Almost everybody who has knowledge enough of Roman law to appreciate the Roman penal system, the
Roman theory of the obligations established by Contract or Delict, the Roman view of Debts and of the
modes of incurring, extinguishing, and transmitting
them, the Roman notion of the continuance of individual existence by Universal Succession, may be

trusted to say whence arose the frame of mind to which the problems of Western theology proved so congenial, whence came the phraseology in which these problems were stated, and whence the description of reasoning employed in their solution. It must only be recollected that the Roman law which had worked itself into Western thought was neither the archaic system of the ancient city, nor the pruned and curtailed jurisprudence of the Byzantine Emperors; still less, of course, was it the mass of rules, nearly buried in a parasitical overgrowth of modern speculative doctrine, which passes by the name of Modern Civil Law. I only speak of that philosophy of jurisprudence, wrought out by the great juridical thinkers of the Antonine age, which may still be partially reproduced from the Pandects of Justinian, a system to which few faults can be attributed except perhaps that it aimed at a higher degree of elegance, certainty, and precision than human affairs will permit to the limits within which human laws seek to confine them.

It is a singular result of that ignorance of Roman law which Englishmen readily confess, and of which they are sometimes not ashamed to boast, that many English writers of note and credit have been led by it to put forward the most untenable of paradoxes concerning the condition of human intellect during the Roman empire. It has been constantly asserted, as unhesitatingly as if there were no temerity in advancing the proposition, that from the close of the

Augustan era to the general awakening of interest
on the points of the Christian faith, the mental energies of the civilised world were smitten with a para-
lysis.   Now there are two subjects of thought—the
only two perhaps with the exception of physical
science—which are able to give employment to all
the powers and capacities which the mind possesses.
One of them is Metaphysical inquiry, which knows
no limits so long as the mind is satisfied to work on
itself; the other is Law, which is as extensive as the
concerns of mankind.   It happens that, during the
very period indicated, the Greek-speaking provinces
were devoted to one, the Latin-speaking provinces
to the other, of these studies.   I say nothing of the
fruits of speculation in Alexandria and the East, but
I confidently affirm that Rome and the West had an
occupation in hand fully capable of compensating
them for the absence of every other mental exercise,
and I add that the results achieved, so far as we
know them, were not unworthy of the continuous
and exclusive labor bestowed on producing them.
Nobody except a professional lawyer is perhaps in
a position completely to understand how much of
the intellectual strength of individuals Law is capable
of absorbing, but a layman has no difficulty in comprehending why it was that an unusual share of the
collective intellect of Rome was engrossed by jurisprudence.   " The proficiency * of a given communi-

ty in jurisprudence depends in the long run on the same conditions as its progress in any other line of inquiry; and the chief of these are the proportion of the national intellect devoted to it, and the length of time during which it is so devoted. Now, a combination of all the causes, direct and indirect, which contribute to the advancing and perfecting of a science continued to operate on the jurisprudence of Rome through the entire space between the Twelve Tables and the severance of the two Empires,—and that not irregularly or at intervals, but in steadily increasing force and constantly augmenting number. We should reflect that the earliest intellectual exercise to which a young nation devotes itself is the study of its laws. As soon as the mind makes its first conscious efforts towards generalisation, the concerns of every-day life are the first to press for inclusion within general rules and comprehensive formulas. The popularity of the pursuit on which all the energies of the young commonwealth are bent is at the outset unbounded; but it ceases in time. The monopoly of mind by law is broken down. The crowd at the morning audience of the great Roman jurisconsult lessens. The students are counted by hundreds instead of thousands in the English Inns of Court. Art, Literature, Science, and Politics, claim their share of the national intellect; and the practice of jurisprudence is confined within the circle of a profession, never indeed limited or insignificant, but attracted as much by the rewards as by the intrinsic

recommendations of their science. This succession
of changes exhibited itself evenmore strikingly in
Rome than in England. To the close of the Republic
the law was the sole field for all ability except the
special talent of a capacity for generalship. But a
new stage of intellectual progress began with the Augustan age, as it did with our own Elizabethan era.
We all know what were its achievements in poetry
and prose ; but there are some indications, it should
be remarked, that, besides its efflorescence in orna-
mental literature, it was on the eve of throwing out
new aptitudes for conquest in physical science. Here,
however, is the point at which the history of mind in
the Roman States ceases to be parallel to the routes
which mental progress has since then pursued. The
brief span of Roman literature, strictly so called, was
suddenly closed under a variety of influences, which
though they may partially be traced, it would be im
proper in this place to analyse. Ancient intellect
was forcibly thrust back into its old courses, and law
again became no less exclusively the proper sphere
for talent than it had been in the days when the Romans despised philosophy and poetry as the toys of a
childish race. Of what nature were the external in-
ducements which, during the Imperial period, tended
to draw a man of inherent capacity to the pursuits of
the jurisconsult may best be understood by considering the option which was practically before him in
the choice of a profession. He might become a
teacher of rhetoric, a commander of frontier-posts, or

a professional writer of panegyrics. The only other
walk of active life which was open to him was the
practice of the law. Through *that* lay the approach
to wealth, to fame, to office, to the council-chamber of
the monarch—it may be to the very throne itself.

The premium on the study of jurisprudence was
so enormous that there were schools of law in every
part of the Empire, even in the very domain of
Metaphysics. But, though the transfer of the seat
of empire to Byzantium gave a perceptible impetus
to its cultivation in the East, jurisprudence never
dethroned the pursuits which there competed with
it. Its language was Latin, an exotic dialect in the
Eastern half of the Empire. It is only of the West
that we can lay down that law was not only the
mental food of the ambitious and aspiring, but the
sole aliment of all intellectual activity. Greek philosophy had never been more than a transient fashionable taste with the educated class of Rome itself,
and when the new Eastern capital had been created,
and the Empire subsequently divided into two, the
divorce of the Western provinces from Greek speculation, and their exclusive devotion to jurisprudence, became more decided than ever. As soon
then as they ceased to sit at the feet of the Greeks
and began to ponder out a theology of their own,
the theology proved to be permeated with forensic
ideas and couched in a forensic phraseology. It is
certain that this substratum of law in Western theology lies exceedingly deep. A new set of Greek

theories, the Aristotelian philosophy, made their way afterwards into the West, and almost entirely buried its indigenous doctrines. But when at the Reformation it partially shook itself free from their influence, it instantly supplied their place with Law. It is difficult to say whether the religious system of Calvin or the religious system of the Arminians has the more markedly legal character.

The vast influence of this specific jurisprudence of Contract produced by the Romans upon the corresponding department of modern Law belongs rather to the history of mature jurisprudence than to a treatise like the present. It did not make itself felt till the school of Bologna founded the legal science of modern Europe. But the fact that the Romans, before their Empire fell, had so fully developed the conception of Contract becomes of importance at a much earlier period than this. Feudalism, I have repeatedly asserted, was a compound of archaic barbarian usage with Roman law; no other explanation of it is tenable, or even intelligible. The earliest social forms of the feudal period differ in little from the ordinary associations in which the men of primitive civilisations are everywhere seen united. A Fief was an organically complete brotherhood of associates whose proprietary and personal rights were inextricably blended together. It had much in common with an Indian Village Community and much in common with a Highland clan. But still it presents some phenomena which we never

find in the associations which are spontaneously
formed by beginners in civilisation. True archaic
communities are held together not by express rules,
but by sentiment, or, we should perhaps say, by
instinct; and new comers into the brotherhood are
brought within the range of this instinct by falsely
pretending to share in the blood-relationship from
which it naturally springs. But the earliest feudal
communities were neither bound together by mere
sentiment nor recruited by a fiction. The tie which
united them was Contract, and they obtained new
associates by contracting with them. The relation
of the lord to the vassals had originally been settled
by express engagement, and a person wishing to
engraft himself on the brotherhood by *commendation*
or *infeudation* came to a distinct understanding as
to the conditions on which he was to be admitted.
It is therefore the sphere occupied in them by Contract which principally distinguishes the feudal institutions from the unadulterated usages of primitive
races. The lord had many of the characteristics of
a patriarchal chieftain, but his prerogative was limited by a variety of settled customs traceable to the
express conditions which had been agreed upon
when the infeudation took place. Hence flow the
chief differences which forbid us to class the feudal
societies with true archaic communities. They
were much more durable and much more various;
more durable, because express rules are less destructible than instinctive habits, and more various,

23

because the contracts on which they were founded were adjusted to the minutest circumstances and wishes of the persons who surrendered or granted away their lands.   This last consideration may serve to indicate how greatly the vulgar opinions current among us as to the origin of modern society stand in need of revision.   It is often said that the irregular and various contour of modern civilisation is due to the exuberant and erratic genius of the Germanic races, and it is often contrasted with the dull routine of the Roman Empire.   The truth is that the Empire bequeathed to modern society the legal conception to which all this irregularity is attributable; if the customs and institutions of barbarians have one characteristic more striking than another, it is their extreme uniformity.

CHAPTER X.

THE Teutonic Codes, including those of our Anglo-Saxon ancestors, are the only bodies of archaic secular law which have come down to us in such a state that we can form an exact notion of their original dimensions. Although the extant fragments of Roman and Hellenic codes suffice to prove to us their general character, there does not remain enough of them for us to be quite sure of their precise magnitude or of the proportion of their parts to each other. But still on the whole all the known collections of ancient law are characterised by a feature which broadly distinguishes them from systems of mature jurisprudence. The proportion of criminal to civil law is exceedingly different. In the German codes, the civil part of the law has trifling dimensions as compared with the criminal. The traditions which speak of the sanguinary penalties inflicted by the code of Draco seem to indicate that it had the same characteristic. In the Twelve Tables alone

produced by a society of greater legal genius and at
first of gentler manners, the civil law has something
like its modern precedence ; but the relative amount
of space given to the modes of redressing wrong,
though not enormous, appears to have been large.
It may be laid down, I think, that the more archaic
the code, the fuller and the minuter is its penal legislation.   The phenomenon has often been observed
and has been explained, no doubt to a great extent
correctly, by the violence habitual to the communities which for the first time reduced their laws to
writing.   The legislator, it is said, proportioned the
divisions of his work to the frequency of a certain
class of incidents in barbarian life.   I imagine, however, that this account is not quite complete.   It
should be recollected that the comparative barren-
ness of civil law in archaic collections is consistent
with those other characteristics of ancient jurisprudence which have been discussed in this treatise.
Nine-tenths of the civil part of the law practised by
civilised societies are made up of the Law of Persons,
of the Law of Property and of Inheritance, and of
the Law of Contract.   But it is plain that all these
provinces of jurisprudence must shrink within nar-
rower boundaries, the nearer we make our approaches
to the infancy of social brotherhood.   The Law of
Persons, which is nothing else than the Law of
Status, will be restricted to the scantiest limits as
long as all forms of status are merged in common
subjection to Paternal Power, as long as the Wife

has no rights against her Husband, the Son none
against his Father, and the infant Ward none against
the Agnates who are his Guardians. Similarly, the
rules relating to Property and Succession can never
be plentiful, so long as land and goods devolve within
the family, and, if distributed at all, are distributed
inside its circle. But the greatest gap in ancient
civil law will always be caused by the absence of
Contract, which some archaic codes do not mention
at all, while others significantly attest the immaturity of the moral notions on which Contract depends
by supplying its place with an elaborate jurisprudence of Oaths. There are no corresponding reasons
for the poverty of penal law, and accordingly, even
if it be hazardous to pronounce that the childhood
of nations is always a period of ungoverned violence,
we shall still be able to understand why the modern
relation of criminal law to civil should be inverted
in ancient codes.

I have spoken of primitive jurisprudence as
giving to *criminal* law a priority unknown in a later
age. The expression has been used for convenience
but in fact the inspection of ancient codes shows that
the law which they exhibit in unusual quantities
is not true criminal law. All civilised systems agree
in drawing a distinction between offences against the
State or Community and offences against the Individual, and the two classes of injuries, thus kept
apart, I may here, without pretending that the terms
have always been employed consistently in jurispru-

dence, call Crimes and Wrongs, *crimina* and *delicta*. Now the penal Law of ancient communities is not the law of Crimes; it is the law of Wrongs, or, to use the English technical word, of Torts. The person injured proceeds against the wrong-doer by an ordinary civil action, and recovers compensation in the shape of money-damages if he succeeds. If the Commentaries of Gaius be opened at the place where the writer treats of the penal jurisprudence founded on the Twelve Tables, it will be seen that at the head of the civil wrongs recognised by the Roman law stood *Furtum* or *Theft*. Offences which we are accustomed to regard exclusively as *crimes* are exclusively treated as *torts*, and not theft only, but assault and violent robbery, are associated by the jurisconsult with trespass, libel and slander. All alike gave rise to an Obligation or *vinculum juris*, and were all requited by a payment of money. This peculiarity, however, is most strongly brought out in the consolidated Laws of the Germanic tribes. Without an exception they describe an immense system of money compensations for homicide, and with few exceptions, as large a scheme of compensation for minor injuries. "Under Anglo-Saxon law,' writes Mr. Kemble (*Anglo-Saxons*, i. 177), "a sum was placed on the life of every free man, according to his rank, and a corresponding sum on every wound that could be inflicted on his person, for nearly every injury that could be done to his civil rights, honour or peace; the sum being aggravated according to adventitious circumstances." These compositions are evidently regarded as a valuable source of income; highly complex rules regulate the title to them and the responsibility for them; and, as I have already had occasion to state, they often follow a very peculiar line of devolution, if they have not been acquitted at the decease of the person to whom they belong. If therefore the criterion of a *delict*, *wrong*, or *tort* be that the person who suffers it, and not the State, is conceived to be wronged, it may be asserted that in the infancy of jurisprudence the citizen depends for protection against violence or fraud not on the Law of Crime but on the Law of Tort.

Torts then are copiously enlarged upon in primitive jurisprudence. It must be added that Sins are known to it also. Of the Teutonic codes it is almost unnecessary to make this assertion, because those codes, in the form in which we have received them, were compiled or recast by Christian legislators. But it is also true that the non-Christian bodies of archaic law entail penal consequences on certain classes of acts and on certain classes of omissions, as being violations of divine jurisprudence and commands. The law administered at Athens by the Senate of Areopagus was probably a special religious code, and at Rome, apparently from a very early period, the Pontifical jurisprudence punished adultery, sacrilege, and perhaps murder. There were therefore in the Athenian and in the Roman States laws punishing *sins.* There were also laws punishing *torts.* The conception of offence against God produced the first class of ordinances ; the conception of offence against one's neighbour produced the second ; but the idea of offence against the State or aggregate community did not at first produce a true criminal jurisprudence.

Yet it is not to be supposed that a conception so simple and elementary as that of wrong done to the State was wanting in any primitive society. It seems rather that the very distinctness with which this conception is realised is the true cause which at first prevents the growth of a criminal law. At all events, when the Roman community conceived itself to be injured, the analogy of a personal wrong received was carried out to its consequences with absolute literalness, and the State avenged itself by a single act on the individual wrong-doer. The result was that, in the infancy of the commonwealth, every offence vitally touching its security or its interests was punished by a separate enactment of the legislature. And this is the earliest conception of a *crimen* or Crime—an act involving such high issues that the State, instead of leaving its cognisance to the civil tribunal or the religious court, directed a special aw or *privilegium* against the perpetrator. Every indictment therefore took the form of a bill of pains and penalties, and the trial of. a *criminal* was a proceeding wholly extraordinary, wholly irregular, wholly independent of settled rules and fixed con ditions. Consequently, both for the reason that the tribunal dispensing justice was the sovereign State itself, and also for the reason that no classification of the acts prescribed or forbidden was possible, there was not at this epoch any *Law* of crimes, any criminal jurisprudence.   The procedure was identical with the forms of passing an ordinary statute; it was set in motion by the same persons and conducted with precisely the same solemnities. And it is to be observed that, when a regular criminal law with an apparatus of Courts and officers for its administration had afterwards come into being, the old procedure, as might be supposed from its conformity with theory, still in strictness remained practicable; and, much as resort to such an expedient was discredited, the people of Rome always retained the power of punishing by a special law offences against its majesty.   The classical scholar does not require to be reminded that in exactly the same manner the Athenian Bill of Pains and Penalties, or *εἰσαγγελία,* survived the establishment of regular tribunals.   It is known too that when the freemen of the Teutonic races assembled for legislation, they also claimed authority to punish offences of peculiar blackness or perpetrated by criminals of exalted station. Of this nature was the criminal jurisdiction of the Anglo-Saxon Witenagemot.

It may be thought that the difference which I have asserted to exist between the ancient and modern view of penal law has only a verbal existence. The community, it may be said, besides interposing

to punish crimes legislatively, has from the earliest
times interfered by its tribunals to compel the wrong-
doer to compound for his wrong, and if it does this,
it must always have supposed that in some way it
was injured through his offence.   But, however rigorous this inference may seem to us now a-days, it is
very doubtful whether it was actually drawn by the
men of primitive antiquity.   How little the notion of
injury to the community had to do with the earliest
interferences of the State *through its tribunals*, is
shown by the curious circumstance that in the original administration of justice, the proceedings were
a close imitation of the series of acts which were
likely to be gone through in private life by persons
who were disputing, but who afterwards suffered
their quarrel to be appeased.   The magistrate carefully simulated the demeanour of a private arbitrator
casually called in.

In order to show that this statement is not a
mere fanciful conceit, I will produce the evidence on
which it rests.   Very far the most ancient judicial
proceeding known to us is the Legis Actio Sacra-
menti of the Romans, out of which all the later Roman law of Actions may be proved to have grown.
Gaius carefully describes its ceremonial. Unmeaning
and grotesque as it appears at first sight, a little at
tention enables us to decipher and interpret it.

The subject of litigation is supposed to be in
Court. If it is moveable, it is actually there. If it
be immoveable, a fragment or sample of it is brought

in its place ; land, for instance, is represented by a clod, a house by a single brick. In the example selected by Gaius, the suit is for a slave. The proceeding begins by the plaintiff's advancing with a rod, which as Gaius expressly tells, symbolised a spear. He lays hold of the slave and asserts a right to him with the words, " *Hunc ego hominem ex Jure Quiritium meum esse dico secundum suam causam sicut dixi ;* " and then saying, " *Ecce tibi Vindictam imposui,* " he touches him with the spear. The defendant goes through the same series of acts and gestures. On this the Prætor intervenes, and bids the litigants relax their hold, " *Mittite ambo hominem.* " They obey, and the plaintiff demands from the defendant the reason of his interference, " *Postulo anne dicas quâ ex causâ vindicaveris,*" a question which is replied to by a fresh assertion of right, " *Jus peregi sicut vindictam imposui.*" On this, the first claimant offers to stake a sum of money, called a Sacramentum, on the justice of his own case, " *Quando tu injuriâ provocasti, D æris Sacramento te provoco,* " and the defendant, in the phrase, " *Similiter ego te,* " accepts the wager. The subsequent proceedings were no longer of a formal kind, but it is to be observed that the Prætor took security for the Sacramentum, which always went into the coffers of the State.

Such was the necessary preface of every ancient Roman suit. It is impossible, I think, to refuse assent to the suggestion of those who see in it a dra-

matization of the origin of Justice. Two armed men
are wrangling about some disputed property. The
Prætor, *vir pietate gravis*, happens to be going by
and interposes to stop the contest. The disputants
state their case to him, and agree that he shall arbi
trate between them, it being arranged that the loser,
besides resigning the subject of the quarrel, shall pay
a sum of money to the umpire as a remuneration
for his trouble and loss of time. This interpretation
would be less plausible than it is, were it not that,
by a surprising coincidence, the ceremony described
by Gaius as the imperative course of proceeding in a
Legis Actio is substantially the same with one of
the two subjects which the God Hephæstus is described by Homer as moulding into the First Com-
partment of the Shield of Achilles. In the Homeric
trial-scene, the dispute, as if expressly intended to
bring out the characteristics of primitive society, is
not about property but about the composition for a
homicide. One person asserts that he has paid it,
the other that he has never received it. The point
of detail, however, which stamps the picture as the
counterpart of the archaic Roman practice is the reward designed for the judges. Two talents of gold
lie in the middle, to be given to him who shall explain the grounds of the decision most to the satisfaction of the audience. The magnitude of this sum
as compared with the trifling amount of the Sacramentum seems to me indicative of the difference between fluctuating usage and usage consolidated into

law. The scene introduced by the poet as a striking
and characteristic, but still only occasional, feature
of city-life in the heroic age has stiffened, at the
opening of the history of civil process, into the reg
ular, ordinary formalities of a lawsuit. It is natural
therefore that in the Legis Actio the remuneration
of the Judge should be reduced to a reasonable sum,
and that, instead of being adjudged to one of a number of arbitrators by popular acclamation, it should
be paid as a matter of course to the State which the
Prætor represents. But that the incidents described
so vividly by Homer, and by Gaius with even more
than the usual crudity of technical language, have
substantially the same meaning, I cannot doubt; and,
in confirmation of this view it may be added that
many observers of the earliest judicial usages of modern Europe have remarked that the fines inflicted by
Courts on offenders were originally *sacramenta*. The
State did not take from the defendant a composition
for any wrong supposed to be done to itself, but
claimed a share in the compensation awarded to the
plaintiff simply as the fair price of its time and
trouble.   Mr. Kemble expressly assigns this character to the Anglo-Saxon *bannum* or *fredum*.

Ancient law furnishes other proofs that the earliest administrators of justice simulated the probable
acts of persons engaged in a private quarrel. In
settling the damages to be awarded, they took as
their guide the measure of vengeance likely to be
exacted by an aggrieved person under the circum-

stances of the case. This is the true explanation of
the véry different penalties imposed by ancient law
on offenders caught in the act or soon after it and on
offenders detected after considerable delay. Some
strange exemplifications of this peculiarity are supplied by the old Roman law of Theft. The Laws
of the Twelve Tables seem to have divided Thefts
into Manifest and Non-Manifest, and to have allotted
extraordinarily different penalties to the offence according as it fell under one head or the other. The
Manifest Thief was he who was caught within the
house in which he had been pilfering, or who was
taken while making off to a place of safety with the
stolen goods ; the Twelve Tables condemned him to
be put to death if he were already a slave, and, if
he was a freeman, they made him the bondsman of
the owner of the property. The Non-Manifest
Thief was he who was detected under any other circumstances than those described ; and the old code
simply directed that an offender of this sort should
refund double the value of what he had stolen. In
Gaius's day the excessive severity of the Twelve Tables to the Manifest Thief had naturally been much
mitigated, but the law still maintained the old principle by mulcting him in fourfold the value of the stolen
goods, while the Non-Manifest Thief still continued
to pay merely the double. The ancient lawgiver
doubtless considered that the injured proprietor, if
left to himself, would inflict a very different punishment when his blood was hot from that with which

he would be satisfied when the Thief was detected after a considerable interval; and to this calculation the legal scale of penalties was adjusted. The principle is precisely the same as that followed in the Anglo-Saxon and other Germanic codes, when they suffer a thief chased down and caught with the booty to be hanged or decapitated on the spot, while they exact the full penalties of homicide from anybody who kills him after the pursuit has been intermitted. These archaic distinctions bring home to us very forcibly the distance of a refined from a rude jurisprudence. The modern administrator of justice has confessedly one of his hardest tasks before him when he undertakes to discriminate between the degrees of criminality which belong to offences falling within the same technical description. It is always easy to say that a man is guilty of manslaughter, larceny, or bigamy, but it is often most difficult to pronounce what extent of moral guilt he has incurred, and consequently what measure of punishment he has deserved. There is hardly any perplexity in casuistry, or in the analysis of motive, which we may not be called upon to confront, if we attempt to settle such a point with precision; and accordingly the law of our day shows an increasing tendency to abstain as much as possible from laying down positive rules on the subject. In France the jury is left to decide whether the offence which it finds committed has been attended by extenuating circumstances; in England, a nearly unbounded latitude in the selection of punishments is now allowed to the judge; while all States have in reserve an ultimate remedy for the miscarriages of law in the Prerogative of Pardon, universally lodged with the Chief Magistrate. It is curious to observe how little the men of primitive times were troubled with these scruples, how completely they were per-suaded that the impulses of the injured person were the proper measure of the vengeance he was entitled to exact, and how literally they imitated the prob-able rise and fall of his passions in fixing their scale of punishment. I wish it could be said that their method of legislation is quite extinct. There are, however, several modern systems of law which, in cases of graver wrong, admit the fact of the wrong-doer having been taken in the act to be pleaded in justification of inordinate punishment inflicted on him by the sufferer—an indulgence which, though superficially regarded it may seem intelligible, is based, as it seems to me, on a very low morality.

Nothing, I have said, can be simpler than the considerations which ultimately led ancient societies to the formation of a true criminal jurisprudence. The State conceived itself to be wronged, and the Popular Assembly struck straight at the offender with the same movement which accompanied its legislative action. It is further true of the ancient world—though not precisely of the modern, as I shall have occasion to point out—that the earliest criminal tribunals were merely subdivisions, or committees, of the legislature. This, at all events, is the conclusion pointed at by the legal history of the two great states of antiquity. with tolerable clearness in one case, and with absolute distinctness in the other. The primitive penal law of Athens entrusted the castigation of offences partly to the Archons, who seem to have punished them as *torts*, and partly to the Senate of Areopagus, which punished them as *sins*. Both jurisdictions were substantially transferred in the end to the Heliæa, the High Court of Popular Justice, and the functions of the Archons and the Areopagus became either merely ministerial or quite insignificant. But " Heliæa " is only an old word for Assembly; the Heliæa of classical times was simply the Popular Assembly convened for judicial purposes, and the famous Dikasteries of Athens were only its subdivisions or panels. The corresponding changes which occurred at Rome are still more easily interpreted, because the Romans confined their experiments to the penal law, and did not, like the Athenians, construct popular courts with a civil as well as a criminal jurisdiction. The history of Roman criminal jurisprudence begins with the Old Judicia Populi, at which the Kings are said to have presided. These were simply solemn trials of great offenders under legislative forms. It seems, however, that from an early period the Comitia had occasionally delegated its criminal jurisdiction to a Quæstio or Commission, which bore much the same relation to the Assembly

24

which a Committee of the House of Commons bears
to the House itself, except that the Roman Commissioners or Quæstores did not merely *report* to the
Comitia, but exercised all powers which that body
was itself in the habit of exercising, even to the
passing sentence on the Accused. A Quæstio of
this sort was only appointed to try a particulai
offender, but there was nothing to prevent two or
three Quæstiones sitting at the same time ; and it is
probable that several of them were appointed simultaneously, when several grave cases of wrong to the
community had occurred together. There are also
indications that now and then these Quæstiones approached the character of our *Standing* Committees,
in that they were appointed periodically, and without waiting for occasion to arise in the commission
of some serious crime. The old Quæstores Parricidii, who are mentioned in connection with transactions of very ancient date, as being deputed to try
(or, as some take it, to search out and try) all cases
of parricide and murder, seem to have been appointed
regularly every year ; and the Duumviri Perduellionis, or Commission of Two for trial of violent
injury to the Commonwealth, are also believed by
most writers to have been named periodically. The
delegations of power to these latter functionaries
bring us some way forwards. Instead of being appointed *when and as* state-offences were committed
they had a general, though a temporary jurisdiction
over such as *might* be perpetrated. Our proximi'y

to a regular criminal jurisprudence is also indicated by the general terms " Parricidium " and " Perduellio," which mark the approach to something like a classification of crimes.

The true criminal law did not however come into existence till the year B.C. 149, when L. Calpurnius Piso carried the statute known as the Lex Calpurnia de Repetundis. The law applied to cases Repetundarum Pecuniarum, that is, claims by Provincials to recover monies improperly received by a Governor-General, but the great and permanent importance of this statute arose from its establishing the first Quæstio Perpetua. A Quæstio Perpetua was a *Permanent* Commission as opposed to those which were occasional and to those which were temporary. It was a regular criminal tribunal, whose existence dated from the passing of the statute creating it and continued till another statute should pass abolishing it. Its members were not specially nominated, as were the members of the older Quæstiones, but provision was made in the law constituting it for selecting from particular classes the judges who were to officiate, and for renewing them in conformity with definite rules. The offences of which it took cognisance were also expressly named and defined in this statute, and the new Quæstio had authority to try and sentence all persons in future whose acts should fall under the definitions of crime supplied by the law It was therefore a regular criminal judicature, administering a true criminal jurisprudence.

The primitive history of criminal law divides itself therefore into four stages. Understanding that the conception of *Crime*, as distinguished from that of *Wrong* or *Tort* and from that of *Sin*, involves the idea of injury to the State or collective community, we first find that the commonwealth, in literal conformity with the conception, itself interposed directly, and by isolated acts, to avenge itself on the author of the evil which it had suffered This is the point from which we start; each indictment is now a bill of pains and penalties, a special law naming the criminal and prescribing his punishment. A *second* step is accomplished when the multiplicity of crimes compels the legislature to delegate its powers to particular Quæstiones or Commissions, each of which is deputed to investigate a particular accusation, and if it be proved, to punish the particular offender. Yet *another* movement is made when the legislature, instead of waiting for the alleged commission of a crime as the occasion of appointing a Quæstio, periodically nominates Commissioners like the Quæstores Parricidii and the Duumviri Perduellionis, on the chance of certain classes of crimes being committed, and in the expectation that they *will* be perpetrated. The *last* stage is reached when the Quæstiones from being periodical or occasional become permanent Benches or Chambers—when the judges, instead of being named in the particular law nominating the Commission, are directed to be chosen through all future time in a particular way and from a particular class —and when certain acts are described in general language and declared to be crimes, to be visited, in the event of their perpetration, with specified penalties appropriated to each description.

If the Quæstiones Perpetuæ had had a longer history, they would doubtless have come to be regarded as a distinct institution, and their relation to the Comitia would have seemed no closer than the connection of our own Courts of Law with the Sovereign, who is theoretically the fountain of justice. But the Imperial despotism destroyed them before their origin had been completely forgotten, and so long as they lasted, these Permanent Commissions were looked upon by the Romans as the mere depositaries of a delegated power. The cognisance of crimes was considered a natural attribute of the legislature, and the mind of the citizen never ceased to be carried back from the Quæstiones to the Comitia which had deputed them to put into exercise some of its own inalienable functions. The view which regarded the Quæstiones, even when they became permanent, as mere Committees of the Popular Assembly—as bodies which only ministered to a higher authority—had some important legal consequences which left their mark on the criminal law to the very latest period. One immediate result was that the Comitia continued to exercise criminal jurisdiction by way of bill of pains and penalties, long after the Quæstiones had been established. Though the legislature had consented to delegate its powers for the sake of convenience to bodies external to itself, it did not follow that it surrendered them. The Comitia and the Quæstiones went on trying and punishing offenders side by side; and any unusual outburst of popular indignation was sure, until the extinction of the Republic, to call down upon its object an indictment before the Assembly of the Tribes.

One of the most remarkable peculiarities of the institutions of the Republic is also traceable to this dependance of the Quæstiones on the Comitia. The disappearance of the punishment of Death from the penal system of Republican Rome used to be a very favorite topic with the writers of the last century, who were perpetually using it to point some theory of the Roman character or of modern social economy. The reason which can be confidently assigned for it stamps it as purely fortuitous. Of the three forms which the Roman legislature successively assumed, one, it is well known—the Comitia Centuriata—was exclusively taken to represent the State as embodied for military operations. The Assembly of the Centuries, therefore, had all powers which may be supposed to be properly lodged with a General commanding an army, and, among them, it had authority to subject all offenders to the same correction to

which a soldier rendered himself liable by breaches
of discipline.   The Comitia Centuriata could therefore inflict capital punishment.   Not so, however,
the Comitia Curiata or Comitia Tributa. They were
fettered on this point by the sacredness with which
the person of a Roman citizen, inside the walls of the
city, was invested by religion and law; and, with
respect to the last of them, the Comitia Tributa, we
know for certain that it became a fixed principle that
the Assembly of the Tribes could at most impose a
fine.   So long as criminal jurisdiction was confined
to the legislature, and so long as the assemblies of
the Centuries and of the Tribes continued to exercise
co-ordinate powers, it was easy to prefer indictments
for graver crimes before the legislative body which
dispensed the heavier penalties; but then it happened that the more democratic assembly, that of the
Tribes, almost entirely superseded the others, and
became the ordinary legislature of the later Republic.   Now the decline of the Republic was exactly
the period during which the Quæstiones Perpetuæ
were established, so that the statutes creating them
were all passed by a legislative assembly which itself
could not, at its ordinary sittings, punish a criminal
with death.   It followed that the Permanent Judicial
Commissions, holding a delegated authority, were cir-
cumscribed in their attributes and capacities by the
limits of the powers residing with the body which
deputed them.   They could do nothing which the
Assembly of the tribes could not have done ; and, as

the Assembly could not sentence to death, the Quæstiones were equally incompetent to award capital
punishment. The anomaly thus resulting was not
viewed in ancient times with anything like the favour
which it has attracted among the moderns, and in
deed, while it is questionable whether the Roman
character was at all the better for it, it is certain that
the Roman Constitution was a great deal the worse.
Like every other institution which has accompanied
the human race down the current of its history, the
punishment of death is a necessity of society in certain stages of the civilising process. There is a time
when the attempt to dispense with it baulks both of
the two great instincts which lie at the root of all penal law. Without it, the community neither feels that
it is sufficiently revenged on the criminal, nor thinks
that the example of his punishment is adequate to
deter others from imitating him. The incompetence
of the Roman Tribunals to pass sentence of death led
distinctly and directly to those frightful Revolutionary intervals, known as the Proscriptions, during
which all law was formally suspended simply because
party violence could find no other avenue to the vengeance for which it was thirsting.   No cause contrib-
ted so powerfully to the decay of political capacity
_n the Roman people as this periodical abeyance of
the laws ; and, when it had once been resorted to, we
need not hesitate to assert that the ruin of Roman
liberty became merely a question of time. If the
practice of the Tribunals had afforded an adequate

vent for popular passion, the forms of judicial procedure would no doubt have been as flagrantly perverted as with us in the reigns of the later Stuarts,
but national character would not have suffered as
deeply as it did, nor would the stability of Roman
institutions have been as seriously enfeebled.

I will mention two more singularities of the Roman Criminal System which were produced by the
same theory of judicial authority. They are, the extreme multiplicity of the Roman criminal tribunals,
and the capricious and anomalous classification of
crimes which characterised Roman penal jurisprudence throughout its entire history. Every *Quæstio*,
it has been said, whether Perpetual or otherwise,
had its origin in a distinct statute. From the law
which created it, it derived its authority; it rigorously observed the limits which its charter prescribed to it, and touched no form of criminality
which that charter did not expressly define. As then
the statutes which constituted the various Quæstiones
were all called forth by particular emergencies, each
of them being in fact passed to punish a class of acts
which the circumstances of the time rendered particularly odious or particularly dangerous, these enactments made not the slightest reference to each
other, and were connected by no common principle.
Twenty or thirty different criminal laws were in ex
istence together, with exactly the same number of
Quæstiones to administer them; nor was any attempt
made during the Republic to fuse these distinct ju-

dicial bodies into one, or to give symmetry to the pro·
visions of the statutes which appointed them and
defined their duties. The state of the Roman criminal jurisdiction at this period, exhibited some resemblance to the administration of civil remedies in
England at the time when the English Courts of
Common Law had not as yet introduced those ficti·
tious averments into their writs which enabled them
to trespass on each other's peculiar province. Like
the Quæstiones, the Courts of Queen's Bench, Common Pleas, and Exchequer, were all theoretical
emanations from a higher authority, and each entertained a special class of cases supposed to be committed to it by the fountain of its jurisdiction ; but
then the Roman Quæstiones were many more than
three in number, and it was infinitely less easy to
discriminate the acts which fell under the cognisance
of each Quæstio, than to distinguish between the provinces of the three Courts in Westmnister Hall.
The difficulty of drawing exact lines between the
spheres of the different Quæstiones made the multiplicity of Roman tribunals something more than a
mere inconvenience ; for we read with astonishment
that when it was not immediately clear under what
general description a man's alleged offence ranged
themselves, he might be indicted at once, or suc·
cessively before several different Commissions, on
the chance of some of them declaring itself compe·
tent to convict him ; and, although conviction by one
Quæstio ousted the jurisdiction of the rest, acquittal

by one of them could not be pleaded to an accusation before another. This was directly contrary to
the rule of the Roman civil law; and we may be sure
that a people so sensitive as the Romans to anomalies
(or, as their significant phrase was, to *inelegancies*)
in jurisprudence, would not long have tolerated it,
had not the melancholy history of the Quæstiones
caused them to be regarded much more as temporary
weapons in the hands of factions than as permanent
institutions for the correction, of crime. The Empe
rors soon abolished this multiplicity and conflict of
jurisdiction; but it is remarkable that they did not
remove another singularity of the criminal law which
stands in close connection with the number of the
Courts. The classifications of crimes which are contained even in the Corpus Juris of Justinian are remarkably capricious. Each Quæstio had, in fact,
confined itself to the crimes committed to its cognisance by its charter. These crimes, however, were
only classed together in the original statute because
they happened to call simultaneously for castigation
at the moment of passing it. They had not therefore
anything necessarily in common; but the fact of
their constituting the particular subject-matter of
trials before a particular Quæstio impressed itself naturally on the public attention, and so inveterate did
the association become between the offences mentioned in the same statute that, even when formal
attempts were made by Sylla and by the Emperor
Augustus to consolidate the Roman criminal law, the

legislator preserved the old grouping. The Statutes of Sylla and Augustus were the foundation of the penal jurisprudence of the Empire, and nothing can be more extraordinary than some of the classifications which they bequeathed to it. I need only give a single example in the fact that *perjury* was always classed with *cutting and wounding* and with *poisoning*, no doubt because a law of Sylla, the Lex Cornelia de Sicariis et Veneficis, had given jurisdiction over all these three forms of crime to the same Permanent Commission. It seems too that this capricious grouping of crimes affected the vernacular speech of the Romans. People naturally fell into the habit of designating all the offences enumerated in one law by the first name on the list, which doubtless gave its style to the Law Court deputed to try them all. All the offences tried by the Quæstio De Adulteriis would thus be called Adultery.

I have dwelt on the history and characteristics of the Roman Quæstiones because the formation of a criminal jurisprudence is nowhere else so instructively exemplified. The last Quæstiones were added by the Emperor Augustus, and from that time the Romans may be said to have had a tolerably complete criminal law. Concurrently with its growth, the analogous process had gone on, which I have called the conversion of Wrongs into Crimes, for, though the Roman legislature did not extinguish the civil rem edy for the more heinous offences, it offered the suf ferer a redress which he was sure to prefer. Still,

even after Augustus had completed his legislation,
several offences continued to be regarded as Wrongs,
which modern societies look upon exclusively as
crimes; nor did they become criminally punishable
till some late but uncertain date, at which the law
began to take notice of a new description of offences
called in the Digest *crimina extraordinaria*. These
were doubtless a class of acts which the theory of
Roman jurisprudence treated merely as wrongs; but
the growing sense of the majesty of society revolted
from their entailing nothing worse on their perpetrator than the payment of money damages, and accordingly the injured person seems to have been permitted if he pleased, to pursue them as crimes *extra ordi-
nem*, that is, by a mode of redress departing in some
respect or other from the ordinary procedure. From
the period at which these *crimina extraordinaria*
were first recognised, the list of crimes in the Roman States must have been as long as in any community of the modern world.

It is unnecessary to describe with any minuteness
the mode of administering criminal justice under the
Roman Empire, but it is to be noted that both its
theory and practice have had powerful effect on
modern society. The Emperors did not immediately
abolish the Quæstiones, and at first they committed
an extensive criminal jurisdiction to the Senate, in
which, however servile it might show itself in fact,
the Emperor was no more nominally than a Senator
like the rest. But some sort of collateral criminal

jurisdiction had been claimed by the Prince from the first; and this, as recollections of the free commonwealth decayed, tended steadily to gain at the expense of the old tribunals. Gradually the punishment of crimes was transferred to magistrates directly nominated by the Emperor, and the privileges of the Senate passed to the Imperial Privy Council, which also became a Court of ultimate criminal appeal. Under these influences the doctrine, familiar to the moderns, insensibly shaped itself that the Sovereign is the fountain of all Justice and the depositary of all Grace. It was not so much the fruit of increasing adulation and servility as of the centralisation of the Empire which had by this time perfected itself. The theory of criminal justice had, in fact, worked round almost to the point from which it started. It had begun in the belief that it was the business of the collective community to avenge its own wrongs by its own hand; and it ended in the doctrine that the chastisement of crimes belonged in an especial manner to the Sovereign as representative and mandatary of his people. The new view differed from the old one chiefly in the air of awfulness and majesty which the guardianship of justice appeared to throw around the person of the Sovereign.

This later Roman view of the Sovereign's relation to justice certainly assisted in saving modern societies from the necessity of travelling through the series of changes which I have illustrated by the

history of the Quæstiones. In the primitive law of
almost all the races which have peopled Western
Europe there are vestiges of the archaic notion that
the punishment of crimes belongs to the general
assembly of freemen; and there are some ·States—
Scotland is said to be one of them—in which the
parentage of the existing judicature can be traced
up to a Committee of the legislative body. But the
development of the criminal law was universally
hastened by two causes, the memory of the Roman
Empire and the influence of the Church. On the
one hand traditions of the majesty of the Cæsars,
perpetuated by the temporary ascendency of the
House of Charlemagne, were surrounding Sovereigns
with a prestige which a mere barbarous chieftain
could never otherwise have acquired, and were com-
municating to the pettiest feudal potentate the character of guardian of society and representative of
the State. On the other hand, the Church, in its
anxiety to put a curb on sanguinary ferocity, sought
about for authority to punish the graver misdeeds,
and found it in those passages of Scripture which
speak with approval of the powers of punishment
committed to the civil magistrate. The New Testament was appealed to as proving that secular
rulers exist for the terror of evil-doers; the Old
Testament, as laying down that " whoso sheddeth
man's blood, by man shall his blood be shed.'
There can be no doubt, I imagine, that modern ideas
on the subject of crime are based upon two assump-

tions contended for by the Church in the Dark
Ages—first, that each feudal ruler, in his degree,
might be assimilated to the Roman Magistrates
spoken of by Saint Paul; and next, that the offences which he was to chastise were those selected
for prohibition in the Mosaic Commandments, or
rather such of them as the Church did not reserve
to her own cognisance. Heresy, supposed to be included in the First and Second Commandments,
Adultery and Perjury were ecclesiastical offences,
and the Church only admitted the co-operation of
the secular arm for the purpose of inflicting severer
punishment in cases of extraordinary aggravation.
At the same time, she taught that murder and
robbery, with their various modifications, were under the jurisdiction of civil rulers, not as an accident
of their position, but by the express ordinance of
God.

There is a passage in the writings of King Alfred
(Kemble, ii. 209) which brings out into remarkable
clearness the struggle of the various ideas that prevailed in his day as to the origin of criminal jurisdiction. It will be seen that Alfred attributes it
partly to the authority of the Church and partly to
that of the Witan, while he expressly claims for
treason against the lord the same immunity from
ordinary rules which the Roman Law of Majestas
had assigned to treason against the Cæsar. " After
this it happened," he writes, " that many nations
received the faith of Christ, and there were many

synods assembled throughout the earth, and among
the English race also after they had received the
faith of Christ, both of holy bishops and of their
exalted Witan. They then ordained that, out of
that mercy which Christ had taught, secular lords,
with their leave, might without sin take for every
misdeed the *bot* in money which they ordained; except in cases of treason against a lord, to which they
dared not assign any mercy because Almighty God
adjudged none to them that despised Him, nor did
Christ adjudge any to them which sold Him to
death; and He commanded that a lord should be
loved like Himself."

INDEX.